CREATIVE ADVERTISING: AN INTRODUCTION

MIRIAM SORRENTINO

LAURENCE KING PUBLISHING

Published in 2014 by
Laurence King Publishing Ltd
361–373 City Road
London EC1V 1LR
United Kingdom
email: enquiries@laurenceking.com
www.laurenceking.com

A catalogue record for this book is available from the
British Library.

ISBN: 978 1 78067 1192

Design: Michael Lenz, Draught Associates
Cover design & illustration: Billie Jean

Printed in China

5405000410415
23nd June 2014

CONTENTS

INTRODUCTION

INTRODUCTION

Advertising interrupts our television viewing, breaks up our articles in newspapers, pops up while we are browsing the Web and falls through our letterboxes. While many might find the way advertising interrupts the landscape irritating, others enjoy it and view it in a lighthearted way. When advertising is done well people often find it entertaining and informative, and consumers are increasingly choosing to interact with it. Today's advertisers have more media at their fingertips than ever before, offering more possibilities for making connections with their audience, yet people are increasingly media savvy and do not easily give product information their undivided attention.

As modern creatives we have to learn about everything: the skills needed to physically create adverts in all the new spaces that have opened up for consumers, as much as the culture, psychology, sociology and technology that make up our lives. Advertising is an industry that always asks itself: how do we engage people? Do we simply entertain them? Or do we encourage them to start a relationship with the brands we develop work for? The working advertiser endeavours to do all of this by being creative, insightful, entertaining and knowledgeable. This is a dynamic and flexible industry; it is always in the process of changing. It needs students and practitioners who are equally flexible and multi-skilled, with plenty of cultural capital at their disposal.

Creative Advertising: An Introduction aims to offer you a contemporary visual guide to the work of advertising creatives, and explores the fundamental principles of advertising and branding practice. Readers are introduced to the advertising process from initial research through to the creation of advertising and branding campaigns. The text is supported throughout by comments and advice from leading industry figures from around the world. What better way to hear what industry wants than from industry itself?

Creative Advertising: An Introduction provides many useful tips and inspirational ideas aimed at assisting the reader to grasp three key requirements:

• Study and understand creative thinking in advertising practice
• Recognize the importance of working collaboratively
• Understand professionalism and best practice in creative advertising

CREATIVE THINKING

One of the main requirements for the advertising industry is creative thinking, no matter which part of the industry you enter. Idea generation inevitably means countless hours and days spent staring blankly into space trying to be creative. There is no quick fix. It is necessary to find ways to cope with dead ends, criticism, frustration and boredom. If you are a student who needs tutors to supply you with 'correct answers' then this industry is probably not right for you. This is not mathematics. There are usually a number of answers that can be reached that could be great. Finding that original thought is the challenge.

Many students embark on advertising courses believing that they can 'just do it'. This is because the professional advertiser makes it appear so effortless. An idea fits so naturally with a brand or product that anyone could have thought of it. Except they cannot.

Thinking creatively, like anything, requires practice. It is easy to believe that thinking is a bit like running; you just get up and go. This is fine if all you want is fun, but it is not all that you need to do for a career choice. We all understand that running competitively takes practice, early mornings, late nights, challenging yourself, disappointments, doing it when you do not want to, continuing when you have used the last of your energy, starting over – in other words, discipline. There is often an assumption that creative thinking should not require all this effort, it should just come easily; after all, we have been thinking all our lives so far. However, in order to succeed in this industry we need to apply the runner's discipline and develop our creative muscles.

Advertising is a good choice for people that like to challenge their thinking, but not so good for those that like easy answers. Consider this honestly before setting out on this path.

CREATIVE PARTNERSHIPS

This is one of the few professions that in many countries operates in creative partnerships. Find out if this is the case in your country. If it is then you need to start looking for a creative partner as you will not be hired as a single person but as a team.

Think carefully about yourself and the type of person that you can work with; in the same way that many good friendships would not make a good marriage, so many good friendships would not make a good collaborative partnership. It may be best, when you first start trying to find a partner, to do some quick creative projects with different people to see whom you gel with.

'I think a good recipe would be: two creative minds, humbleness, some sense of professionalism and the right personal chemistry.'

MIA ROBERTSSON, COPYWRITER, FAMILJENPANGEA, STOCKHOLM

I went into the industry partnered up with one of my best friends. We had a common language and a set of shared jokes and references. We also had licence to get fed up with each other and lose our tempers yet still know that we would be friends at the end of the day. Advertising is a highly pressurized industry and choosing your partner is one of the most important decisions you will make.

You will need to have skills that complement each other's, with enough common ground to be able to have meaningful conversations. A shared sense of humour is a lifesaver, as are similar political and moral views. Ads can be risqué in all sorts of ways and if you are both not comfortable in what you are creating then your partnership will ultimately fail.

You need to value each other's input without one always trying to have the upper hand. Listening is key to any relationship, and in this partnership you actually have to hear what the other person is saying and try to develop it further, not just spend your time waiting to express your own ideas. Being honest yet tactful is another valuable skill to develop, as sometimes your partner's idea might not be great but they may be stuck on it: find ways to suggest that they could come back to it later but in the meantime they should look at some other thoughts.

'First of all, you need to feel great with your teammate. You spend lots of hours with them. So you have to be sure that they are a good person, besides having good creative skills. I can't imagine working with a bad person. Second of all there must be a confidence in the team. Sometimes during the creative process you can say things that sound really stupid, so you need someone who can listen and remove the stupidity out of what you said to extract what's worthwhile. Third: you need someone with the same passion as you.'

MARIO CRUDELE, SENIOR COPYWRITER, PONCE BUENOS AIRES

Even within a team there will be times when your partner is ill or on holiday and you will be required to answer briefs on your own or to team up with someone else in a similar position. At times I've been teamed up with someone I didn't know and this can be great fun. You can't become so dependent on a partner that you can no longer work without them. It can be quite liberating coming up with ideas on your own. However, most people who work in creative teams understand that the sum total of the team creates more than the parts it is made from.

'I don't want to see two individuals in a team — I want to see the potential of the third person that they make when together.'

JUSTIN TINDALL, GROUP EXECUTIVE CREATIVE DIRECTOR, LEO BURNETT LONDON

> **TASK**
> Conduct a personal audit. What are your strengths and your weaknesses? Be honest. Are you someone that starts ideas or finishes them? Do you quickly understand a brief or are you good at pitching an idea? Identify the areas where you could use some help and see if the people that you are considering partnering up with supply those skills.

As with any relationship, you have to work at it. If you take each other for granted, do not respect each other or would rather not be in the same room as each other, you need to find a new partner. Even within a good relationship there are times when one of you wants to work and the other one does not or has a prior engagement. Matching diaries, energy levels and interest requires perseverance and flexibility from both parties. If you want to work with each other you should be able to find a way to compromise; if not you may need to reconsider your choice of partner.

PROFESSIONALISM

An essential thing to remember is that advertising is part of business and consequently you will spend large portions of your working life working with people in suits who look at figures, sales and logistics dispassionately. They understand that the jobs of countless other people and the profits of their company rest on their choices and they will act accordingly. It is important that you take this element of your career choice just as seriously as everything else. Though you may spend most of your time in jeans and a T-shirt, you are nonetheless a business person, supplying creative solutions to other business people. This needs to be reflected in your behaviour and presentation and through an understanding of the purpose of advertising in business. Balancing these requirements with excellence in creativity is not an easy challenge but it can be done with a positive attitude, perseverance, tenacity, an ability to take criticism and a willingness to constantly learn new things.

HOW THE BOOK IS STRUCTURED

PART ONE_____

CHAPTER 1 - THE BUSINESS OF ADVERTISING begins by exploring advertising as part of business.

CHAPTER 2 – THE DEVELOPMENT OF ADVERTISING looks at advertising history, the emergence of 'creatives', current trends, and how we 'read' adverts.

CHAPTER 3 – A BRANDED WORLD introduces readers to the fundamentals of understanding what a brand is and the importance of developing tone of voice.

PART TWO_____

CHAPTER 4 – STARTING A CONVERSATION investigates how research into consumer behaviour is used to develop a strategic insight.

CHAPTER 5 – THINKING OF WHAT TO SAY introduces readers to idea creation

CHAPTER 6 – HOW WILL YOU SAY IT? This chapter explains how different types of media are applied in practice and looks at the impact of different media on advertising campaigns.

PART THREE_____

CHAPTER 7 – CRAFTING YOUR IDEAS covers skills building, focuses on how we can utilize the cultural cues that unite us and how we can craft ideas in copy and art direction. Also takes a look at why particular software is used in the industry, with examples of student work.

CHAPTER 8 – EXECUTING THE EXECUTIONS explores presenting to and working with others on an advertising campaign and in a professional capacity.

CHAPTER 9 – CAREER PLANS details the skills and competencies required of those seeking a career in creative advertising, with a number of tips on creating a portfolio and how to get a career in the industry.

A 2012 ad by Brazil's Z+ Comunicação for Baruel foot deodorant.

WHO IS THIS BOOK FOR?

Advertising has always been a competitive profession and it is becoming increasingly so. In the past people could become creatives after pursuing other careers and having some life experience. Today it is much more common practice to take in graduates.

While there are multiple undergraduate paths to an advertising career, there are only a handful of crossover texts. On the market a number of specialist books are available that explore marketing, research, media theory, design and copywriting. Also available are a variety of interesting and vibrant memoirs from great advertising figures, and beautiful books tracking advertising through history. More recently there have been some useful books looking at how to generate advertising ideas and how to break into the industry. Books can also be found that critique advertising, branding and capitalism, explaining theory as distinct from practice.

When I began teaching I felt that what was missing was a book that presented an overview, that drew in some of these various strands and presented a rounder picture of what the advertising industry is and how creative work is made. In reading through this text you will see how the remit of advertising has changed from the stereotype of a 30-second television ad. Unfortunately, in providing such an overview, I cannot pursue every avenue of enquiry in each area of advertising, so to this end I have included further reading for each chapter at the end of the book. Readers might think that I have overlooked some great campaigns, but in certain cases clients and agencies have been unable to track down historical ads, or an agency and client have parted company and neither has access to the original work. At other times, ads are omitted because they did not particularly resonate with me; this does not make those ads any less significant, it is simply that every compilation is subjective.

Advertising crosses a number of academic disciplines and there are a variety of courses that offer a way into the industry. There are some stand-alone courses in advertising offered at university/college level as either a degree, MA or portfolio classes. A streamed degree is also an option, such as within design, where students opt into advertising in their second year. Introductory courses to the field are offered at many universities either as a short course or a module. A number of advertising students reading this book will not be on a degree but in independent workshops or company schemes. Some students may be on business and marketing courses but specializing in advertising. Others that enter advertising, but perhaps go into planning or account-handling departments, may have pursued degrees in humanities or social sciences, and still others will have entered production departments through media studies. There is a rich variety of people who enter the profession and a myriad things to discover and learn about communication for business. It is this exploration of creativity, technology and psychology that makes the job so rewarding.

'Creatives must always be aware of the flow and form of communication media. This ever-changing and reformatting phenomenon inspires us to explore new design thinking across varying channels and technologies. How we communicate today may be different tomorrow. Educating the new designers and creatives to these possibilities is at the heart of Greenwich philosophy.'

NICKIE HIRST, DESIGN FUTURES PROGRAMME LEADER, UNIVERSITY OF GREENWICH, LONDON

THE
BUSINESS
OF
ADVERTISING

1

1 THE BUSINESS OF ADVERTISING

THE CURRENT CONTEXT

Advertising is often seen as an extension of the entertainment industry, and in many ways it is, in that directors, artists, designers and writers work in it. Work is made in media that are viewed and noticed by huge numbers of people. It can have a certain amount of glamour, and a great number of motivated, intelligent and creative people are drawn towards it. But advertising is also a business.

An advertising agency can be large or small. It can be a traditional agency or a new hybrid communications agency. Whatever the size, it is a company that delivers a product to others. Like other businesses it is interested in profit, efficiencies, processes, partner businesses, quality of product, distribution and suppliers. It has a long-term strategy, competitors, a target market, internal communications, PR and branding.

The advertising industry generates enormous profits and creates many jobs, and other companies invest large sums of money in it.

When considering advertising, critics tend to think about it in terms of exploitation and profit, business people in terms of predictability and sales, and creative people in terms of ideas and craft. None of these positions in isolation is helpful if you want to understand how advertising works.

Advertising is all around us, even in a magazine in a piazza in Italy.

2010	COUNTRY	ADSPEND	2013	COUNTRY	ADSPEND
1	USA	151,519	1	USA	164,844
2	Japan	43,267	2	Japan	45,300
3	Germany	24,631	3	China	34,236
4	China	22,606	4	Germany	26,508
5	UK	18,047	5	UK	19,678
6	Brazil	14,243	6	Brazil	18,662
7	France	12,875	7	France	13,825
8	Italy	10,753	8	Russia	12,228
9	Australia	9,394	9	Italy	11,734
10	Canada	8,867	10	Australia	10,981

ABOVE
Our exposure to TV
advertising begins early.

LEFT
Top ten ad markets,
in US$ million at
current prices.
Currency conversion
at 2009 average
rates. Advertising
statistics courtesy of
ZenithOptimedia.

LEFT
Traditional and digital
billboards in the
Shinjuku district of Tokyo.

BOTTOM LEFT
Storefront advertising in
a shopping centre
in Singapore.

BELOW
We see advertising even
while using Facebook.

BOTTOM RIGHT
Times Square, New York,
is well known for its
advertising hoardings.

THE MARKETING FAMILY

Advertising sits under the umbrella of marketing, although it is often the only marketing activity that the public are aware of. Marketing is any activity whose purpose is to sell the products or services made by a company, and includes distribution of product, agreement on promotional activity, staff training and product improvements, as well as more consumer-focused activities. There are many different methods and tools available to market products or services, such as experiential, sponsorship, PR, websites, social networking, events and advertising. Some of these marketing activities now fall under the expanding auspices of advertising, particularly in 360-degree communications companies that are multifunctional, hybrid businesses, though the larger traditional advertising agencies are also adapting their approach (see Chapter 6). For the marketing manager these activities form part of an integrated marketing plan designed not only to get their product or service across in the most effective way but also to make the most of their budget. Because many advertising agencies now use a mix of marketing activities it is important to understand the different elements of marketing.

PACKAGING
Packaging occupies a rather unusual position in the marketing family as it not only provides a surface, or medium, on which a company can tell consumers about the goods inside – for instance whether they are luxury, value or fun items – but it is often integral to the product. It is hard to imagine shampoo, cereal or coffee without packaging.

EXPERIENTIAL MARKETING
Advertising isn't necessarily the best way of getting across what a brand stands for to potential customers. It depends entirely on the brand and what kind of impression they want to give – branding will be covered in greater depth in Chapter 3. Brands focus a lot of their activities on environments, experiences and events, where consumers directly interact with products, rather than television, newspapers and magazines. Sometimes it is not the product but the product's attributes, such as lightness or fun, that will be the main focus. An experience can be created that is all about this lightness, perhaps involving trampolines and balloons. Alternatively, talking to consumers about the need to protect tooth enamel from fruit acids could involve a

'That's the nature of experiential stuff, you're not pushing it on people, you're letting them stumble across it, play with it and have fun with it.'

AARON SEYMOUR-ANDERSON, ART DIRECTOR, FALLON MINNEAPOLIS

stunt in which large fruits appear to attack customers in shops. These experiences and events can be hugely involving and attract a lot of media attention – the UK-based flash mobs for the T-Mobile communications company that can be viewed on YouTube are a good example of this. The opportunity to get involved with media that is more theatrical and artistic has started to be explored by many agencies.

The 2009 John Lewis 'Harmony House' experiential interactive installation, by Adam & Eve, London.

SPONSORSHIP

Sponsoring can enhance brand image and shape consumers' attitudes towards a product. Client organizations use sponsorship to support those events that they feel can influence consumer opinions.

In 2008 Puma became one of the sponsors for the Volvo Ocean Race, one of the world's toughest sailing races. This event represented the ideal global platform to promote Puma's first ever range of sailing and lifestyle wear. They entered a yacht, *Il Mostro* – 'the monster' in Italian – named after an iconic Puma training shoe. *Il Mostro* was designed by London-based design agency GBH to look like a running shoe with the Puma formstripe on one side, a textured red shoe strap on the other and the sole wrapping around the bottom. During the following nine months, the 11-strong crew visited ten countries, finishing in second place. With their legitimate involvement in race activities, Puma used the 11 stopover ports to stage 'Puma City', designed by Lot-Ek and GBH. This unique retail space utilized 24 shipping containers that could be assembled and disassembled to travel to each port in time with the race. Over five million people watched *Il Mostro* and visited the Volvo Ocean Race villages at stopover ports. Sales on one day in the Boston Puma City were greater than any daily sale in any Puma store ever. Media coverage exceeded $50 million in advertising value. In 2012, the 2008 version of *Il Mostro* was auctioned while GBH worked on designing a new yacht with Puma maintaining sponsorship to build upon the interest generated.

TASK
You have to promote a clothing range of skateboarding shorts. Choose three marketing activities that you need to utilize to launch this product onto the market and write down the advantages they each bring.

The 2008–10 Puma sponsorship of *Il Mostro* in the Volvo Ocean Race. The GBH design made the yacht stand out from its competitors.

PUBLIC RELATIONS

The hugely influential marketing strategists Al and Laura Ries, who have acted as consultants to many Fortune 500 companies, suggested in 2002 that clever PR will change the future of advertising. This can be seen when you consider how subtle and clever a good PR campaign can be. SK-II is a brand of premium skincare products that was originally developed by Procter and Gamble in Japan. The scientists from SK-II started studying the skincare properties of yeast in the 1990s after observing the youthful-looking hands of elderly sake brewers. This led to the creation of a 'myth' that Japanese monks had discovered their particular serum as a by-product of the sake-making process, a story that instantly creates an image in the mind's eye that is considerably more appealing than the thought of scientists studying a refined, purified strain of yeast. Selected beauty magazines ran the story as breaking news, giving it a credibility that an advert could not achieve. A brand that had comparatively little exposure in the mid-1990s became one of the world's most expensive skincare brands. The PR worked so well I went straight out and bought the serum after reading an article! What is important to remember is that the story itself is true – a group of Japanese monks did have more youthful hands through handling this material, even if the product we buy is not created through this process. The implied narrative of the monks' discovery leading to the product's subsequent release into the world is fictional.

SK-II serum. The packaging and typography is kept minimal to keep with the 'Zen'-like feel.

ADVERTISING

Making a human connection is primarily
what is paid for in advertising, perhaps
more so than in some of the other types of
marketing activity previously mentioned.
Some critics of advertising see this point,
where previously nonexistent meanings and
connections are made between the product
and the consumer's life, as exploitative
and cynical. However, as a creative, the
individuality of your connections is what
makes for interesting campaigns, is
ultimately what will get you a job and is
what keeps the advertising business going.

TEAMWORK

The business of idea creation in advertising
is a team process. In many parts of the
world this often happens in the collaborative
partnership of a creative team – a copywriter
and an art director. However, traditional team
structures are giving way to more flexible
working. In many countries people are
employed as individuals. In some agencies,
a senior team comes up with the big idea
and other teams work on the executions.
In other agencies there is cooperative work
in larger groups, separating into smaller
teams when it comes to specific executions.
The advantage is that this collaborative
approach can result in a large number of
ideas being generated quickly. However,
a large team can also be a good place for
weaker members to hide.

    The larger agencies worldwide still
favour the traditional creative team, finding
it a predictable and effective way of
generating ideas. Ideally the creative team
will have developed confidence in working
with each other, will be supportive of each
other and will present a united front to the
rest of the agency and clients. There is truth
to the idea that there is strength in numbers.

    Whether your agency does creative
work in teams or people work individually,
eventually the project has to be discussed
with and agreed by other members of
the agency.

Art director Carole
Davids drawing up
scamps.

Creative team
at Leo Burnett.

The usual structure of a
traditional advertising
agency.

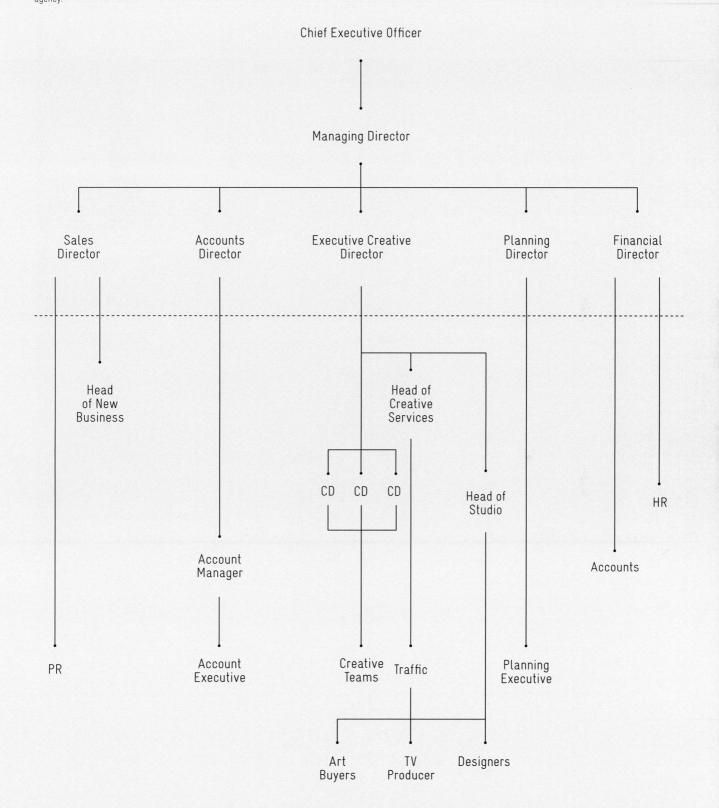

THE LARGER CREATIVE TEAM

On the creative floor a junior team may start by showing their work to a group head. This is a more senior person who has specialist knowledge of that particular account. If the group head agrees this work then it can go on to be presented to the creative director. Sometimes, depending on the size of the agency, this group head position is given to a creative director (CD) who, in turn, works for an executive creative director (ECD).

If there is a more senior team or person willing to act as a mentor it is worth showing ideas to them when you think they have potential. You do not always get the response that you want but it is better to know that something is not working and have a chance to come up with a better idea than it is to take a selection of bad ideas to your creative director.

The creative director or the executive creative director is in charge of the standard of creative output of the agency. Any campaign, or indeed any single small press ad, will have to be agreed by this person. They are the person who hires and fires on the creative floor. It is therefore important to establish some kind of rapport with them.

The creative floor does not work in isolation. When you start in an agency you are given a brief to answer. This does not simply arrive on your desk as a piece of paper – you will be briefed in person by the strategy and account-handling departments and by a traffic person or project manager from the creative services department.

TOP
Creative team, Ian Mitchell and Kevin Travis, presenting to creative director Garry Munns at Arc Worldwide.

ABOVE
Creative team briefing at the Leo Burnett agency: Anna Sweet and Pansy Aung with account director Rob Cooling.

CREATIVE SERVICES

There are a number of roles that are part of the creative services department. The purpose of creative services is to enable the creative department to complete work to schedule. The head of creative services is responsible, alongside the creative director, for deciding which creative gets which brief. They arrange briefings, formal meetings with the CD or group head, and they will personally come and check on how you are doing and see if you need any help or information.

'For me a team will not only be top of class in creative excellence but will appreciate time management, adherance to deadlines, collaborative working, appreciation of budgets, big business thinking and the economic environment.'

STEVE FREEDMAN, GROUP CREATIVE SERVICES DIRECTOR, LEO BURNETT LONDON

TRAFFIC/PROJECT MANAGERS
Traffic, or project managers, are there to manage your time and see each job through to completion. If you establish a good relationship with the traffic department they will let you know when choice briefs are coming in. These might be more interesting briefs allocated to more senior teams that you can do in your own time when you are not finishing work specifically given to you by the agency. Cracking these extra briefs could get you noticed by the creative director, and potentially by the awards panels that are the mark of success in advertising.

If you consistently fail to meet deadlines or cannot be relied upon to complete work to a good standard then traffic will pass this information on to the CD. Once the client has approved the work, traffic often supervise the production, art buying and studio work.

THE PRODUCTION TEAM
The production team is made up of television and radio producers, who will be assigned to you by traffic. You will naturally develop favourites; producers that have a great relationship with production companies, or ones that are mad and fun, or a producer that can always be relied upon to have taxis waiting when necessary. Your favourite may not be the agency favourite or the one that is assigned to you; however, whoever you find yourself with, they are your link to the production company and post-production facilities (editing companies) that you will be using.

THE ART BUYER
The art buyer deals with stills imagery for press, posters and any other application where a photographer, illustrator and typographer are needed. They know and have relationships with a great number of image makers through the huge variety of ads that they have created for all the teams within your agency and any previous agencies.

THE STUDIO
Depending on the size and nature of the agency there is often a studio. This is where designers, illustrators and retouchers will sit. If there is a studio you will inevitably end up in it, as that is where all still imagery is finished.

FROM THE TOP
Leo Burnett group executive creative director Justin Tindall organizes the week's creative schedule, with creative services director Steve Freedman and marketing director Katie Lee.

TV producer Lou Pegg.

Art buyers meeting with a photographers' agent.

The design studio: designer James Long at work.

STRATEGY AND CLIENT MANAGEMENT DEPARTMENTS

THE PLANNING DEPARTMENT

The account planner is in charge of the strategy behind the brief. The role of the planner is to understand the lives, aspirations and purchasing intentions of the intended audience for the product or service and to understand the product or service itself. Planning is research-based and many planners were once researchers themselves. A planner needs to make sense of research and turn it into something that the creative may be able to use to make a connection with their audience.

In a briefing it is often the planners who will make the most insightful comments, the kind of comments that can light that little spark in a creative's head. Often creatives have a lot in common with planners because many creatives are also great strategists.

ACCOUNT HANDLING

Account handlers have the difficult balancing act of keeping both clients and creative teams happy, which often involves relaying information that the other side does not want to hear. They represent the client within the agency. If the client is unhappy they might leave the agency. Sometimes it is not a change in creative direction that splits a client from their agency but a lack of chemistry between the account team and their opposite numbers at the client organization. This relationship is at the heart of the account handler's role, and they also manage the process and the budgets.

A vital element of the account handler's job is presenting creative ideas to clients. Many clients want essentially non-creative advertising and a good account handler will brief the creative department about that to begin with so that no time is wasted. Meanwhile the account handler works behind the scenes to open more creative opportunities with that client. Some very good creatives started out as account handlers, because they understand the strength of good ideas and understand that they are in the business of selling.

MEDIA PLANNING AND BUYING

Media space such as billboards or radio is bought and its use planned by an independent company before a creative brief is written (see Chapter 4). Often the client will have a relationship with a media buyer for a number of their brands. This media buyer may also work for rival agencies or sister agencies under the same parent/holding company. For the client this allows for economies of scale in terms of purchasing media space, as the buyer can leverage beneficial deals with media owners for multiple clients. High-spending clients will have their media choices decided a year in advance based on data collated from previous years. To an advertising creative this can feel odd because the media choice comes before the creative idea.

The media buyer has to think about the brand personality; should they shout their message or whisper it? Is there going to be a rich variety of media directing consumers from one to another? Will everything start at the same time? Will it be all outdoor posters in urban locations or on bus sides? This level of creative planning can make a creative campaign (see Chapter 6).

Leo Burnett account director Lizzie Dixie.

CLIENTS

Client companies come in all shapes and sizes, from huge multinationals with multiple brands and products to small local chains or charities. When it is time for awards the smallest clients of all will appear, such as window cleaners, searched out by the creatives themselves in order to be able to create interesting advertising. These small clients are usually happy to have any advertising at all and would not ordinarily be able to afford it, and so are likely to let the creative be as 'creative' as they wish.

Within a client organization, the advertising agency talks to the marketing manager, who is essentially the face of the client; often the agency will never meet the MDs or CEOs who make the final decisions on a campaign. The marketing manager is responsible for selling the work internally. Many MDs feel sceptical about marketing activity in general, even their internal marketing activity, wanting to see ROI (return on investment) in hard data.

'I think the struggle that a marketing department has within the client organization is that they're talking to an MD who's done an MBA who knows more about marketing than their brand manager does and looks for the contribution marketing makes to profits.'

NICK STRINGER, STRATEGIC BUSINESS LEAD, BBH LONDON

Some client companies have a strict hierarchy and no one down the line will approve brave advertising because it risks their job – brave advertising will sometimes make fun of the product or be extremely subtle in its use. Often clients think that creatives are interested only in awards and not in improving sales, and this is true of a number of creatives.

'The worst part is when the client has a strong idea of what they want, but cannot describe their vision early in the process.'

MATTIAS CEDERFELDT, ART DIRECTOR, POND, STOCKHOLM

A good client can create a great campaign. They are often aware of the innovative ways in which their competitors are reaching their audience and want to be part of it.

A single integrated brand message through all media is arguably the best way of communicating effectively to a target audience. This involves a number of agencies working in partnership with each other. The best clients understand that they are the reference point for all their marketing agencies; they are able to make decisions and are good at communicating their objectives to all the agencies involved. They understand that while their agencies all work for them they are also businesses in their own right and will each want a bit more of the others' work. These relationships need to be managed by the client.

A GLOBAL BUSINESS

As advertising developed, small advertising agencies often grew into networks – that is, a number of agencies working under the same name and with the same ethos over several cities or countries. Now we have big global owners that have swallowed up not just individual agencies but whole networks, and we also have huge merged networks. The largest owners at the time of writing are Omnicom, Interpublic, WPP, Havas, Hakuhodo and Dentsu. To give an example, WPP owns the global networks Young & Rubicam Brands, Ogilvy Group, JWT and the Grey Group, among many others. This system provides relative financial safety to the agencies within these global companies as they are backed by large funds. In the choppy waters of advertising, which are tied to economic well-being, this can be the only way to weather financial storms. It can also have an effect on the work: for example, a situation could arise where DDB, AMV and TBWA, all owned by Omnicom, were all pitching for the same account. Omnicom would not need to be concerned, as they would gain financially whichever agency won. This can lead to a lack of drive from the ultimate owners for great creative work.

For the multinational client a multinational network arrangement suits. The fact that their advertising agency is owned by an even larger company may have little impact on their choices, or they may feel reassured that the agency will be able to operate in any market through sister agencies or networks. In terms of the work, the brand management team can agree a strategy and creative campaign locally and feel assured that it will be implemented globally. They will feel that the particular things they want communicated will be communicated in the way that they want, with the brand colours and tone of voice. It feels like a controllable process.

CREATIVE DIFFERENCE

It is pointless to pretend that there are not still some glaring inequalities within advertising agencies. In the vast majority of agencies across the world there is still a disproportionate number of 30-year-old and younger men working in the creative departments. In the Western world they are almost exclusively white. A late-night, laddish culture persists in many creative departments that can make working difficult if you do not fit that profile. There can be a general perception that it is better to stay late and be seen, even if only emailing, than to go home. However, as any good creative director would tell you, you need to have a life outside the office in order to put something of interest into your adverts.

'Because of the way this business is set up, the placement system in particular, you tend to get a lot of richer, middle-class junior teams, almost exclusively white. At this stage, there'll be a reasonable amount of female teams, but as soon as they reach middleweight level they seem to mysteriously disappear and get replaced by younger versions. It's difficult to think of any female teams who've made it to the very top. Senior female creatives who negotiate four day weeks and don't socialize regularly tend to be the subject of a fair amount of bitching from their male counterparts.'

ADAM TUCKER, CREATIVE DIRECTOR, LEO BURNETT LONDON

Women are often marginalized to 'women's products', effectively excluding them from the accounts most likely to allow great creative work, and therefore awards. Senior men tend to judge awards and select the output from creative departments. They also select who works there. Many male creatives do not appreciate the ads that women write or that female consumers like, which is curious considering which gender does the majority of the shopping – in Britain 80 per cent of all purchasing decisions are made by women. In 2005 *Adweek* reported that in the United States only four out of all agencies had flagship offices with women as creative directors. Worldwide this is slowly improving, with such agencies as JEH United in Thailand led by the well-respected female creative director Jureeporn Thaidumrong, Adam & Eve/DDB UK by Emer Stamp, and SapientNitro New Zealand by Nancy Hartley.

African American men and women can also find themselves marginalized, but this time to the 'ethnic market'. In 2009 American advertising agencies faced legal action over the findings of a report showing that black college graduates earned only 80 cents for every dollar earned by white staff. In 2006 in England just under 7 per cent of all creative departments was made up of people of colour.

Further up the agency ladder there is even less representation. Until relatively recently, many agencies in Asia and Africa had creative directors shipped in from North America or Europe. However, this is changing – for example, Piyush Pandey is the Executive Chairman and National Creative Director of Ogilvy & Mather India. In 2008 Ogilvy & Mather was the first ad agency both in the United States and Europe to appoint an Asian ad man, Tham Khai Meng, as its worldwide creative director. It would have been hard to refute his credentials, as revenue at Ogilvy & Mather Asia-Pacific had doubled to $500 million a year during his tenure as regional creative director. In 2011 Global Advertising Strategies, a leading cross-cultural marketing agency, hired the highly respected African American Ola Kudu as creative director. As an agency it seeks to speak to a variety of cultural and social identities of consumers worldwide.

'When I first got into advertising, I was aware that I was one of only a handful of European creatives of African Caribbean origin. Now, thankfully, the industry is much more diverse, with many ethnic men and women, working across all roles and genres.'

JON DANIEL, EXECUTIVE CREATIVE DIRECTOR, EBB&FLOW, LONDON

As people get older within the advertising industry other problems arise. Combining work with having a family can be very difficult, for men as well as women. Some creative departments make it tougher by demanding physical presence rather than allowing their creatives to use modern media channels to work; this is rather surprising for an industry that prides itself on understanding how modern people need to live and work. However, there are encouraging signs that a number of agencies are moving with the times and letting creatives work a day from home, or fewer days in the week.

Many of today's creative directors are relatively young. They have grown up with modern media and like the idea of its effective integration into working practice. These CDs are likely to have young families themselves and have a mixed social circle that includes men, women and people of a variety of races, and do not see why a diverse group of people should not be employed. They understand that they will get a richer, more varied and more culturally appropriate range of symbols, references and signs in the adverts produced by their creative department. This allows for better, more effective communication to a variety of target markets, which ultimately generates more profit.

THE BUSINESS OF BUSINESS

The business of business is to generate profit and create better working lives for all. Companies that make more money will invest part of their profit into their workforce and their company. The more profit is generated and ploughed back into society and workers' lives, the more extra money ordinary people will have to spend. This is what underpins our Western free market economy.

A successful advertising campaign can give a product or brand the edge it needs to increase profits and, following the ideals of the liberal economy, this is for the benefit of all. It seems so straightforward, so why isn't it?

CAPITALISM

To understand advertising as a business, it is worth examining briefly the economic system from which the advertising industry developed. Capitalism is an economic system in which the production and distribution of goods and services for profit is privately owned by individuals or corporations. Goods and services are defined as products.

For the greater part of the twentieth century there were worldwide changes in political, economic and religious governance of states; for example, changes from dictatorships to socialist states, and democratic movements and civil protests that formed new independent states. These upheavals kept the general public aware of the economic systems in which we live and trade, at least on a surface level. As the century came to a close many states had either converted to capitalism or engaged with global capitalism. Capitalism has become so widely established that it remains largely unquestioned by the developed world. Students often enter higher education unaware that they are part of this structure; creatives entering advertising agencies rarely give it any thought. The economic and moral criticism levelled against capitalism, mostly around issues of greed and cultural colonialism, and thence against advertising, therefore comes as a surprise.

The German philosopher, historian and revolutionary socialist Karl Marx, in his wide-ranging work the *Grundrisse* (rewritten and published in 1867 as *Capital*), offered what is still one of the clearest critiques of capitalism. Contrary to popular belief, Marx was not against capitalism in its simplest form – when goods are produced as a 'commodity', labour is used as a 'commodity' and the new goods are purchased as a 'commodity', and an exchange value is agreed based on the amount of the commodity called 'labour' used to create it. For example, an apple pie may be exchanged for five apples. Yet Marx identified the potential for imbalance in a capitalist system resulting in exploitation when the value of the labour of the people producing the goods was no longer factored into the exchange value. The exchange value then becomes set by people speculating on how much others are willing to pay for a given thing. Hedge funds and other financial institutions that speculate on the market consider that the act of speculation harms no one and creates economic growth. Marx argued that profit cannot materialize from nowhere: any money created must be taken from somewhere else in the process – from the labourers that create the commodity in the first place. The desperate living conditions of some of the world's poorest people have been linked, rightly in some cases and no doubt wrongly in others, to capitalism and the effects of profiteering.

The anti-capitalist movement, encompassing a broad collective of ideas and attitudes that oppose capitalism, picks up on the extremes of global capitalism, pointing to countries where daily wages have remained the same or actually decreased while corporations seem to have ever-increasing profits. Few people would argue that there should not be improvements in global labour rights and environmental conditions, though some argue that it is governments that are responsible for solving the larger social problems.

The anti-globalization/anti-capitalism agendas not only cover wages and conditions but also embrace the idea that society should not be based on consumption. They take the view that consumers are manipulated into buying unnecessary goods set at whatever prices multinationals speculate will be most profitable. The Canadian sociologist Andrew Wernick termed this 'promotional culture', suggesting a link between our contentment and our consumption. Other critics, such as the French socialist and philosopher Pierre Bourdieu, suggest that as people we now know how to differentiate ourselves from others only through our consumption. This position suggests that the advertising of products does not help the consumer make a purchase based on rational commodity-based information but merely seduces them. This creates a work–spend cycle that people are locked into so that they are always consumers, unable to resist the power of advertising.

The presumption of greed, manipulation, overindulgence, capitalist excess and general bad behaviour follows advertising around, but there are also benign services that advertising provides, such as public service films and broadcasts financed by the multinationals. These include HIV/AIDS awareness initiatives and Nike's 'Girl Effect' campaign to tackle female poverty.

'There are some cases when advertising can do something really responsible for society; a good case that comes to my mind is the Tap Water Project.'

MARIO CRUDELE, SENIOR COPYWRITER, PONCE BUENOS AIRES.

There are also specific businesses whose activities have social benefit, such as *The Zimbabwean*, with its efforts to remain a free-speaking paper. The purpose of its advertising is to raise revenue, and its recent campaign (see page 129) was paid for rather than created without payment (pro bono), yet such campaigns are obviously beneficial regardless of where one might sit on the issue of consumption.

> **TASK**
> In small groups think of five advantages and five disadvantages of global capitalism. Back up your discussion with hard facts.

OPPOSITE
An anti-capitalism march. There have been a number of marches in cities around the world in recent years.

SEAT LEON.
WHERE HEART OF RACER MEETS TECHNO FREAK.

SCAN QR CODE WITH YOUR MOBILE DEVICE AND DISCOVER ALL HIDDEN
FEATURES OF SEAT WEBSITE.

MEMBER OF THE VOLKSWAGEN GROUP

ABOVE

Adverts are created to entice people to buy more products. These ads highlight new features that some argue don't need to be developed. Grey Argentina created this print ad, entitled 'Bold', in 2011 for Cover Girl mascara, highlighting how thick they make your eyelashes.

RIGHT

The 2011 press campaign by Brazil's Longplay 360 makes a feature of the camera's waterproof and shatterproof qualities.

OPPOSITE

Jandl developed the 2011 QR code press campaign for the SEAT Leon, emphasizing the product's technological features.

Strong resistance stands up rugged weather easily.

FUJiFILM

• Waterproof to 3 meters • Shock and fall-resistant to 1.5 meters • Resistant to cold weather to 14 °F • Dust-resistant

FINEPIX XP10
More than you imagined.

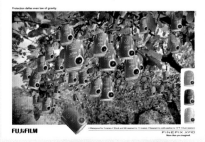

CREATIVITY

'I get paid to sit and think all day. I sit and scribble random thoughts. I type and I draw. I brainstorm with my mates. I go on shoots all over the world with brilliant directors, photographers and designers. Then when all that's done I see my work on telly, in store or in magazines. Can you really think of a better job?'

MADELEINE MORRIS, CREATIVE DIRECTOR, GREY LONDON

For visual people, ideas people and storytellers, advertising can offer a highly creative and fulfilling career.

Unlike in many jobs, the work involved in advertising can be different every day. As a creative you could be brainstorming one day and on the other side of the world on a shoot the next. As an account person you could be talking to clients on a video conference in the morning and managing an enormous budget in the afternoon.

As a planner you could be investigating the brand preferences of a particular group on Monday, and on Tuesday you could be sitting behind a two-way mirror listening to a completely different group of people. As a media planner you are confronted with new developments in technology and media opportunities with increasing regularity. It is an industry in which you are challenged to think in creative ways all the time.

It is also an industry in which you can craft your work. In fact, the greatest proportion of the money spent on campaigns, after the huge media spend has been deducted, is on the physical creation of the work. There are few opportunities for a working life in the creative arts where an ability to draw, use colour, create texture, play with composition and create narratives will be paid for. Unsurprisingly, therefore, there is a huge number of visual, eloquent, thoughtful and culturally switched on people working in advertising agencies.

Who could argue with the value of advertising for public information? This integrated 2009 advertising campaign for the Metropolitan Police by Abbott Mead Vickers encouraged participants to 'choose a different ending' to the violent option.

THE DEVELOPMENT OF ADVERTISING

2

2 THE DEVELOPMENT OF ADVERTISING

EARLY ADVERTISING

Rather than being a modern phenomenon, as is often thought, advertising dates back to early mercantile societies. The ancient Egyptians inscribed sales messages on papyrus, while in Pompeii, the Roman town that disappeared under the volcanic ash of Mount Vesuvius in AD 79, there is evidence on a wall of early tourism advertising. Many critics of marketing imagine the ideal society to be without advertising and promotion, but it is actually hard to find times in which some form of it was not practised.

Before mass advertising could begin there needed to be significant developments in both technology and society. In China the invention of paper in the second century AD and the development of woodblock printing meant that imagery could be reproduced on a stable, easily manufactured surface. The *Diamond Sutra*, printed in China in AD 868, is the oldest surviving printed book. By the eleventh century printing with movable type had been developed in China, and we can see evidence of advertising in the Asia-Pacific region from as far back as the Song Dynasty (960–1260), from which there are still some surviving copper printing plates.

In the thirteenth century the Goryeo Dynasty in Korea invented metal movable type in order to print books, but the technique did not spread as it would in Europe, some two hundred years later, after Johannes Gutenberg invented the printing press around 1439. Gutenberg's invention, based on the technology of screw presses, used a movable type made of metal alloy. During the Renaissance a working screw press could print 3,600 pages a day – a major leap from hand-copying each page. With the spread of the printing press and of paper mills, news sheets began to appear. In 1605 Johann Carolus printed what is widely acknowledged as the first newspaper, in Strasbourg.

The first English newspaper, *The Weekly Newes of London,* was published in 1622, and its first advertisement is said by historian Henry Sampson to have been an ad for the return of a stolen horse. In 1631 came the first weekly newspaper in France, *La Gazette*, created by Théophraste Renaudot. It ran many ads and public announcements. During the Great Plague of London in 1665–66 newspapers carried ads for preventatives and cures.

The inventions of the Industrial Revolution in Britain from the 1750s on, and the huge numbers of people that moved to the cities to service the mass production industries, led to an escalation of mass media and advertising through newspaper production and distribution. As the market began to be dominated by mass-produced goods it became in the interests of businesses to differentiate their products from one another and encourage their use on a larger scale. The urbanization of the population also opened up a market interested in information and gossip, which was catered to by magazines and newspapers. Urbanization also brought many more people into contact with printed words and imagery; while not everyone might have been able to read a book, almost all could follow simple headlines and images.

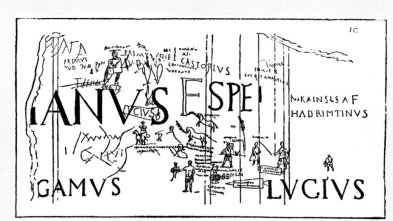

ADVERTISEMENTS ON THE EXCAVATED WALLS OF POMPEII

In 1786 the earliest acknowledged advertising agent, William Taylor of London, advertised himself as 'Agent of the Country Printers, Booksellers etc'. The agency's role was to buy space for adverts that were produced directly by clients. Realizing that there was profit to be made, in 1800 the Englishman James White founded an advertising company, which moved to Fleet Street in London and became R. F. White & Son Ltd. In 1842 the first French advertising agency, Publicis, opened. On the other side of the world Volney B. Palmer opened the first American advertising agency in 1850. Soon after, in 1864, William James Carlton opened an agency in New York, which was bought by his leading salesman, James Walter Thompson, in 1868. It was Thompson who first hired writers and artists to form one of the earliest creative departments in an advertising agency. JWT and Publicis still operate today as two of the leading global communications networks.

Thompson realized that his agency could sell more advertising space if they developed the actual adverts as well. This move to creating adverts within the agency led to greater creativity and increased sales. Strong creative talents such as Stanley Resor and Helen Lansdowne began to stand out. In 1908 the Cincinnati office of JWT opened. Lansdowne was one of the first women to present work to large clients. In 1910 she purportedly increased sales for Woodbury's facial soap by 1,000 per cent with her 'The skin you love to touch' ads. By 1927 Resor's leadership of JWT had led to more than $100 million in billings.

ABOVE
1896 Paul Sescau
Photographe poster
by Toulouse–Lautrec.

RIGHT
Helen Lansdowne's 1911
Woodbury Soap ad for
the J. Walter Thompson
Company.

SOCIAL ADVERTISING

Advertising skills were not only used to sell products but were also used for social ends. In England in the 1910s, Mary Lowndes and Emily Harding Andrews, among others, created dramatic posters for the suffragettes, a politically active group in Britain that lobbied successfully for the right of women to vote.

Social advertising created with a political aim in mind is known as propaganda. Propaganda seeks to change people's views on particular issues in order to facilitate political change. Sometimes this went through advertising agencies but more usually this was work commissioned by government departments from individual designers and illustrators.

With the advent of World War I the advertising poster was enlisted to promote government policies. In Britain in 1914, Alfred Leete created a cover illustration for the *London Opinion* magazine using an image of the Secretary of State for War, Lord Kitchener. This was then turned into recruitment posters for the army using the words 'Your country needs you' and '(Lord Kitchener) Wants You'. The aim of the posters was to persuade, and perhaps emotionally pressurize, the men of Britain to join the army. In 1917 a similar message was used in the United States on James Montgomery Flagg's 'I want you for the U.S. Army' poster, of which there were more than four million copies printed.

In Germany, by the start of World War II in 1939, Adolf Hitler's Reich Ministry of Public Enlightenment and Propaganda employed two thousand people. Its head, Dr Joseph Goebbels, a former journalist, exploited many media, including film, radio, newspapers and poster arts, to deliver Nazi propaganda and influence public opinion. The Propaganda Ministry systematically reinforced the Nazi policy that Jews were second-class citizens and the enemies of ordinary Germans.

The power of advertising to promote political change was used in the Russian Revolution of 1917, which led to the overthrow of the tsars; in the Soviet propagandist posters that followed in the 1930s; and during the Cultural Revolution in China from 1966 to 1976. The changes in both Russia and China were supposed to empower the ordinary person, taking power away from the privileged aristocracy. Common propaganda themes included the new, happier, ideal society, and the struggle itself for this utopian dream, in which workers were portrayed as the heroes. The political leaders of the Soviet Union (Vladimir Lenin, followed by Joseph Stalin), and of China (Mao Zedong), were frequently portrayed in these posters, and as icons they achieved an almost religious significance. This was advertising, but the product was an ideology and the leader a symbol of that ideology. The visual look of these ads has been referenced on many occasions since.

Alfred Leete's 1914 posters for the British army clearly influenced James Montgomery Flagg in 1917 for his American army poster.

Mary Lowndes'
powerful 1912 poster
for the National Union
of Women's Suffrage
Societies, using the
well-established
symbol of Justice to
question the purpose
of excluding women
from the Reform Bill.

LEFT
Modern techniques such as collage were used in this 1931 poster to show the modern revolutionary movement in the USSR.

LEFT
Nazi propaganda, much like its communist counterpart, served to iconise the party leader.

OPPOSITE
Armando Testa of Milan, Italy, uses the symbolism of Socialist revolutionary propaganda in this press campaign for Meltin'Pot clothing.

东方红

毛主席是我們心中的紅太陽 68.9

THE EMERGENCE OF CREATIVES

During World War II, product-based advertising was still formulaic and conservative. It would be changed dramatically by the meeting of two creatives in the American agency William H. Weintraub. At the start of the 1940s, graphic designer Paul Rand and copywriter Bill Bernbach worked together on the brochure 'Mechanized Mules of Victory' for the AutoCar Company of Ardmore, Pennsylvania. Although their working relationship was extremely brief, the creativity generated in this partnership sparked the drive towards creative teams and away from people working in isolation. Rand and Bernbach added to each other's work, enhancing its meaning. They brought strong creativity and visual flair to an industry that had quickly developed conventions for itself. They were conventions that clients liked to follow because it made them feel comfortable, but which were still a hangover from the days of shouting out your wares from a market stall – promotions-led, lacking subtlety and nearly always exaggerated.

Rand was heavily influenced by the fun and play of Modernist movements such as Dada, often mixing collage, typography and photography in his layouts, and the minimalist European aesthetic of the Swiss Style. His compositions were less cluttered and formal than those of his counterparts and surprised his audience. He was keenly aware of the power of creating a 'branded' look, a visual language and tone of voice that could be 'owned' by the brand. His El Producto cigar campaign provides a good example of how a visual territory can be defined and maintained. The cigars are personalized by quirkily drawn hands, feet and accessories.

Bill Bernbach left William H. Weintraub and went on to co-found Doyle Dane Bernbach in 1949. DDB's style marked a step change for advertising, with adverts for Volkswagen® such as 'Think small', created by Helmut Krone and Julian Koenig, and its follow-up, 'Lemon'. These adverts were dramatic because they were not full of hyperbole, they did not shout, they had a sense of humour and they perfectly fused art direction with copy. The client was instrumental in making this campaign great, plucking the 'Think small' line from a number of Koenig's lines. Like Rand, Krone was a revolutionary art director, often just leaving wide expanses of white page, or using a photograph in place of a logo, or not showing the product at all. Krone and Koenig together took the advertising world by storm and DDB became the most talked about and emulated agency.

'Bill Bernbach always spoke about the importance of looking deeply into a product as the answer to your problem lies within the product.'

SIMON HIGBY, CREATIVE DIRECTOR, TRIBAL DDB STOCKHOLM

OPPOSITE
This 1942 brochure for the AutoCar Company of Ardmore, Pennsylvania, called 'Mechanized Mules of Victory', was created at the William H. Weintraub agency by Paul Rand and Bill Bernbach.

BELOW
Paul Rand was in control of the William H. Weintraub art department. His designs were simple and fun, with a strong visual brand identity.

MECHANIZED MULES OF VICTORY

THE AUTOCAR COMPANY
ARDMORE, PENNSYLVANIA

LEFT
The 1948 De Beers
campaign by US
agency N. W. Ayer &
Son developed the idea
that a diamond is a
symbol of eternal love.

¼ carat (25 points) $90 to $200
½ carat (50 points) $225 to $450
1 carat (100 points) $570 to $1150
2 carats (200 points) $1365 to $3300

In April, 1956, jewelers throughout
the country were asked for the
prices of their top-grade engagement
diamonds (unmounted) in the
weights indicated. The result is a
range of prices, varying according to
the qualities offered. Exceptionally
fine stones are higher priced.
Add Federal tax. Exact weights
shown are infrequent.
N. W. AYER & SON

Message of Love—painted for the De Beers Collection by Pierre Ino

The miracle of love

A girl's joy, flowering like a rose, is radiant and full in the
lovely miracle of love awakening. And for her a star,
blazing bright as her dreams, will recall this moment always.
Her engagement diamond, fair spark of eternity,
reflects the light of her happiness in changeless splendor,
and treasures its tender message of love until the end of time.

Remember, color, cutting and clarity,
as well as carat weight, contribute to
a diamond's beauty and value.
A trusted jeweler is your best adviser.
Extended payments can usually be arranged.

a diamond is forever

De Beers Consolidated Mines, Ltd.

POT-AU-FEU
MAGGI

LEFT
Designed by Raymond
Savignac, the well-
repected French graphic
artist, this Maggi poster
from 1959 created a
strong branded identity.

OPPOSITE
The groundbreaking
1959 'Think small' ad
for Volkswagen from
Doyle Dane Bernbach.

© 1962 VOLKSWAGEN OF AMERICA, INC.

Think small.

Our little car isn't so much of a novelty any more.

A couple of dozen college kids don't try to squeeze inside it.

The guy at the gas station doesn't ask where the gas goes.

Nobody even stares at our shape.

In fact, some people who drive our little flivver don't even think 32 miles to the gallon is going any great guns.

Or using five pints of oil instead of five quarts.

Or never needing anti-freeze.

Or racking up 40,000 miles on a set of tires.

That's because once you get used to some of our economies, you don't even think about them any more.

Except when you squeeze into a small parking spot. Or renew your small insurance. Or pay a small repair bill. Or trade in your old VW for a new one.

Think it over.

Mary Wells is another DDB creative who made a dramatic impact on advertising. After seven years at DDB, she went on to open her own agency, co-founding Wells Rich Greene in 1966. She not only conceived ad campaigns but also rethought products, creating, in effect, brand extensions for companies – the idea of selling Alka-Seltzers in handy two-packs, for example. The Alka-Seltzer account brought in $20 million in business to the agency. WRG's New York State Board of Tourism work became one of the best loved and most enduring identity campaigns, with Milton Glaser's famous 'I ♥ NY' design. This creative, almost entrepreneurial way of thinking is one of the ways that we work in advertising today. Mary Wells offered media-neutral, totally integrated campaigns before anyone even knew those terms.

The other side of this creative revolution was the drive to become ever more scientific, accountable and measurable within a profession that arguably was as much art as business. In the 1950s Rosser Reeves was the vice-president and copy chief of Ted Bates & Co. He believed in the science of measurability and predictability and believed people would buy products if you offered them rational arguments. He turned this into his concept of the 'unique selling point' – the USP. This is an idea that has lasted to this day.

Currently many creatives and planners argue that products are becoming homogenous, with little difference among them except for an emotional difference created by adverts. There is also debate about whether consumers buy products based on rational sales messages at all, which would mean that there is little point in a rational USP.

Another leading figure in the 1950s advertising scene was David Ogilvy. He founded the New York-based ad agency Hewitt, Ogilvy, Benson & Mather in 1948 after a number of years working for Gallup Research. Unlike some agencies, his took the audience seriously and assumed that they were intelligent. He wanted to inspire people to buy things by creating a mystique, a story. Like Rand, he believed in the importance of creating a strong brand image, famously giving brand identities to Schweppes, Hathaway shirts and Dove soap among many others. He believed that 'every advertisement should be thought of as a contribution to the brand image'. For the campaign 'The man in the Hathaway shirt', for example, Ogilvy created a sophisticated gentleman who wore an eyepatch, giving him a rakish air. The man, known as the Baron, embodied the brand identity. The Hathaway ads ran from 1951 to 1990. In 1965 Ogilvy merged his company with Mather & Crowther, his London backers, to form what would become the famous international company Ogilvy & Mather.

A USP consists of three parts:

- **There must be a proposition –**
  'Buy this product and you get these benefits'

- **The proposition must be unique,**
  and distinct from its competitors

- **The proposition must be strong enough**
  to attract new customers

BOTTOM LEFT
One of the best-known pieces of brand building in the world, designed by Milton Glaser in 1976 for Wells Rich Greene. I LOVE NEW YORK is a registered trademark and service mark of the New York State Department of Economic Development; used with permission.

BELOW
In this 1965 Clio Award-winning ad from Wells Rich Greene, a man recounts a story in which a waiter insists he should try a particular dish. 'Try it, you'll like it' passed into popular culture as a common phrase as a result.

The man in the Hathaway shirt

AMERICAN MEN are beginning to realize that it is ridiculous to buy good suits and then spoil the effect by wearing an ordinary, mass-produced shirt. Hence the growing popularity of HATHAWAY shirts, which are in a class by themselves.

HATHAWAY shirts *wear* infinitely longer—a matter of years. They make you look younger and more distinguished, because of the subtle way HATHAWAY cut collars. The whole shirt is tailored more *generously*, and is therefore more *comfortable*. The tails are longer, and stay in your trousers. The buttons are mother-of-pearl. Even the stitching has an ante-bellum elegance about it.

Above all, HATHAWAY make their shirts of remarkable *fabrics*, collected from the four corners of the earth—Viyella, and Aertex, from England, woolen taffeta from Scotland, Sea Island cotton from the West Indies, hand-woven madras from India, broadcloth from Manchester, linen batiste from Paris, hand-blocked silks from England, exclusive cottons from the best weavers in America. You will get a great deal of quiet satisfaction out of wearing shirts which are in such impeccable taste.

HATHAWAY shirts are made by a small company of dedicated craftsmen in the little town of Waterville, Maine. They have been at it, man and boy, for one hundred and twenty years.

At better stores everywhere, or write C. F. HATHAWAY, Waterville, Maine, for the name of your nearest store. In New York, telephone OX 7-5566. **Prices from $5.95 to $20.00.**

YOU DO NOT HAVE TO BE YOUR MOTHER UNLESS SHE IS WHO YOU WANT TO BE. YOU DO NOT HAVE TO BE YOUR MOTHER'S MOTHER, OR YOUR MOTHER'S MOTHER'S MOTHER, OR EVEN YOUR GRANDMOTHER'S MOTHER ON YOUR FATHER'S SIDE. YOU MAY INHERIT THEIR CHINS OR THEIR HIPS OR THEIR EYES, BUT YOU ARE NOT DESTINED TO BECOME THE WOMEN WHO CAME BEFORE YOU. YOU ARE NOT DESTINED TO LIVE THEIR LIVES. SO IF YOU INHERIT SOMETHING, INHERIT THEIR STRENGTH. IF YOU INHERIT SOMETHING, INHERIT THEIR RESILIENCE. BECAUSE THE ONLY PERSON YOU ARE DESTINED TO BECOME IS THE PERSON YOU DECIDE TO BE.

World domination without the laser death ray masterplan.

The Economist

LEFT AND BELOW LEFT
Director Tony Kaye shot
this surreal ad for Dunlop
tyres in 1993, cutting
through the rest of the
ads on TV in the UK.

ABOVE
In the UK this irreverent
1992 Tango ad by HHCL
created the 'water-
cooler effect' that many
clients and agencies
seek. Its style has been
imitated by many
others since.

VISUAL ADVERTISING

The visual approach pursued by Rand in the 1950s was an approach that was also favoured by leading European advertisers such as Armando Testa, from the Armando Testa Group, in Italy. Testa created designs with humour and simplicity. He loved art, particularly minimalism, often creating his own art and design pieces, and this passion is shown in his advertising designs. The agency has produced work for clients such as Pirelli, Lavazza, San Pellegrino and Fiat Lancia and is still fiercely independent. Both Rand and Testa showed how advertising could be simple, playful and dramatic using imagery, perhaps even leading with a visual rather than simply illustrating the copy.

This visual approach was more fully developed as a worldwide phenomenon in the 1970s. The first agency founded by partners from different countries, TBWA, made up of a Frenchman, a Swiss, an Italian and an American, created the dramatic Absolut Vodka campaign in 1980, using the bottle as the centrepiece and hero of every advert. Since then there have been more than 1,500 adverts in the campaign.

In his 1978 campaign for Bombril, a brand of household products, the great Brazilian advertising creative Washington Olivetto took visual executions further, allowing the image to become more surreal. The campaign showed the Brazilian comedian Carlos Moreno impersonating famous figures, including the former US President Bill Clinton. These ads were so popular that they were even scheduled in television listings. Brazil, in particular, specialized in visual advertising owing to the diversity of languages spoken within Latin America – this lack of words, which avoided the need for translation, opened the door to pan-Latin-American contracts. This later led on to lucrative international advertising contracts and awards.

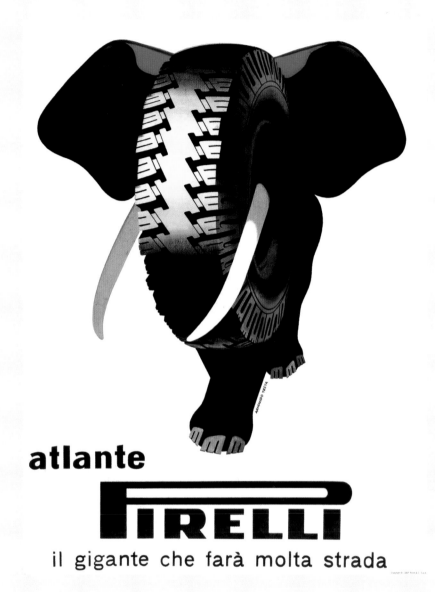

Armando Testa's simple graphic style and great lateral thinking came together in this 1955 Italian ad for Pirelli.

LEFT
This 1978 ad for Bombril
had comedian Carlos
Moreno imitate the
Mona Lisa.

ABOVE
Every year Lavazza
releases a calendar of
stunning images evoking
the essence of Italy, its
people and its coffee.
These images are then
repurposed as posters.
Created by the Armando
Testa advertising agency,
this 2010 calendar was
shot by Miles Aldridge
and is based on famous
Italian songs.

Agencies in South America, South Africa and Asia have since excelled at visually led advertising. The person who undoubtedly influenced the advertising for the whole Asia–Pacific region was British advertising executive Neil French, when he worked for the Ball Partnership Singapore in the mid–1980s. For their Kaminomoto campaign, French had to work with complex Singaporean laws that did not allow for a description of the product (hair restorer) or images of men with or without hair, as it would imply hair growth. French's solution was to show hair growing on normally 'bald' objects, such as eggs and snooker balls. The endline was: 'Be careful with the Kaminomoto.'

The practice of having a single campaign or advert that can be shown across the world as a global communication can be linked to the rise of simple visually led advertising, together with the desire of global clients to retain full control over their brand identity. However, many cultures do not have a tradition of simple graphics; this is a modern Western phenomenon, and this level of minimalism and surrealism in visual communication is something that has to be learned, both to create and to understand it. Some advertising theorists, such as Chris Hackley, point out that global work can smack of cultural colonialism, with advertising campaigns making the world's people seem all the same, having the same concerns, interests and beliefs. Though visually led advertising has limitations, it is the holy grail of judging panels at awards shows, as a quick look through the most recent award annuals will reveal. When visual advertising works, it really works [see p63]. The simplicity and drama of a strong, simple visual can be persuasive. But largely it struggles to communicate a deeper human observation or truth.

Boddington's 1992 'Ice Cream Cone' press ad from 'The Cream of Manchester' campaign by BBH London.

 THE CREAM OF MANCHESTER.

Boddingtons Draught Bitter. Brewed at the Strangeways Brewery since 1778.

THE RETURN OF WORDS

'It's very rare and very difficult to communicate a human truth about anything other than sex and death with just visuals; it's a very modern disease to think you can. You just can't assume that someone in China views life in the same way I do: you end up with lowest-common-denominator ideas.'

JUSTIN TINDALL, GROUP EXECUTIVE CREATIVE DIRECTOR, LEO BURNETT LONDON

The explosion of digital content on the Internet has created a revolution in the way words are used to communicate a message. There are now countless ways for advertising and marketing messages to be communicated digitally via emails, RSS feeds, instant messaging services and social media networks such as Facebook and Twitter. Online advertising language is designed to capture and hold our attention, words are still of crucial importance. For advertising creatives the digital revolution offers new opportunities for expression, whether on a blog or YouTube video; words can be used in an approachable, personal and persuasive format, making the reader feel like they're involved and encouraging audience participation.

The Internet has changed what contemporary marketers and advertisers aspire to create. When ordinary people rather than businesses choose their preferred format, a more even mix of word and image seems to emerge. The written blog is a powerful social tool for sharing opinion and life experience, with a role as important as those of YouTube, Flickr and Picasa as image-based social tools. And we mustn't forget Twitter, a platform used by individuals, companies and advertisers alike to share ideas in 140 characters. This really is where the power of the right choice of words can be seen – in follower numbers. Although there is the opportunity to attach images to tweets, users tend not to, preferring the immediacy and brutality of words constrained by 140 characters.

'There is a new expression. A bit quicker, more blog-ish, if you know what I mean. I see that as liberating since there is room for more influences now.'

MIA ROBERTSSON, COPYWRITER, FAMILJENPANGEA, STOCKHOLM

To stay ahead of cultural trends, advertising and marketing need to reflect this word and image mix – to feel less like 'advertising'.

'Language cannot be ignored. Bear in mind that language is alive in itself, changing form and content as we move along in time. It adapts. So it is not an obsolete piece that we can write off as part of the history. True, images are powerful. But I believe all this "visuals taking over" thing is a bit hyped up.'

ERGIN BINYILDIZ, EXECUTIVE CREATIVE DIRECTOR, GREY ISTANBUL

LEFT
Words take centre stage in this advert for Nike where, despite the large amount of text, the message is always clear.

LEFT
This ad for the Cinéglobe film festival cleverly combines words and images to connect cinema with science.

In 2012 DDB London developed a print campaign for VW's BlueMotion series. Developed by creative director Jeremy Craigen, it perfectly illustrates how a sign can convey meaning or an idea. The message highlights the efficiencies of the Bluemotion technology reflected by the economic use of letters rearranged to create a 'flower' symbol.

VOLKSWAGEN'S BLUEMOTION RANGE.
LESS FUEL. FEWER EMISSIONS.
Think Blue.

THE SEMIOTICS OF ADS

The difference in cultural mores from country to country can lead to difficulties in global campaigns. A brand in the West may stand for the empowerment of women but might come across differently within other markets. If advertisers impose their Western viewpoint they can be criticized for showing a lack of cultural sensitivity; however, if they fail to promote their message then they can be criticized for not standing true to their values. What is a sign of something in one country might be a sign of something else in another country. How advertising is read is key to understanding how it works and how it should be developed. Analysing how it is read also highlights the limitations of global advertising campaigns. One way of doing this is through semiotics.

Semiotics is the theory and study of signs and symbols. It looks at how meaning is constructed within a culture and how an idea becomes associated with words, images and objects. At the point when the word, image or object (for example, the colour red) stops being simply what it is and a group of people agree that it has a particular meaning for them (for example, danger) it becomes a sign. However, that meaning is fluid and subject to change. For a different group of people the meaning may be something entirely different – the colour red may be a sign of passion. Anything can be a sign if there is another person who interprets it as 'signifying' something other than itself (that is, the word 'red' cannot be a sign of the colour red). As a group we come to this interpretation largely through cultural convention, habit and association and it is mainly an unconscious process.

The theory of semiotics developed in the early twentieth century from the work of two men. The Swiss linguist Ferdinand de Saussure (1857–1913) developed the school of thought that would become known as structuralism, based on the role of signs as part of human life, and called his new theory 'semiology'. Meanwhile, the American logician and philosopher Charles Sanders Peirce (1839–1914) developed the theory of 'semiotics'.

Peirce believed that a sign was made up from:

• **a sign, or representamen** – the word, image, sound or thing that does the representing

• **an object** – the thing that is being signified, the subject matter of the sign

• **an interpretant** – the meaning of the sign

Peirce pointed out that signs can appear in three different forms: *iconic signs*, which imitate the thing they are representing, for example photographs; *indexical signs*, which demonstrate a physical connection, for example a cough to illness; *symbolic signs*, which develop meaning through convention and habit, for example thumbs up to mean good. For him signs have fluid meanings.

Saussure believed that a sign consists of:

• **the signifier** – the word, image, sound or object that does the representing

• **the signified** – the meaning/idea it represents

Saussure noticed that signs, particularly when words are mixed with images, can have a number of different meanings.

The music cassette tape in this press ad from BAR, Lisboa becomes symbolic not only of life in the 1980s but also of the youth of the target market. Making the tape out of the product allows the bubble gum to become a symbol of our 1980s youth.

The literary theorist Roland Barthes, the philosopher Jean Baudrillard and the writer and critic Judith Williamson extended semiotic theory to the study of media and brand communication, and this is the theory most commonly applied to advertising. They take ideas of denotation (literal meaning) and connotation (any idea or feeling that can be associated with it), which are terms describing the relationship between the signifier and its signified, and apply them to mass marketing techniques. While Saussure kept his analysis to the obvious, literal (denotative) meaning, these writers give more weight to connotative meaning, which allows for a more subjective and personal understanding of each sign as the viewer brings their own meanings to it.

Williamson's examples of the way in which colour is used in adverts as a sign is perhaps one of the clearest examples of signs in action. She identifies an advert that evokes richness by using the colours brown and gold, and an advert that evokes sophistication by limiting the palette to black, white and silver. Both adverts describe a whole world in a snapshot and use colour to control meaning and mood. There are many ads that you will be able to recall that use white to connote purity and innocence, though white is not intrinsically 'innocent' and innocence is merely an idea that we have learned to associate with it. Within the advert, white would represent those values and anyone then wearing or using it would come to embody those values by association. However, although white is the colour of purity and innocence in the West, in Vietnam it is associated with funerals and in Nicaragua with peace. Colours have different connotations in different cultures – a global campaign would have to research the meanings of a specific colour carefully if it was to be used as an important sign.

In advertising we create environments through imagery, sound and narrative that enhance a product's or brand's relationship to its customers' lives. We do this by referencing the many objects, behaviours, rituals, people and symbols that exist within our society. In putting everyday things in the context of an advert we turn them into a sign of something else. The minute we reference a sign or borrow a sign, we are creating a communication that contains multiple signs with multiple meanings all linked to each other by a common denominator – the product or brand.

'The message becomes a play of complicity between the one who observes and the one who communicates. We all know that a comedian is a well-paid actor who has studied his part well, but this does not make us feel prejudiced towards him or stop us from smiling.'

LUCA D'ALESIO, CREATIVE DIRECTOR, TOUCHÉ ADVERTISING, BOLOGNA

When advertising really works it communicates to people at a deeper level than even the original intention. The signs resonate, the execution entertains. It then becomes something owned and liked by the audience on their own terms. It becomes part of popular culture and is even at times displayed and celebrated as a form of popular 'art'.

Publicis Conseil created this ad for the Renault Mégane convertible cabriolet. Because of the lack of a roof the driver can see up the angels' dresses. Their innocence, virtue and angelic nature are symbolized by the colour white even while their expressions and body language show that they are compromised by their desire to look at the car, and therefore the driver.

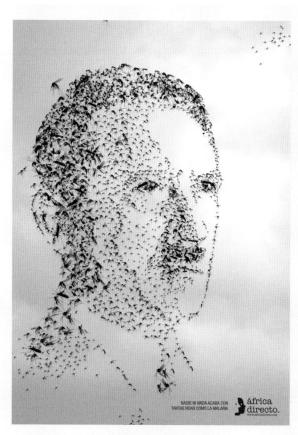

NADIE NI NADA ACABA CON
TANTAS VIDAS COMO LA MALARIA

áfrica
directo.

Da Domopak Spazzy, sacco Maxi Strong:
doppio spessore, capiente fino a 150 litri, riciclabile e prodotto con il 100%
di plastica riciclata. Maxi Strong fa parte della nuova gamma Domopak Spazzy:
sacchi nettezza per ogni esigenza, resistenti, funzionali e attenti all'ambiente.

Resistente ed Ecologico. 100% PLASTICA RICICLATA

Remember.

ADVERTISING AS POPULAR ART

The fact that advertising focuses on the financial value of any subject, is so ruthlessly targeted, and is often arrived at by committee renders it, for some, incapable of being an art form. The accepted view is that art speaks about what it is to be human without commercialism at its heart, and that the subject is respected for its innate worth. Yet some pieces of advertising quickly become culturally relevant and do attain the status of popular art. There is perhaps a debate to be had about whether people can judge for themselves what is and is not art, as well as whether there ever was a time in which some of the works recognized as art were not hand in hand with commercialism and client interest.

It has often been pointed out that some of the great artistic works of the Renaissance had a client, for example the Vatican. It could be argued that there was a brand message, a brand tone of voice, and mandatory colours and symbols, and that the artists could be sent back for alterations if any of the required elements were missing. Working artists through the centuries have had clients that they had to please; they were not in charge of what to paint or how to paint it. François Boucher's portrait of the courtesan Marie-Louise O'Murphy, for example, was purportedly part of a 'marketing' campaign to raise the interest of King Louis XV of France.

In Europe and North America people have always been able to find 'art' that they liked in places that were not traditionally approved of. Instead of buying artworks or visiting galleries in the late nineteenth century, households of more modest means would take out prints from magazines to frame as art for their walls. This imagery became popular art though it derived from a commercial context. In the 1930s the Shell Corporation placed commissioned artworks on the side of delivery vehicles; some of these posters were high art acting as commercial art. Some old posters for companies such as Guinness are framed and put on walls in people's living rooms as 'art'. This is part of Modernism's legacy.

The start of Modernism at the end of the nineteenth century marked a change in attitudes towards the differentiation between high art and low art. Ideas of subjectivity rather than objectivity took hold and people became more concerned with their own views on the world. It also led to an awareness of the media in which things are created, the surface, the materials and their innate meaning, which has been called self-consciousness. All of this led to experimentation by artists in the form, function, materials and processes used and an increase in the use of collage and fragmented surfaces.

Both Judith Williamson and the art critic John Berger have pointed out the conceptual similarities between advertising and particular art movements – for Berger it was Realism and for Williamson, Surrealism. These and other art movements inevitably influenced advertising, being the culture that the creatives saw, understood and were taught themselves.

Modernism gave way to Postmodernism, in which techniques of pastiche, collage, parody and irony are commonplace. Copying, or 'repetition', is part and parcel of Postmodernism – to represent old ideas as 'new'. Postmodern artists even use adverts themselves as part of art pieces. Copying, referencing and reframing are also essential elements of advertising. Adverts also refer to other adverts as social commentary, or to add 'texture' in the same way that Postmodern art does. It becomes difficult to draw a line between what is and is not art, and therefore what has cultural significance.

Cadeau, created by Man Ray in 1921, would seem to have directly inspired the 1991 Saatchi & Saatchi ad entitled 'Iron'.

LOW TAR As defined by H.M. Government STOPPING SMOKING REDUCES THE RISK OF SERIOUS DISEASES
Health Departments' Chief Medical Officers

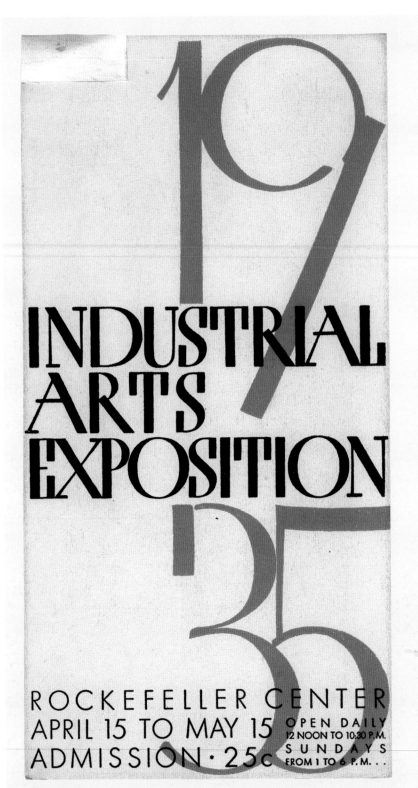

The 1935 Industrial Arts Exposition poster by Paul Rand took a less cluttered approach to design but was clearly inspired by the colours and play of Dadaist pieces such as Kurt Schwitters' and Theo van Doesburg's 1922 lithograph *Small Dada Evening*; below.

CREATING CULTURE

Like most people, creatives tend to reflect the society and culture that they come from. In a process known as referencing, they draw inspiration and take from a number of cultural sources, using not only the classics in art and literature but also popular culture, the news, television shows, modern art and film, how we behave, the clothes we wear and where we go out.

Such critics as Stuart Ewen, William Leiss, Stephen Kline, Grant McCracken and Judith Williamson argue that this lends a certain social value to products that they have not earned, because not only do they lack the context in which the original works were created but they have emptied out the meanings from the original – any genuine feeling, intent or belief. These critics consider this form of referencing to be cultural theft. There has been criticism when artists have done this in the past as well, such as Marcel Duchamp's parody of the *Mona Lisa*, though this was not for the benefit of a corporation.

'It steals from it. Rarely adds anything. I think the way advertising adds to culture is only at a point in the future when people want to look back on a culture and understand what that culture was like. Advertising will be a really wonderful way of looking at that.'

JUSTIN TINDALL, GROUP EXECUTIVE CREATIVE DIRECTOR, LEO BURNETT LONDON

It is the creative's job to sit and imagine situations or moments in which the brand, product and consumer fit together in a memorable way. It could be argued that all the cultural references within an ad work as signs and the meanings of all signs are fluid. A different meaning from the 'original' cultural meaning is suggested by the advertiser, and the viewer agrees to it. This then can create new pieces of popular culture. When this works well it creates what is called the 'water-cooler effect', in which people (gathered round the office water cooler or coffee machine) talk about the advert, thereby giving it a life beyond the ad spend. This can dramatically influence the commercial success of a campaign.

An integrated advertising campaign created by VCCP broke in the UK in January 2009 for the price comparison website comparethemarket.com. The ads focused on a fictional, similar-sounding website, comparethemeerkat.com, with its founder, an aristocratic Russian computer-generated meerkat named Aleksandr Orlov, and a catchphrase, 'Simples'. People not only talked about it but repeated the catchphrase, bought a book about Alexsandr's life and followed him on Facebook and Twitter. When people like a campaign this much it can create popular culture. But this is not the aim of an advert - it needs to reach its marketing objective. The 'Compare the Market' campaign achieved this - in the first nine weeks quotes increased by 80 per cent and there has been a year on year increase in sales.

At its best, advertising creates culture. Gives people new ways to think about things, new insights into the things that matter to them, or creates new storylines to follow. Advertising that just reflects culture is usually just lazy.'

JOHN PATROULIS AND SCOTT DUCHON, EXECUTIVE CREATIVE DIRECTORS, AGENCY215, SAN FRANCISCO

For the creative this process of creating culture is part of the return; it is the job satisfaction and creates part of the fun of the job. You have made something that everyone likes. You have spoken to the people you were trying to reach, your target market, in a way that is memorable and appropriate, and they have appreciated it and interacted with it. Yet it is this perceived desire to create 'culture' that can attract the most intense criticism.

René Magritte's work approached the ideas of reality and illusion through the seemingly illogical placing of people and everyday objects, an idea that this ad for bathroom fixtures is also playing with.

A
BRANDED
WORLD

3

3   A BRANDED WORLD

WHAT IS A BRAND?

Like early advertising, branding was in use thousands of years ago. The ancient Egyptians, Greeks, Romans and Chinese used seals on packaged goods to let others know who owned and made them, acting as an indication of their quality. Governments quickly saw the benefit of this because if they knew who had made a product it was easier to demand taxes from them. In the mid-1800s manufacturers started to use the term 'brand', a word that originally referred to the hot metal stamp used on livestock. The purpose of a brand was then to identify the livestock's owner; now, a brand aims to create a human connection in a market filled with mass-produced goods created by unknown people. This is visually embodied by the logo, but a brand is more than just its physical appearance: it also comprises its tone of voice and the way in which it is experienced in the real world by consumers.

A brand can differentiate one product from another and create a personality and set of associated values. It changes what was just a commodity into something that has value beyond the labour it took to create it. It can therefore command more money than a non-branded product. As consumers we like brands because we feel we are getting more than merely the commodity. Businesses like branding because it helps to protect the manufacturer from a single product's potential failure in the market, as a brand is more than just an individual product.

A brand is also applicable to organizations, services and even personalities. Brands are also relevant to a concept such as sustainability, rather than a specific product. Consumer items such as products and services are what a brand represents. In today's branded world, it could be argued that the management of a brand's image has become more important than the production of the item, which that brand represents.

The American branding consultant Alycia de Mesa (who has also written under the name Alycia Perry) suggests that 'a brand is a promise of a relationship and a guarantee of quality'. The American critic and cultural analyst Naomi Klein, who has critiqued the excesses of global capitalism for more than a decade, maintains that we 'think of the brand as the core meaning of the modern corporation', and makes links between brands and corporate responsibility.

De Mesa believes brand creation is necessary for businesses to speak to their customers in a common language. This allows businesses to grow, profits to roll in, jobs to be created and commercialism to prosper. It allows for consumer choice. In contrast, Klein identifies the move from companies proudly manufacturing their own wares to their focusing on 'myth' creation as the start of the branding project. She believes the outsourcing of all product creation to the cheapest supplier has led to less accountable business practices and 'proper' job losses. De Mesa and Klein are each right in many ways but they come to the branding agenda from very different points of view.

Both Klein and De Mesa are clear that we should think about a brand not as a product but as a set of ideas in which products feature. This could be one product or a series of products. It allows the company behind the brand to be flexible in what it offers rather than fixated on a given product; in particular it allows it to create brand 'extensions'. These are products that are related in some way but are not necessarily just upgrades of the main product for which the brand is known. For example, if a brand is known for 'antibacterial cleaning' rather than for a particular liquid then it is free to create household wipes, sprays and antiseptic gels. In this example it is important that all the brand-building focus is on 'antibacterial cleaning' rather than the original liquid product.

A successful brand will have scope in that it will be developed within an expansive campaign where the brand is extended across multiple media. This extension doesn't just sell more products but helps to reinforce the brand's success and ensures a higher degree of recognition from consumers. The convergence of social and mobile technologies has seen the

In 1929 Reckitt & Sons (UK) developed Dettol antiseptic disinfectant liquid. The company, now Reckitt Benckiser, has since developed a number of brand extensions.

number of points of contact between a brand and consumers grow exponentially. These brand and customer touch points can be defined as any contact or interaction point between a consumer and a brand or company. Touch points help the brand to develop and the most successful brands are those that take all touch points into consideration. There is a fundamental shift taking place in the way that brands communicate and build relationships with customers. Social media allows brands to talk to consumers 24 hours a day wherever they are in the world. Twitter and Facebook allow consumers to engage with brands and participate directly in advertising campaigns. IKEA, the world's largest furniture retailer, have created the Share Space website where customers can post pictures of rooms they have redecorated.

A good example of consistent branding and brand building is the UK brand Innocent. Innocent based its identity on the drinks that the founding three friends first made in 1999. They saw a gap in the market for pure, 100 per cent fruit smoothies, but it was not just the drink that excited them, it was the idea of the purity of the drink. This led them to trade with suppliers in an ethically and environmentally aware manner, an idea that was true to their values and also fairly rare in business at the time – the Body Shop was the only other large UK business pursuing this strategy.

The company promotes the idea that to be 'Innocent' is to be honest, natural and engaging; every communication must answer these brand values. To create the Innocent identity the company used a felt-tip-drawn face with a halo as their logo, kept the signature lower-case and wrote playful copy on their labels, website and other branded material. Innocent also organizes thoughtful events such as the annual 'Big Knit', when the public is asked to knit tiny bobble hats to be sold on smoothie bottles and the money raised is given to charities helping the aged. This action is 'on brand' precisely because it is honest, natural and engaging.

Through clever and creative marketing, Innocent extended their initial branding on bottles to branding in multiple media, such as poster and TV advertising and signage on vans, developing a recognizable tone of voice that has made it possible for people to recognize the difference between an Innocent smoothie and the average smoothie. Such successful brand building has enabled them to dominate the market. At the time of writing Innocent have a 63 per cent share of the £111 million UK smoothie market and they have been able to brand-extend into veg pots as well as other drinks.

The Innocent brand has been thoughtfully developed and expressed through a variety of media, maintaining a consistent tone of voice throughout.

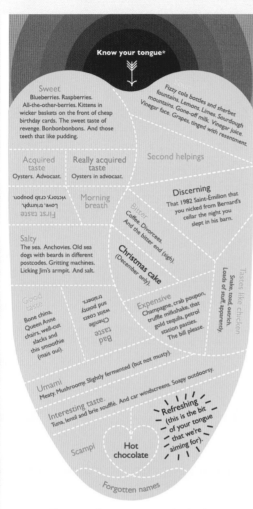

Know your tongue*

Sweet
Blueberries. Raspberries. All-the-other-berries. Kittens in wicker baskets on the front of cheap birthday cards. The sweet taste of revenge. Bonbonbonbons. And those teeth that like pudding.

Fizzy cola bottles and sherbet fountains. Lemons. Limes. Sourdough mountains. Gone-off milk. Vinegar juice. Vinegar face. Grapes, tinged with resentment.

Second helpings

Acquired taste
Oysters. Advocaat.

Really acquired taste
Oysters in advocaat.

First taste
Love, triumph, victory, crab poupon.

Morning breath

Discerning
That 1982 Saint-Émilion that you nicked from Bernard's cellar the night you slept in his barn.

Bitter
Coffee. Divorcees. And the bitter end (sigh).

Salty
The sea. Anchovies. Old sea dogs with beards in different postcodes. Gritting machines. Licking Jim's armpit. And salt.

Christmas cake
(December only).

Tastes like chicken
Snake, toad, ostrich. Loads of stuff, apparently.

Good taste
Bone china, Queen Anne chairs, well-cut slacks and this smoothie (mais oui).

Bad taste
Chenille waist coats and pointy trainers.

Expensive
Champagne, crab poupon, truffle milkshake, that gold tequila, petrol station pasties. The bill please.

Umami
Meaty. Mushroomy. Slightly fermented (but not musty).

Interesting taste
Tuna, lentil and brie soufflé. And car windscreens. Soapy outdoorsy.

Refreshing
(this is the bit of your tongue that we're aiming for).

Scampi

Hot chocolate

Forgotten names

Your tongue has got more zones than London Underground. And it's demanding – sometimes it wants sweet, sometimes it wants sour, sometimes it wants to lick an old sailor's beard. But if you really want to treat your tongue right, please refresh it daily. And feel free to use this specially invented smoothie recipe – we made it because we were after something a little more refreshing. Hope it does the job.

fancy a chat?

Us too. Just pop in to Fruit Towers, 1 Goldhawk Estate, Brackenbury Road, London, W6 0BA or ring the banana phone on 020 8600 3993. In Ireland, visit us at Fruit Towers, 46 Mountjoy Square, Dublin 1 or call 01 879 6600. Otherwise email doormat@innocentdrinks.com, or even join the family at www.innocentdrinks.com/family

Swallowing the pips: would it be all that bad to have a tree growing inside of you

?

The Pros

Birdsong on tap (if you tended to the branches outside your ears)

Supply of wood whenever you burped

Great way to use up CO_2

Free entry to all parks

The Cons

You'd be dead

Where would the roots go?

Lightning conductor

Would the roots come out of your bottom?

Splinters

Owls keeping you up

Us too. Just pop in to Fruit Towers, 1 Goldhawk Estate, Brackenbury Road, London, W6 0BA or ring the banana phone on 020 8600 3993. In Ireland, visit us at Fruit Towers, 121 Lower Baggot Street, Dublin 2 or call 01 664 4100. Otherwise email doormat@innocentdrinks.com or join the family at www.innocentdrinks.com/family

protects what's good
Tetra Pak

helpful little hats

25p per hatted bottle goes to Age UK

The Big Knit has begun. Over the past few weeks, lovely people across the country have knitted thousands of little woolly hats. For each bottle/hat combo sold, 25p will be given to Age UK, to help make winter warmer for older people. Available now in Sainsbury's and Boots stores. To find out more visit **www.innocentdrinks.co.uk/bigknit**

 Age UK (Charity no.1128267) is the new force combining Age Concern and Help the Aged.

banana free

innocent®
pure fruit smoothie
kiwis, apples & limes

Brand building can help to reinvigorate a well-known brand. Established brands need to be ever more imaginative in extending their brand while still remaining consistent to their core brand values.

In 2009, BBDO New York and the Barbarian Group, created an award-winning brand image campaign called Cube Film Installation for the independent premium cable channel HBO (Home Box Office). The objective was to reinvigorate HBO's core brand values of storytelling, original programming and delivering innovative content. As an independent cable channel, it is vital for HBO to attract and retain subscribers.

In New York, Philadelphia and Washington, D.C. they installed a four-panel video installation called the HBO Cube. Designed to enhance the storytelling experience, it screens four different interpretations of one story simultaneously, from four distinct perspectives. Each side of the cube stands alone as an engaging film, and as a piece of a much larger plot. The audience moves around the cube; they watch the story unfold from different angles, forming different viewpoints of the characters and story. It features two films especially created for this event, *Heist* and *The Affair* by Noam Murro of Biscuit Films. Each film is two minutes in length and played twice successively on a rotating basis. Both films stood on their own as embodiments of the brand, but were also later revealed to be part of a larger narrative experience on the campaign website.

The aim of unfolding the larger narrative online was to engage people in storytelling in a way that let them explore the content. The Barbarian Group created the campaign website HBO Imagine, which features an interactive storytelling experience where users can choose what films they want to see. The website promotes the HBO brand concept of 'It's more than you imagined' and helps to extend the HBO brand by encouraging users to connect on a deeper level.

The Cube installed in Washington, D.C.

BRAND BUILDING

'In an entire day, we're likely to see 3,500 marketing messages.'

OWEN GIBSON, MEDIA CORRESPONDENT FOR *THE GUARDIAN*, 19 NOVEMBER 2005

To put this statement into perspective, Gibson was writing about a day that involved walking around a media-saturated environment, the centre of London in the UK. He wore a gadget called the Eye Contact, which captured everything he saw. This figure would not be the same if he had walked around Ravello, a small village in the south of Italy, or Poughkeepsie, USA, yet this statement is probably indicative of most industrialized cities in the world.

As consumers the marketing messages we predominantly come into contact with are 'brand building'. Brand building encompasses every communication that is designed to reach the consumer before they directly experience the brand, such as the logo, packaging, retail environments and advertising. As creatives in the advertising industry, our job is to get into the consumer's psyche before they have formed an impression of the brand, or if they have a poor impression of the brand, to change their feelings about it (change the existing 'brand image', which is how the brand is actually seen and performs). As David Ogilvy believed (see Chapter 2), we are in the business of bringing to life a 'brand identity' – to make an existing brand more attractive to its target audience, or if there is none, to create it with our mix of word and image.

'When people see something interesting (because they consider it funny, intelligent, moving, or, what is more, they can't explain it) they engage with brands much more effectively.'

MARIO CRUDELE, SENIOR COPYWRITER, PONCE BUENOS AIRES

Today it is rare that we are asked to create new brand identities from scratch as this is no longer seen to be within the remit of a traditional advertising agency. To understand why this is we need to look at the development of design agencies and influential branding consultants, such as Wally Olins. Olins is now Chairman of Saffron Brand Consultants of London, New York, Mumbai and Madrid and is one of the world's leading practitioners in corporate identity. He started as an ad man. After a stint of heading Ogilvy, Benson & Mather in Mumbai, Olins came back to England and co-founded the hugely influential Wolff Olins design consultancy in 1965. He took the work traditionally created by advertising agencies, which threw in logo design and packaging for free, and created a separate paying market for it. Olins understood the potential financial value of a 'brand' to corporations, and as an agency Wolff Olins began to focus on branding. Olins understood the power of symbolism in brand and corporate design. He instinctively knew it was part of advertising even while taking it away from traditional advertising agencies, whereas many branding agencies saw it as a distinct practice.

'To create a bond with the audience, brands make use of insights. Some are based on primitive human truth, some on cultural facts. In other cases, it reflects unconventional ways of living, looking for and communicating inspiration, or transforming society.'

ERGIN BINYILDIZ, EXECUTIVE CREATIVE DIRECTOR, GREY ISTANBUL

In the 1980s the branding scene expanded. Everything had a brand: new companies, old companies, service companies, utility companies. Traditional advertising agencies found that large portions of their work were being farmed out to new design consultancies specializing in brand communication, as if this was a speciality that differed from advertising's original intent, or certainly from Ogilvy's view on what advertising should be – that every advertisement should contribute to the brand image. Since then, advertising agencies have had to redefine their offering in order to remain viable.

'The type of work changes on a daily basis; what we now call brand activation, but used to call below the line and was done at other agencies, is done here. Everyone works on everything. It's one big creative department and we like to think creatives should be able to work in any media. We are hoping that more work comes to us with a completely open media brief.'

STEVE FREEDMAN, GROUP CREATIVE SERVICES DIRECTOR, LEO BURNETT LONDON

But it is not just advertising agency thinking that is changing: there has also been a change in the kind of work design consultancies do. Just as advertising agencies are taking back some of the work design consultancies do, so designers are taking advertising campaigns on.

'To be honest I don't see a difference [between branding campaigns and advertising campaigns]. Everything we do contributes to how a brand is perceived in the marketplace. Whether doing a TV ad or designing brown paper bags we should be looking to communicate a consistent tone of voice and building a stronger brand presence for our client.'

SHANE BRADNICK, CREATIVE DIRECTOR, BMF, AUSTRALIA

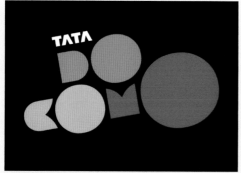

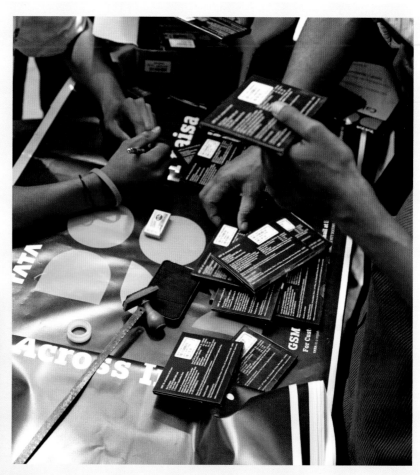

When India's Tata Group partnered with Japan's NTT DOCOMO in 2012, Wolff Olins was engaged to develop the identity and advertising for the new brand – Tata DOCOMO. The identity is friendly and gives plenty of opportunity for designers and users to play with it. Try looking at Tata DOCOMO on YouTube.

Brands require a set of guidelines determining how their separate elements should be used to ensure a strong, consistent identity. These guidelines show how the logos, type and images making up the Tata DOCOMO brand identity should be deployed.

BRAND VALUES

Every brand has brand values. Research a company online or look through an annual report and pretty soon you will encounter this term, but what does it mean? Put simply, brand values are the principles and philosophy that a brand advocates. Alycia de Mesa uses the example of different cell phone networks to illustrate how their positioning starts to indicate what their values might be; for example, some might offer the most innovative products, other mobile networks will promote integrity, operating in an ethical way that ensures fairness for customers. Brand values help to differentiate one brand or company from another and should stem from elements of the business itself, such as the business model, employee/employer relationships, research and development departments, customer service as well the type of relationship a brand would like to have with its consumers. A good branding agency is able to identify these key aspects and illustrate them evocatively in word, colour and form. Well-defined brand values create a brand identity critical for successful customer communications. We respond differently to a brand that suggests it is pioneering to one that suggests it is caring. It is the precision used in identifying believable, recognizable values that creates a brand that resonates with consumers. Even a value such as humour could be specified as wry, witty, playful or jolly. Each of those words are unique, they evoke different colours, imagery and sentence structures and consequently customers will respond to each word differently. A brand is made up of a small number of brand values in order to create a unique character and these values can be at the forefront or in the background of a communication at any time but whatever their format, they are the things that give a brand its worth and help put a product or concept deep into the hearts and minds of the consumer. These mobile network brands may also express similar positions in different ways to reflect their brand values, one brand being 'cheap and cheerful' and another 'financially astute' or 'no one's fool'.

In 2009, BMF Australia won a D&AD Yellow Pencil award for printed material in branding and a Silver Pencil award at the One Show for point of purchase for their Tooheys Extra Dry (TED) 696 project. The client, Lion Nathan Australia, wanted to launch a larger beer bottle, known as a longneck beer, but BMF saw two main problems in the longneck beer market: one was the competition and the other was the fact that longneck beers are put in brown paper bags at purchase. So, they turned the problem on its head and saw it as an opportunity. They asked well-known local and international artists to design paper bags incorporating the numbers 696. These paper bags were delivered to shops, which wrapped them around any longneck beer bottle sold. BMF also launched a website inviting the public to design a version of the bag, using the numbers 696 in the design. This then became a fully integrated branding campaign. To find out more you can view the case study online at Vimeo. This campaign worked because as a brand Tooheys Extra Dry is known for its edgy and surprising creative advertising and because its brand values are evocative, collaborative, fresh and innovative.

A number of alcohol brands have built up sponsorship relationships with the music or art scene over a number of years. Tooheys Extra Dry has a well-recognized relationship with the music scene in Australia that allowed for an easy and believable link with MTV for the culminating exhibition, allowing even more of their target audience to see their message and participate in the campaign.

'An idea like this could not work without the participation of a lot of people, from the clients being brave enough to put their brand in the hands of its consumers, to the agency giving the idea the freedom it needs to live.'

SHANE BRADNICK, CREATIVE DIRECTOR, BMF, AUSTRALIA

The 2009 'TED 696 Project' by BMF, Australia, used multiple media to engage both their customers and designers worldwide in a collaborative and innovative brand experience.

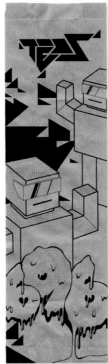

TED696 PROJECT
FINALISTS

WINNING DESIGN BY
MICHAEL WATT

TARGET MARKETS

'Everything you create for any brand is a direct expression of that brand. So without question it needs to reflect who they are and what they stand for.'

JOHN PATROULIS AND SCOTT DUCHON, EXECUTIVE CREATIVE DIRECTORS, AGENCY215, SAN FRANCISCO

The core essence of a brand and the values attached to it attract different target markets (see Chapter 4). Simply put, a 'target market' is a group of customers to which a company has decided to direct its marketing and its products. These groups of customers are defined by a number of distinct aspects, which may be geographic, demographic, behavioural or product-related.

Similar products can have very different brand attributes and propositions and therefore different target markets. Each target market has different priorities and sensibilities as each is composed of individuals. With regard to mobile phone networks, for example, I may need great coverage and not be that concerned about the cost of it, while my friend may want a good-value deal; my mother has no interest in using the Internet yet I cannot imagine life without it. We are all in the mobile phone market but belong to different 'target markets'. So a brand has something it wants to say about itself and somebody it wants to say it to, and the best way to make a connection is to make sure that the brand has a personality that people respond to – a personality that is true to the brand's values, positioning and products.

BRAND PERSONALITY

De Mesa's description of how a brand lives and breathes is very useful: 'Much like a person, a brand has a fundamental identity, a projected image, perceptions about it held by others, and relationships to parents, siblings, and those we want to get to know and impress.' It is essential to understand this personification of brands in order to work on branded products effectively.

Every modern brand will have a brand personality, sometimes known as 'communication attributes', which provides guidelines for the tone of voice used in the brand's marketing. The main personality attributes for two different software producers might be 'serious and knowledgeable' and 'visionary and connected'. The way in which these two companies speak to you and show understanding of your life and needs will be very different. Their distinct tones of voice are evidence of their different brand personalities.

Think back to Innocent, with their natural fruit smoothies. They endeavour to be honest, natural and engaging. This is their brand personality. If a piece of brand communication, whether verbal or visual, is not in this tone of voice, it is not Innocent. This starts with the logo and continues through to the advertising.

A brand's personality can be deciphered by looking at all their communications (logo, packaging, advertising, retail environments, point of sale) and deciding what impression they give you. Although you may not get the exact wording you should be able to get close enough if all the agencies are communicating effectively. If you are not the target audience, however, you may have a different response from that of those it was intended for; you may find something twee and someone else may find it nostalgic. How it is communicated also reveals who it is for.

TASK
Find advertising for a product that you like and write a list of ten words or attributes that you think describe how the brand is trying to portray itself. For example, you may find the product, such as a running shoe, comfortable, but the brand communications may be about sport and winning.

WORKING IN AN AD AGENCY ON A BRAND

Bigger brands tend to be like the more popular kids in the playground – the other kids already know who they are and some of them know that they will like what they have to say. This means that the kids will at least keep an open mind to the thing the brand wants to communicate. Consequently the client is very invested in the identity that they have taken time to build, the personality that they have created. Some clients will have spent a good deal of time getting to know their target market, so they have some understanding of their responses and preferences.

As advertising creatives, there is a reason why we get excited about working on big brands, why we want to work on Calvin Kleins and not Calvin Clones. It is because we are not immune and we have bought in to the brand idea too. We, too, perceive an added value, and understand that some brands are just 'cooler', even when their products are pretty similar to their competitors'. Sometimes the products developed by a brand you are working on will initially make you cringe. Yes, there might be a more creative 'opportunity' on the incontinence underpants brief, but where is the glamour? The attraction of working on big brands is that there is also likely to be a bigger budget and more consumer acceptance, which means advertising will have an impact and we will be able to work in the more expensive media choices.

For an advertising creative, working on any brand, from the most glamorous ones to the more mundane ones, has challenges. Working on the better-known brands means you have to deal with the existing brand image (how the brand is actually perceived by the consumer) as well as the brand identity (how the clients think the brand should be perceived). These are often two vastly different things. A consumer experience of a customer help desk, for example, may be very different from how the MD of that company imagines it, yet it creates the brand image.

Naomi Klein argues that ad agencies have envisioned themselves as guardians of the brand personality and value. Advertisers have adopted the role of protecting, enhancing and delivering a particular tone of voice and brand values. In practice, for creatives, this means that while you may have a great idea that you believe will sell the product, unless that idea is considered right for the brand it will not get past account handling, who stand up for the brand values of the client.

Sometimes it appears that the brief we have been given does not take the existing brand image into account. Consequently we may find that we do not understand or agree with the proposition as, in our opinion, we cannot say what the client and agency team want to say about the brand in a way that connects truthfully with the audience. Often, at some point in the creative process, we end up shouting at the brief that it is mad or just downright stupid. But the fact of the matter is that we have to answer the brief that the client has agreed. And we have to answer it in the right tone of voice, enhancing all of the brand values, and we have to trust that the clients and planners have researched the target market more thoroughly than we have. No matter how funny your script is the client will not budge from their main points of differentiation and their values, though they may allow you to take a different slant than usual, provided it still feels 'on brand'.

Jim Aitchinson points out in *Cutting Edge Advertising* that clients are only too aware that 'Brands can be *reframed*, so people see them differently.' This allows the advertiser to take a brand that is no longer communicating with its customers and re-engage them. Generally it is not our job to change the product or question it but to re-present it to the target market.

COMMUNICATING FOR A BRAND

Imagine that the brand you have been given to work on is 'Bob'. For this example, 'Bob' can be personified as a school kid with a hobby. We can see that there are some issues with Bob but we are not allowed to change them, we simply have to explain to the other kids in the playground that Bob could be their friend too. We need to find a way of relating Bob to them. Bob may be fully convinced that everyone will find his indexed collection of matchsticks interesting; you may be convinced that everyone will not find it interesting, they will just find it odd, and he certainly will not get a girlfriend (or the female market).

Your job, however, is not to jump up and down on his matchsticks and tell him that he should throw them away. The matchsticks are part of Bob just as the scientific research that helped create many products are part of those brands. Perhaps Bob does not need to run up to everyone and try to explain the value of his matchstick collection over and over again; perhaps he just needs to be 'reframed' as a kid that is dedicated and knowledgeable. These may already be his brand values but no one can really see it. This level of dedication can make him interesting or quirky and the creative needs to evoke that part of Bob's brand personality. That is the job of advertising: to find a way of engagingly communicating on a brand's behalf to its audience. In fact many technology-based products such as cars do just that, showing research labs filled with staff obsessed with perfecting their product in a humorous yet empathetic way. This delivers the dedicated side of a personality while also showing a more humble side through self-deprecating humour.

DEVELOPING TONE OF VOICE FROM BRAND VALUES

Working in an agency inevitably means working on brands and understanding brand personality. Everything must be delivered in the right tone of voice. Understanding that you are communicating on behalf of a brand and not yourself is key. This almost always starts with a written tone of voice, as an art director or designer's job is often to find the right visual tone to apply to words that must be included. If you are already working in a copywriter/art director team then you will be considering your copywriting at the same time as any visualizations. If not, and you are an art director working on your own, you need to start thinking about which words you will use and how you will use them, as this creates a tone of voice.

'You have to find the tone of voice for the brand. It can't be yours, or all your work will sound the same (obvious, but surprisingly common). If the tone is reassuring and measured like John Lewis, then that tells you how the ads should sound. If it's Tango, then zany is good. No one wants a hilarious Save the Children ad and, likewise, no one wants a heartfelt Peperami ad.'

ADAM TUCKER, CREATIVE DIRECTOR,
LEO BURNETT LONDON

Creatives think about the brand's personality and the brand's values and create a tone of voice that is right for the people that they wish to communicate with, the target market, while being true to the brand. Often, they will approach the subtle differences between brands as an opportunity to be a little bit wittier or friendlier or more empowering than another similar brand.

'Most people would probably get the same feeling for both Volvo and Nissan based solely on their company profile — it is the tonality that makes the difference.'

MIA ROBERTSSON, COPYWRITER,
FAMILJENPANGEA, STOCKHOLM

There are many different tones of voice and many nuances within them. You will become skilled in delivering them as you study and work. Just as people are friendly in different ways, so are brands: even within a tone of voice that is 'open, honest, friendly and humorous' there are subtleties in delivering it that make it feel more like a particular brand's personality.

'Certain brands use particular tones of voice because it fits their brand attributes. For example toothpaste often feels clinical, Ryvita — chatty and matey, BMW — exciting, M&S food — mouth-watering.'

MADELEINE MORRIS, CREATIVE DIRECTOR,
GREY LONDON

Common tones of voice include scientific, caring, matter-of-fact, sensual, fun, child-like, concerned, friendly, knowledgeable mentor, authoritative, challenging, urban youth, informative and empowering. Finding adverts that you think deliver these tones of voice will help you understand them better.

As your creative skills develop you will become confident with the use of colour, layout and typography, which all contribute to the overall tone of a piece of communication. Written tone of voice can sometimes be overlooked in the design process. Achieving the right tone of voice in your copy can make a vital difference in successful communications and presents a unique challenge in persuading audiences to read what you have to say. Copywriters are highly skilled individuals who use a written tone of voice to communicate a brand's personality.

TASK

'Find an existing advert. Rewrite the same copy in three or four different tones of voice — do it conversationally, do it matter of fact, do it lightheartedly, do it youthfully — and then describe how you would change the image to match.'

BRENDAN WILKINS, CREATIVE DIRECTOR,
EURO RSCG, LONDON

OPPOSITE
This 2009 John Lewis ad by UK agency Adam & Eve has a cultured, understanding, discerning and middle-class tone of voice.

Joseph Joseph nest £35, Chef 'n g'rabbit junior £18, Laguiole cheese knives £24

John Lewis
johnlewis.com

The Adam & Eve 2010
TV ad 'Always a Woman'
is credited with turning
around the fortunes of
the John Lewis stores.

WE MUST MAKE THIS A THING OF THE PAST

CHILD SOLDIER
Democratic Republic
of the Congo c.2000

It's frightening to think children today are still recruited as soldiers, employed as prostitutes, or don't have access to clean water. These are some of the many issues Save the Children is working to make obsolete. Don't miss our unique **'Make it a thing of the past'** exhibition. For details in your capital city, visit savethechildren.org.au

Save the Children
savethechildren.org.au

ABOVE
This ad by M&C Saatchi Australia for the charity Save the Children is plain-speaking, authentic and distinctive, making its activism evident to the viewer.

RIGHT
This 2007 Peperami salami ad from Lowe London is part of a long-running campaign using variations on the endline 'Peperami: It's a Bit of an Animal' for Unilever's various Peperami products. The character 'The Animal' encapsulates an approach that is fun, tongue-in-cheek, masculine and naughty. Its tone of voice is now so embedded in the public's imagination that Unilever have been able to make the move to crowd-sourcing the advertising.

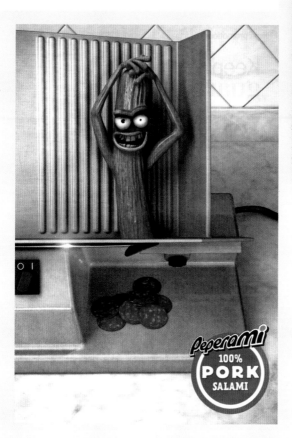

Peperami
100%
PORK
SALAMI

inspired by
everything everywhere

Good news! Orange customers can use T-Mobile's signal as well.

You can now call and text in more places
Visit t-mobile.co.uk/share to sign up

Life's for Sharing

T··Mobile··

inspired by
everything everywhere

And vice versa (which is Latin for right back at you).

You can now call and text in more places
Visit orange.co.uk/share to sign up

together we can do more

orange

ABOVE
Fallon and Saatchi & Saatchi collaborated in the UK to create a linked campaign for the T-Mobile and Orange phone networks. Their distinctive written and visual tones of voice are evident.

USING VISUAL TONE OF VOICE

Consider the way you would describe to your friends how good a party was. It is possibly not the same way that you would describe the same party to your parents, or grandparents, or doctor. It is not just the vocabulary that would change, but potentially the entire contents of the conversation. Now start to think as an art director: the visual tone of voice is just as important as the verbal tone of voice. Imagine which party photos you would show to your different audiences.

At the time of writing, mobile phone giant Vodafone is the UK's most valuable brand and is the world leading telecommunications company, ranking seventh most valuable brand in the world. The Partners, UK, have recently created a range of packaging for Vodafone, making use of visual language based on metaphors to promote specific product benefits, for example bees implying busy, hardworking people, and shoals of fish implying sociability.

The work needs to be able to communicate internationally because Vodafone is a worldwide brand and this packaging is to be used worldwide. 'Red, Rock Solid and Restless' are Vodafone's brand values and personality. 'Red' stands for passion and spirit, 'Rock Solid' means dependable and empathetic, and finally 'Restless' is always striving to improve and be funny. The Partners' work is colourful, bold, modern, understanding, playful and stylish, and thus fits Vodafone's brand personality beautifully.

A good example of the visual brand elements (brand personality traits) of an identity communicating a message is Vodafone's acquisition of the Hutch network

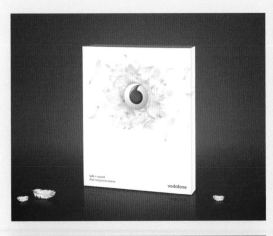

in India. This is also a good example of colour as a sign (see Chapter 2). Hutch was personified as a pug dog that faithfully follows its owner around and this was summed up in the advertising endline 'Wherever you go our network follows'. Hutch's primary brand colour was pink. Vodafone's primary brand colour is red and although it is dependable and empathetic, it has to challenge itself to improve. But humour is also a part of the Vodaphone brand personality; it cannot challenge itself to improve in a dry, robotic way, it is 'restless'.

The launch campaign showed the Hutch pug dog in its pink, solid but slightly old-fashioned kennel; the dog then went out for a day's play and on its return home discovered a new, red, kennel. This kennel was designed to be fun, with multiple exits and entrances, but it was also solid, dependable and modern, perfectly embodying what a dog would want. The change from pink to red was a quickly understood message, and reinforced by the endline 'Hutch is now Vodafone'. The launch advert can be viewed on YouTube. The rebranding and brand-building project involved block-booking all advertising time on the Star Network for 24 hours on launch. The network conducted day-after research with viewers on the Star Gold channel (a Hindi film channel) with the advert scoring 88 per cent in brand awareness, a previously unheard of figure.

Thus, tone of voice dictates many aspects of advertising. If a brand personality is serious, caring and empathetic, as you would imagine a nurse to be, then it is pointless delivering stand-up routines to the client.

The Partners 2010
packaging for Vodafone.

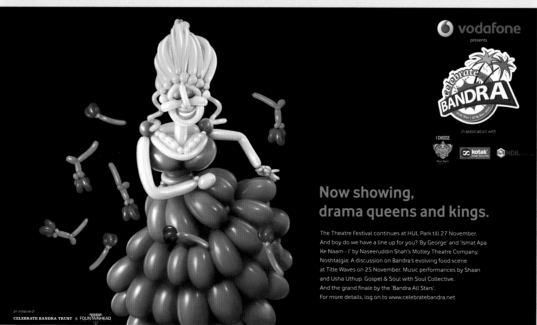

Now showing, drama queens and kings.

The Theatre Festival continues at HUL Park till 27 November. And boy do we have a line up for you? 'By George' and 'Ismat Apa Ke Naam - I' by Naseeruddin Shah's Motley Theatre Company. Noshtalgia: A discussion on Bandra's evolving food scene at Title Waves on 25 November. Music performances by Shaan and Usha Uthup. Gospel & Soul with Soul Collective. And the grand finale by the 'Bandra All Stars'. For more details, log on to www.celebratebandra.net

LEFT
Ogilvy & Mather Mumbai's 2011 Vodafone campaign to celebrate Bandra is passionate, empathetic and funny, and uses a limited range of colours so that the red zings.

When Hutch's brand colours changed from orange to pink, the pug – Cheeka, symbolizing the brand's values – was shown in a variety of ads with a pink nose or a pink bone.

OPPOSITE
Cheeka demonstrated the smooth transition from Hutch to Vodafone while maintaining all the customer-focused service that consumers expected.

Hutch is now Vodafone

For years you have come to expect good things from Hutch. And now that we are Vodafone, with over 200 million customers in 25 countries, we will bring in a host of exciting products, thoughtful services and relevant solutions. And as always we'll do our best to live up to your expectations.

www.vodafone.in | 98200 98200

vodafone

STARTING
A
CONVERSATION

4

4 STARTING A CONVERSATION

TARGET MARKETS

Because we — the client and the advertising agency — are not necessarily members of the target market that we want to speak to, we need to collect information about its habits, preferences, sensibilities and culture in order to become more knowledgeable. At the heart of this drive is research, which will be conducted by research companies, by the planners within an advertising agency and by the creatives themselves.

Advertising and marketing are displayed in public places visible to everyone, so you might be forgiven for thinking that they are aimed at everyone. However, you only need to think about the adverts that you notice – some of them are funny, entertaining or impactful, while some do not even register – to realize that they are not all created with you in mind. If you are male the chances are you do not even glance at the ads for super-length mascara, and why would you? You are not targeted.

People are individuals and so advertising needs to be carefully targeted. Ideally, advertising wants to talk to as many people as possible in one communication. However, this aim conflicts with our true experience of life, in which the people that surround us reflect a range of views, beliefs, preferences, finances and life experience; 'the public' is fragmented. All the people on a bus may be unified in the activity of using public transport, but they come from different backgrounds and lead different lives and so cannot necessarily all be targeted in the same way. The global market only serves to highlight the differences among people.

Although there clearly is not a single public with which to initiate a conversation, there are distinct groupings of people that come together for one product or activity, perhaps forming different groups for another product or activity. To take the example of being on a bus, we might not all be going for an important job interview, yet we may all share the experience of waiting endlessly for a bus only for three to turn up at once, as the old cliché goes.

We also all like to feel that we belong to a culture, as it gives us a sense of community and citizenship. For example, we might be part of student culture, business culture, skateboarding culture or new-mum culture. We recognize the signs that are shown to us in adverts, feel as though our lives are reflected in the advertising and are glad someone is on our wavelength.

In accepting that we are not all part of one big group and that it is not financially feasible for business to speak to us individually, we need to understand that we will be categorized into broad groups, becoming more closely targeted as each of the categorization methods is applied.

RIGHT
How a client reaches
the consumer through
their ad agency.

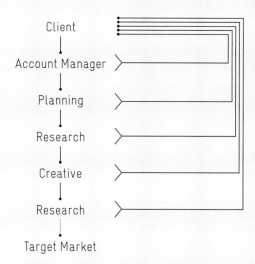

Client

Account Manager

Planning

Research

Creative

Research

Target Market

Presentations
of findings and
agreement to
proceed

RIGHT
Are you attracted by
this 2003 DDB Helsinki
press ad?

Fortunately you do not have to settle for mouse grey.

The new, bigger Polo

RIGHT
Do you identify with this
1998 Discover Brokerage
ad by US agency Black
Rocket?

YOU'RE NOT YOU WHEN YOU'RE HUNGRY.

Are you targeted by these ads for Snickers?

STANDARD CATEGORIZATION METHODS

In describing the target market on a brief all of the following methods can be used in conjunction with one another. However, they are quite basic tools. The planner will also use more in-depth research methods to analyse the behaviours of the target market.

SOCIAL CATEGORIZATION

The A, B, C1, C2, D and E categories may be something with which you are already familiar. They appear on most briefs and are a description of the jobs, and therefore income, that a household has. The presumption is that the occupation of the earner can describe their buying habits. However, this is a very blunt tool. My first creative partner and I had the same occupation – advertising creative – and were at the same level, yet I bought a house in the suburbs and filled it with a mix of second-hand and IKEA furniture and she bought a flat in the city and filled it with designer pieces. Not everyone in the same income bracket behaves in the same way.

LIFE STAGES

The life stages method of categorization is a relatively new field in market research, borrowed from sociology. It describes people as they move through the relationships in their life, from being a young single person with substantial freedom through to being widowed in late life. This presumes that everyone at a given stage in his or her life will act in a similar way. It is true that it can describe action – I moved to the suburbs when I had a young family and had less disposable income than my creative partner. However, although I had fitted the vision of the 'bachelor stage' when younger (a young, single person with disposable income), I also had friends of the same age who bought their own home, thereby drastically reducing their income and changing their spending habits. Not everyone at the same life stage behaves in the same way.

BRAND RELATIONSHIPS

Another method of categorization that is looked on favourably at the moment is a person's brand relationships. Researchers have found that brands can help in explaining a person's preferences, in bringing that person to life for other people. For example, a person may be described as wearing Nike shoes, an O'Neill's top and Ted Baker jeans while listening to his iPod. It is quick and easy shorthand as it paints an understandable picture. It is flexible as it can describe both a 14-year-old schoolboy and a 40-year-old man. They share a liking of the same products and brand messages though do not share the same income or life stage. A brand tells you about your target audience's values and helps with targeting and strategy. However there is a danger of being too simplistic with it; people cannot be tied down so easily.

'In Germany there has been a backlash against being so easily pigeonholed with the emergence of the "canny" shopper. This is a phenomenon where someone will go to Waitrose and to Lidl and this makes them feel clever; they are knowingly saving money.'

ALI BUCKNALL, FREELANCE CONSULTANT STRATEGIST, LONDON

TASK
Look at your own family and categorize the members according to each of these methods. Do you all neatly slot into a single section or do you cross many categories?

OCCUPATION GROUPS

A
Business people – directors, CEOs, very senior managers,
highest level civil servants

B
Business people – qualified middle managers of large businesses
Owners of middle to small businesses employing a number of staff
High-level civil servants, educationalists and local councillors

C1
Non-manual managers/junior management
Owners of small businesses employing small staff/no staff
Varied qualifications

C2
Skilled manual workers
Supervisors of other manual workers

D
Semi-skilled or unskilled manual workers
Trainees for skilled manual work

E
State dependency for over 6 months – unemployed, sickness, other reasons
Casual workers

LIFE STAGES

The bachelor stage
Young single people

Newly married
Young co-habiting couples without children

The full nest 1a
Young co-habiting couples with dependent children under 6 years old

The full nest 1b
Young co-habiting couples with dependent children over 6 years old

The full nest 2
Older co-habiting couples with dependent children

The empty nest a
Older working co-habiting couples with no children living at home

The empty nest b
Older retired co-habiting couples with no children living at home

Solitary survivors a
Older working single people

Solitary survivors b
Older retired single people

RESEARCH METHODS

The following are three principal research methods, helping the client and the advertiser to know their market. You might ask why companies need to know their customers in such detail. The answer is to communicate effectively. Think for a moment about the target market 'students'. There is a widely held assumption that students are poor, and if you ask students they will say that they are poor. If you look at objective data students do not have much money going in and out of their accounts, they are often in debt and they talk to each other about how poor they are. However, although they might perceive themselves as poor, many own iPods, laptops and smartphones. To talk to this group a brand cannot just talk to 'poor' people.

QUANTITATIVE RESEARCH

Quantitative research samples the responses of a number of people to given questions and represents the answers numerically. Quantitative market research gauges, describes and forecasts behaviour in large numbers of people. It is a good tool for tracking studies, for example to trace how brand perceptions change over time. Through the data you can track the market's view of your brand in comparison to similar brands. It uses a range of sampling strategies including online, mail and telephone surveys and personal quantitative interviews. All of these techniques use closed questions – that is, questions that require yes/no answers and are aimed at generating figures and graphs as their outcome.

A common criticism of this method is that quantitative market research studies often project their results on to the entire marketplace whereas in practice they have only sampled a relatively small number of people and that number is made up of people who like answering questionnaires. Another criticism is that the use of multiple closed questions as a methodology never gets to the reasons why people like or dislike things. This could lead to avoidable and damaging results such as, for example, a television show being cancelled when it needed only to be played half an hour later. A closed question such as 'Do you watch the *Star Show*? Answer: Yes/No' does not leave room for the question 'Why?'.

QUALITATIVE RESEARCH

Qualitative research is carried out by talking to small groups of people in informal environments and asks 'open' questions that invite them to explain what they mean and to provide full answers. Focus groups are an example of qualitative research – a small number of people in a room critiquing an idea or product. The researcher will look at what resonates in the group, their body language and their use of description, rather than just at straight statements. This combination of in-depth questioning and behavioural analysis helps write the sections of the creative brief that require information about the target market's habits and beliefs. Common criticisms of qualitative research are that the sample size is too small, participants can be critical for the sake of being critical, and group dynamics can sway the outcome.

THE RISE OF ETHNOGRAPHY

Ethnography, derived from social anthropology, is increasingly used as a qualitative research method. It is a process or method of research that aims to scientifically describe specific human cultures. Ethnography goes out into the field – into more natural environments.

'The principle of ethnography is really valid; if you want to understand the lion you don't go and look at it in the zoo.'

ALI BUCKNALL, FREELANCE CONSULTANT STRATEGIST, LONDON

To talk to people about breakfast cereals a researcher using the ethnographic approach would go to a person's home at breakfast time rather than asking them to sit in front of a two-way mirror one evening to talk with strangers. This puts people at their ease and they act more naturally. The person's breakfast habits are researched in the context of their family, their home, the contents of their fridge and how they really eat breakfast, not how they think they eat breakfast when asked to think about it out of context.

'Certainly ethnography is used in a commercial context in the insight stage as well as looking at individual psychology. It's not like the academic world where one might spend six months on a South Sea Island; this is more like one day in someone's home — it's a bastardized form of the academic approach.'

PETER TOTMAN, DIRECTOR OF QUALITATIVE RESEARCH, JIGSAW RESEARCH, LONDON

Common criticisms of this methodology are that it assumes that the researcher understands the language of the group they are observing, and that the group being observed will change its behaviour through the very act of being observed.

HOW RESEARCH HELPS DEVELOP STRATEGY

The purpose of strategy is to make a brand's marketing objective relevant to its target market.

'The best way to think about strategy is to think about an inverted pyramid. You have your business objective then your marketing objective then your advertising objective and then your advertising strategy and then your proposition.'

ALI BUCKNALL, FREELANCE CONSULTANT STRATEGIST, LONDON

'The task of any communication from a communications agency is to build stories that are capable of including and amusing a brand's audience and, in the end, for that message to be captured in their memory. It's something beyond the search for originality, and above all is much more than gratuitous offense or provocation for its own sake. It is part of a communication strategy that focuses on the product or the service in question, attempting to point out the unique properties of the product in a memorable way.'

LUCA D'ALESIO, CREATIVE DIRECTOR, TOUCHÉ ADVERTISING, BOLOGNA

Let us take an imaginary brand, 'Bob', as an example, and consider that the client who owns brand Bob has a business objective to increase sales. The marketing objective may then be to target new customers for brand Bob. The advertising objective may then be to get target market X to think about the product, brand Bob, in a new way. The advertising strategy that is developed is all about how to get the target market to the point where they re-evaluate Bob. What can we say and what insight into the target market will generate this response?

Agency planners are responsible for developing strategy and they utilize research to ensure that the advertising communication is as effective as it can be. There is a research cycle that most agencies follow to hone and assess this strategy.

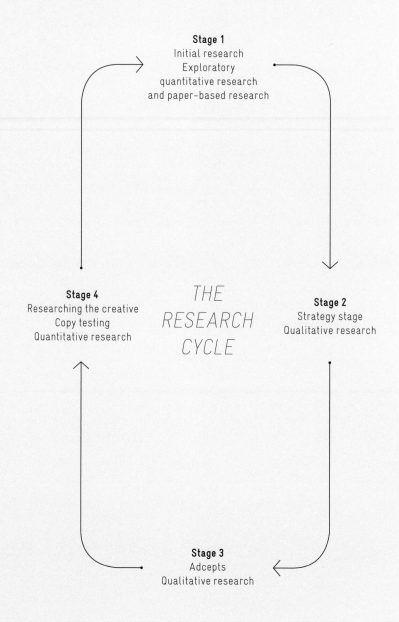

Stage 1
Initial research
Exploratory
quantitative research
and paper-based research

THE RESEARCH CYCLE

Stage 2
Strategy stage
Qualitative research

Stage 3
Adcepts
Qualitative research

Stage 4
Researching the creative
Copy testing
Quantitative research

STAGE 1 – INITIAL RESEARCH

The planner starts with desk research. The client provides a small bundle of information and the planner works in circles around it brainstorming, ending up with some answers and usually with further questions that need more research. The planner then looks at market research reports, press cuttings on any of the suggested areas of interest and things that expert eyewitnesses have said. After all this is done the planner can see what is missing from their knowledge. Commissioned research from specialist research companies may follow.

STAGE 2 – STRATEGY

The planner then starts to think about strategy, considering different possible positioning for a product. For example, strategies for Bob may be challenging ('Use Bob for two weeks and see the change'), or perhaps more empathetic ('Bob can help you live your life the way you want'); perhaps competitive ('Bob knows more than Tim'), historical ('Bob's knowledge is built on information he's collected for years'), or thinking of life without Bob ('What will happen to the things you care about without Bob?'). Other common strategies include: turning negative associations into positive ones ('The scientific data that Bob has is revolutionary'); focusing on real changes or customer service in store, often by looking at the owner or staff ('Bob has had a makeover'); or commenting on the price – which could be value or premium ('Bob may be a bit more expensive than Tim but you know you're getting quality').

> **TASK**
> Take five existing adverts for cars and work out the strategy they are using.

STAGE 3 – ADCEPTS

This is a qualitative stage, as what is needed is in-depth responses from the target market in order to discover which strategy it favours. People are invited to a research facility or the advertising agency research room to form part of a focus group to look at several different campaign concepts, often called 'adcepts'. These might be a sentence within a visual or a whole range of examples of all the possible campaign ideas. Ideas can be both tested and developed in these meetings, and ideas can also die here. Planners can

be under enormous agency pressure for a particular ad to 'win', so they may try to mitigate the risk inherent in the way in which the groups are run by focusing more on favoured routes.

STAGE 4 – EFFECTIVENESS

This stage often warrants the most criticism as it habitually uses a quantitative technique, which gives yes/no answers, rather than a qualitative technique, which elicits more in-depth and meaningful responses. In addition, this stage of the research cycle often uses methodologies that were in use 20 years ago, which are seen by many as outdated. These methods purportedly measure advertising's effectiveness.

Almost all clients require pre-testing (checking the effectiveness of an advert before it is aired) to be conducted. The majority require tracking studies after the adverts have aired to check if people have seen them. The client's internal marketing team are then able to show they exercised due diligence and mitigated risk when presenting within their client organization. If a campaign is to be launched internationally, then pre-testing must be undertaken in the relevant countries. Research is big business in its own right.

Global clients like global research systems and most global advertising companies own a research company. These research companies have their own proprietary systems. One of the largest research companies in the world, with 78 offices in 54 countries, is called Milward Brown, part of the WPP group. They use a system called Link™, which has a fixed number of criteria that they score adverts against. This is the most common system used in the UK.

In the United States there are a number of research companies, such as Gallup & Robinson, which is one of the oldest and largest, and they use several different research systems. One of the most popular is a process called the persuasion copy-testing system, or persuasion shift. These tests give one-number results and the number result has to show an increase in persuasion above the baseline number. Another US system scores against previous campaigns to see if the new campaign will outperform the old campaign.

All quantitative systems perceive effectiveness if an above-average number of people recollect the brand and advert and believe it may lead to a purchase.

Although clients like these processes because they feel very scientific, many

planners and researchers feel that they are too blunt a tool and do not capture enough in-depth information, nor observe how people react to ads that they see over and over again. Many clients also use them as a pass/fail test. It is torture for planners, as lots of campaigns die at this stage or come back to the agency for endless tweaking – but tweaking without in-depth information from the target market.

Econometric modelling is a more subtle approach. It originated as a tool that economists used to forecast developments in the economy. Advertisers use econometric modelling to factor in some of the variables in people's lives, such as their monthly finances or exposure to certain media.

'Econometric modelling is all about working out the return on investment, and if you build the model well enough with all the right variables mixed in you can discern the effect of what posters contributed on top of TV or how brand measures have tracked against sales, so it's all about defining how what we do delivers value.'

NICK STRINGER, STRATEGIC BUSINESS LEAD, BBH LONDON

Other, more tailored, nuanced approaches are used by some quantitative companies, such as Hall and Partners in the UK, and planners tend to prefer applying these methods. They involve testing the actual marketing objectives that the advertising is working to and judging whether the ads are answering them – if it is all about driving sales is the advertising in line with the marketing objectives? If it is about enhancing a brand's personality attributes, such as empathy, does it do this? The business strategy is not always to increase sales: sometimes it is to enhance brand awareness or decrease costs. Why is it important to understand the business and marketing objectives? Because advertising should be judged against these initial objectives to see if it is effective, not standardized ones that the campaigns were not designed to answer.

Effectiveness tracking is changing thanks to such developments as social media and interactivity with branded products, content and advertising. This can help clients, creatives and, in particular, the target market – who come back for more of what they like. The effectiveness of an ad is then fed back into the initial development of the next ad or a new campaign.

So chocolatey it's dangerous   Brand ⊗

An adcept can be as simple as a working endline with the simplest of executions. The problem at this stage is that if the presentation is too basic then it doesn't get the idea across, and if it is too finished, it gets judged as though it's a real advert.

At last a chocolate biscuit that's good for you!

DEVELOPING A STRATEGY

Developing a strategy requires insight into the target market and an understanding of the marketing objectives. The role of the planner is to make those two distinct things meet in the middle, somewhere where a conversation can start. Clients often have something they want to say that is not necessarily what anyone else finds interesting.

'What happens a lot is that what clients think is interesting, compelling and motivating is not what the public thinks is interesting, compelling and motivating and when those two things don't line up then that's when it's tough to do something good with the brief — where perception and reality aren't the same thing. The person that you're talking to decides what they want to listen to; you really have to understand your audience.'

MATT MACDONALD, EXECUTIVE CREATIVE DIRECTOR, JWT NEW YORK

The agency planner has the difficult role of translating the client-perceived benefit to something perceived by the target market as a benefit.

'The most important part of any brief is the insight, otherwise you'd just go with the name of the product and run with it. As creatives we don't need another creative thought but what we do need is insight: often it's difficult to have that insight for yourself.'

BRENDAN WILKINS, CREATIVE DIRECTOR, EURO RSCG LONDON

When Fallon Minneapolis developed the multi-award-winning campaign 'Alice – Follow the White Rabbit' for the science fiction channel Syfy, they used a key insight to make a connection with the audience while at the same time allowing creative freedom. Rocky Novak, director of digital development at Fallon Minneapolis, explained: 'We did some quantitative and qualitative research early on to find the most iconic pieces of the [*Alice's Adventures in Wonderland*] story, and what came back pretty loud and clear was that regardless of what remake and version of the story people were familiar with they all recalled the White Rabbit really really clearly. The coolest part was that in the version we were reading and seeing – pilots of the Syfy remake or re-imagination – he couldn't have been more different. He was an assassin. So that became a really nice spot for creative leverage.'

Sir John Tenniel's original 1865 illustration of the White Rabbit from *Alice's Adventures in Wonderland*.

Fallon Minneapolis
revisits the White Rabbit
for their 2009 'Follow the
White Rabbit' campaign
for the Syfy channel.

THE PROPOSITION

In most agencies the proposition is a single sentence that sums up the strategy; it is agreed with the client and creative director and it is the statement that the creative team must deliver to. An example of a single proposition is 'Brand X chocolate biscuits are fun to eat'. The strategic direction determines the idea of 'fun' as opposed to 'healthy' or 'energizing'.

'The planner's job is to try and simplify the strategy as much as possible: they don't always have to give you a proposition, you don't need it in five words, but give us a simple direction and agree it with the client. That's the best thing. The worst briefs are always where the client wants to say three or four things and you get into a mess.'

ANGUS MACADAM, EXECUTIVE CREATIVE DIRECTOR, DENTSU LONDON

That is not to say that you cannot imply a number of things within the single proposition, but every creative and planner will tell you that being single-minded in your communication is essential. A good example of offering a direct thought but suggesting other values is the advertising by the UK-based supermarket Tesco, in which their strategy and advertising proposition is clearly that they are a customer-focused business. They have an ongoing campaign that is cleverly encapsulated by the endline 'Every little helps'. This is a summation of Tesco's philosophy: value, customer ethos, trust and likeability encapsulated in three little words. It is astonishingly simple. In 1993 Tesco launched this customer-focused strategy to its staff and created many new offerings in its stores to help its customers – among them baby changing-rooms, extra checkout operators when there are queues, no-quibble exchange policies and a Clubcard. In the period from 1990 to 1995 the campaign attracted 1.3 million new customers and turnover increased by 38 per cent. In the period from 1995 to 1999 the campaign delivered incrementally more than £2.2 billion of turnover. Tesco tracked it all using econometric modelling but it considers what the UK-based IPA call 'likeability' to be the most clear predictor of advertising effectiveness.

'Top advertising companies nowadays mock themselves, utilize understatement and have a laugh with their audience. Superficially it would appear that modern advertising acts in a simplistic way, but the true power of an advert derives from this simplicity. Our function is to build a simple message, but not a dull one; one that is easily comprehensible, effective and, especially nowadays, optimistic and positive.'

LUCA D'ALESIO, CREATIVE DIRECTOR, TOUCHÉ ADVERTISING, BOLOGNA

There will be times when you have to work to double propositions in your career, but what tends to happen is that you focus on one and push back on the other. An example of a double proposition is 'Brand X chocolate biscuits are fun to eat and they also lower cholesterol'. The challenge is to decide which one to focus on.

Other problems might be hidden within a proposition. Sometimes the phrase that masquerades as a proposition is not really a proposition but a creative idea. You can waste a lot of time on a brief like that because it was quite creative to begin with.

'You get a proposition which is almost giving you the endline sometimes and you think "well, I know what you needed to say", so there's not enough room to move. All the ideas methodology is stripped away from you because it gets taken away from you at brief stage.'

BRENDAN WILKINS, CREATIVE DIRECTOR, EURO RSCG LONDON

'If 50 per cent off is the strategy but it is written as "gives you more" as the proposition then you have problems. "Gives you more" is already a creative idea. But if the proposition had been left at "50 per cent off" you might have fun with media – with only half-finished radio ads or half-billboards.'

SHANE BRADNICK, CREATIVE DIRECTOR, BMF, AUSTRALIA

Granny Smiths.

What's the difference between ours and our competitors'?

Not much really.

They're the same quality as Waitrose.

And the same price as Asda.

Comparison based on loose Granny Smith Apples.
Asda price checked at Leyton Store 26.09.05.
Price comparison excludes Express, Metro and IOM.

TESCO | *Every little helps*

A 2006 Lowe print ad
for Tesco, the British
supermarket chain.

THE BRIEF

The brief is written by the lead planner with input from the account handler and creative director. It is signed off by the client and forms the contract of trust between the client and the agency. The brief exemplar here is for an imaginary beer, Briaska, and is typical of brief formats in leading agencies, though exact phrasing will vary.

The first page acts as a summary of the purpose of the brief, identifies all the key players and dates and specifies the media. The subsequent pages are designed to answer many of the questions that the creative may have when working on the brief. The marketing objective is made evident under 'Why are we advertising?', the target market is made three-dimensional with 'Who are we talking to?' and the tone of voice is described in 'What is the brand's tone of voice?'. The proposition is delivered by 'What should the advertising say?' and supported by 'Why should they believe it?'. In the case of Briaska Beer, highlighting how the brand is prepared to stand up for freedom of expression may be a viable route, particularly if it can be backed up with real examples. A section that identifies problems and opportunities for the brand may be included. Mandatories and considerations are always made explicit. An important section that is not always on agency briefs is: 'What does the client expect?' This is almost as helpful as being in a meeting with the client as it suggests how creative, experimental or pragmatic the client wants to be with this campaign.

MADE UP AGENCY
CREATIVE BRIEF

Client – Briaska Beer	Project – Cultural Festivals
Job No. – 01020304	Brief Received – date
Creative Time – 2 weeks	Client Presentation Date - date
Account Exec – Jack Green	Internal Review Date – date
Traffic – Jane Blue	Creative Group Head – Jennifer Orange
Planner – Joe Pink	Creative Teams – Sandy & Timo, Phil & Alex

Overall Intention

Get; confident free-thinking cultured 25 – 45-year-old people

To; see that Briaska adds to their cultural experience

By; highlighting Briaska's 10 years of cultural sponsorship

Requirement
Radio, Posters, Press, Digital
Production budget £250k
Media budget £2.5 million

Originated by Joe Pink

Why are we advertising?
To open up a new market for Briaska while maintaining their values.

Who are we talking to?
Confident, free-thinking and independent-minded individuals who regularly take part in cultural activities. They go out rather than stay at home and have a busy social calendar. They are educated, articulate and marketing savvy so are not easily persuaded. They like to experiment with new, challenging events and activities and enjoy being part of the avant garde. They may only just be aware of the brand as it hasn't entered this market yet; they may have come across it on holiday.

What problem or opportunity does the brand have with the consumer? Briaska has been involved in cultural events in Russia for the last 10 years.

What would we like consumers to think about the brand? It's a progressive, independent-minded, cultured brand

What should the advertising say? For the last 10 years we've been integral to avant garde Russian culture.

Why should they believe it? Briaska has facilitated cultural events, even when they have run contrary to Government desires.

What is the brand's tone of voice? Provocative, educated and innovative.

What does the client expect? A campaign that links innovation and taste to cultural value.

What are the mandatories? Timings mean we need to focus on outdoor first.

Considerations
We have access to their archive of cultural event photography.

EMPATHIZING WITH THE TARGET MARKET

'I was writing copy for a cancer mouthwash. A lot of people had been trying to write it before and they were trying to be witty or edgy and that is so not appropriate to someone in a cancer waiting-room; they wanted work that was more empathetic to their situation. So I made it really matter of fact and straightforward and simply gave them the details. I didn't go all sympathy, sympathy, because that wasn't what was needed, and a caring tone of voice is easy to misinterpret as patronizing. Empathy means putting yourself in someone else's position so you're coming from their point of view.'

MADELEINE MORRIS, CREATIVE DIRECTOR, GREY LONDON

To be empathetic is to understand and identify with another person's situation and feelings. The key to empathy is research, observation, imagination and an open mind. In advertising, you will find that you are usually selling to someone that you do not immediately identify with. Empathizing with somebody does not mean patronizing them. Helping you to understand the target market and being able to empathize with it is key to a planner's role.

It took 74 people to put a smile back on my face

This UK National Health Service recruitment ad from D'Arcy juxtaposes the woman's slow smile with the noises and people involved in the healing process. The tone, words and imagery all show empathy with the people's situations.

> **TASK**
> 'To get into someone else's head it helps if you can picture who they are. Think of a type of person that is nothing like you – it doesn't need to be extreme, like an astronaut, it could be a lady on a checkout with two kids at home. Read about people that might be like that in magazines and newspapers, read books written from that point of view and then write a description of a day and a night in their lives.'
>
> MADELEINE MORRIS, CREATIVE DIRECTOR, GREY LONDON

HOW INSIGHTS INFORM CREATIVE IDEAS

Account planners in agencies work closely with creatives on projects to shape the briefs behind the creative ideas, researching and turning their findings into actionable insights. In addition to the research on the creative brief, planners will work hard to supply further insights throughout the duration of the campaign. Planners have a unique role in an agency as they are the closest to the consumer and are responsible for understanding the position of a brand in the minds of consumers. Social and digital media have given planners a new platform for listening to and engaging with a target audience.

In 2005 UK creative team Angus Macadam and Paul Jordan created a dramatic advert for teen road safety. Research by the Department for Transport had revealed that teenagers often come out of school and step out on to the road without looking. The brief was to trigger teenagers to think twice at the roadside. The creative team observed that teenagers behave in certain ways around their friends and this insight formed the crux of the campaign. The planner, Becky Barry, summarized this insight as 'autopilot'. By watching the behaviour of teenagers outside schools the team came up with a multi-award-winning campaign. Barry didn't just brief the team and then leave them to be 'creative', she worked with them, honing the insight, ensuring the creative team were bringing that insight to life. It is the insight in any brief that offers the opportunity to make outstanding work that not only resonates with the target market but can also gain attention from awards panels.

'At the time we kept talking about how teenagers almost have their own language, almost as if they're talking in another language like French, so we thought we should talk to them in "French". Capturing it all on a mobile and making it feel as authentic as possible was our way of allowing them to pay attention to the message.'

PAUL JORDAN, EXECUTIVE CREATIVE DIRECTOR, DENTSU LONDON

The story was simple – a group of friends walk down the street filming each other on their mobile phones and one of them gets knocked down by a car – but the insight and the way it was executed brought it chillingly to life. The film was left as an unbranded video on a website and teenagers passed it around their friends, resulting in 29 per cent of all UK teens seeing the viral in just five days.

Your job as a creative is to translate the proposition, thinking about what it could mean for the target market and trying to incorporate the product into that story. You need to understand the strategy and, where possible, find out what the original marketing or business objectives were. You need to empathize with your target market. At the end of all of this you will need to come up with a campaign idea.

'It all comes down to some basic principles. Knowing whom we're talking to, finding a strategic insight to latch on to, then finding the most exciting and unique way of expressing that insight.'

JOHN PATROULIS AND SCOTT DUCHON, EXECUTIVE CREATIVE DIRECTORS, AGENCY215, SAN FRANCISCO

In this Leo Burnett 2005 TV ad for the UK Department for Transport, part of the 'THINK!' campaign, a group of teenagers are filming themselves on their mobile phones until one gets knocked down. The ad replicated the low-resolution appearance of footage shot on a mobile phone to great effect.

THINKING
OF
WHAT
TO
SAY

5

5 THINKING OF WHAT TO SAY

THE IDEA

When a creative team is briefed by the planner and the account executive, the target market, strategy, proposition, product and tone of voice are explained at great length. The team is then left with the hallowed piece of paper, the brief, in a room on its own for a finite amount of time, during which it is expected to brainstorm until it comes up with a great idea. This is where the hard work for the creative team starts.

'In today's world advertising amuses, it plans surprises for people and in cases like Volkswagen's Fun Theory, it even changes people's behaviour.'

ERGIN BINYILDIZ, EXECUTIVE CREATIVE DIRECTOR, GREY ISTANBUL

You cannot just tell people about the product, you need an engaging idea. But what is an advertising idea, and how do you come up with one?

For a creative, an idea is a thought, concept or theme that links the product to the target market. Ideas come in many forms; you might get a single image in your head, a single word, a well-known phrase, a song lyric, a philosophical point, you might remember something you have seen or heard or just have a random silly thought.

'Because TED 696 was a bigger version of the original we had a variety of ideas to do with big; blurry photos of Bigfoot holding bottles of TED [Tooheys Extra Dry], other ideas of big hands and big mouths; we thought about beer enlargement pumps like a direct response campaign. We went round the houses before we ended up with our idea.'

SHANE BRADNICK, CREATIVE DIRECTOR, BMF, AUSTRALIA

An idea is perhaps best described as a route or a path that you can follow. To take the example described by Shane Bradnick, you could follow the path about beer enlargement pumps, but alternatively you could follow a path about owning all bags for longneck beer bottles – which was the idea the TED 696 campaign eventually settled on (see Chapter 3). From initial routes other paths can be found until an idea emerges that feels interesting.

However, you do not stop there. The whole point of brainstorming is to develop the habit of having lots and lots of ideas, not just 10 or 20. Every creative would love to have produced an answer straight away or in the first hour, but it does not quite work like that. We all have to work pretty hard at it. Sometimes the first or second thing we write down is our 'big idea' but it becomes this only after investigating many other routes and then revisiting it with a new understanding of everything it could mean. Sometimes a particular route needs a little work in order to find out if there are any ideas there that are not immediately evident. If it feels interesting, explore it, but do not spend too long on it – learn to recognize that some thoughts are just dead ends. Say your ideas out loud and bounce them off your creative partner. What might seem boring to you might spark an idea in them; what seems great to you may make no sense to them.

These three ads from the 2005 DDB London press campaign for the Harvey Nichols department store express different ways in which a person might deny themselves day-to-day necessities in order to buy that one great item.

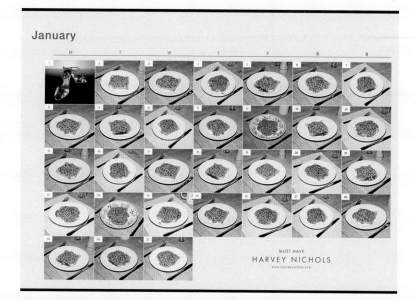

An important point to grasp when working as an advertising creative is that ideas also have to be different from each other. When advertising students first start trying to generate ideas they tend to have one idea and repeat it in slightly different ways, and they consider this to be a list of different ideas rather than different executions of the same idea. For example, a student might think that they have created three ideas: 1) Bigfoot holding a huge beer bottle; 2) a giant holding a huge beer bottle; 3) a dinosaur holding a huge beer bottle. The problem here is that our student has got so engrossed in the idea that only a creature so large can make the bottle look normal size that they have not noticed that it is in fact just one idea expressed in different ways – in other words three executions – and have failed to think of other ideas or to consider that this idea may not be the best one.

Once you are happy that the idea that you have found is interesting and can be developed further then you need to explore your root idea with executional ideas.

'Everyone can come up with ideas. As creatives we have to decide which is the best and grow it.'

HIROKI NAKAMURA, HAJIME YAKUSHIJI, SHINSAKU OGAWA, HIROSHI KOIKE, TSUBASA KAYASUGA, CREATIVE TEAM MEMBERS, DENTSU TOKYO

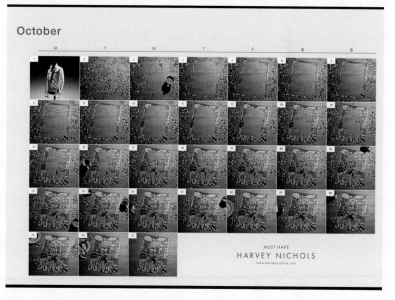

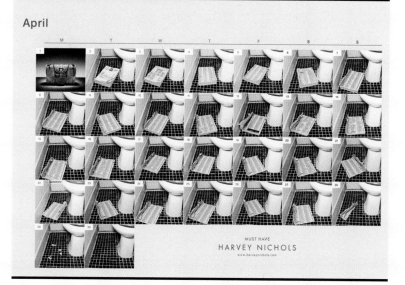

5

THE EXECUTIONS

THINKING OF WHAT TO SAY

The execution is your advert – though at this stage it is not in its finalized form. Executions require you to think of the different ways that your idea can be expressed. Often exaggeration is employed through humour to get the point across. For example, a 2005 press campaign by DDB London for high-class store Harvey Nichols had one execution in which various meals of beans on toast were shown, another with a jigsaw puzzle being completed on a table, and yet another with a phone book being slowly used up instead of toilet roll.

'The Harvey Nichols calendar campaign has a simple human truth at the heart. It was a very satisfying process: it came from the planner, who was a massive fashionista – she came from Greece I think. She told us a story about going to university, getting her grant on day one, and just blowing the lot on a dress she'd seen. She said, "I just told myself that I'd live on baked beans for a month." It was a story that stayed with us.'

JUSTIN TINDALL, GROUP EXECUTIVE CREATIVE DIRECTOR, LEO BURNETT LONDON

The idea was that people will do without anything in order to buy the things they really want; the potential consequences were exaggerated to add humour and impact; the visual theme running through the executions was a calendar month. It is essential in a campaign that each ad is not simply a repeat of the first with, for example, beans on toast, egg on toast, and cheese on toast, or the campaign will quickly become boring.

USING HUMOUR

Humour can be shown in all sorts of ways, but usually jokes have to be structured in order to work. Imagine that whatever you want to say in your execution is the set-up to a joke and your visual, headline or endline is the punchline. For example if you want to say that X brand chocolate biscuits are the most chocolatey biscuits available, you might envisage that to mean that they are dangerously chocolatey; this becomes the joke but it currently is not very funny so you work on it some more. If we put any more chocolate into X brand chocolate biscuits then you 'open the packet at your own risk'. From this we can visualize a number of executions, for example a posh house party that, upon the arrival of brand X biscuits, suddenly has an eruption of chocolate everywhere, covering the posh guests with chocolate; or the biscuit held in a stasis field as the density of the chocolate ingredients might cause a black hole. Write your set-up and then write the word 'then' or 'so' to help you deliver a punchline.

Using existing jokes can also help. You use them as a structural base and alter the characters, the products and the situations one by one to get closer to a believable scenario for your brand but without losing the essential jokiness.

TASK
Look at a well-known comic strip, such as *The Far Side*, and try to change elements within the jokes. Mix up the media a bit; try watching stand-up routines and identify a particularly interesting scenario and try to change elements within it.

OPPOSITE
The 2012 ad for National Geographic's *Dog Whisperer* show is a great example of the use of humour in advertising. A joke doesn't have to be hammered home – it can be quite subtle.

112.113

Dogs have issues too

DOG WHISPERER
with CESAR MILLAN

NATIONAL GEOGRAPHIC CHANNEL

THE CAMPAIGN

An advertising campaign is a series of adverts that share a single idea and theme. Campaigns are what creatives want to work on as they are more substantial, show the breadth of an idea and stand more chance of winning awards. The critical part of making an advertising campaign is determining the idea and establishing a tone of voice, as this sets the parameters for the individual ads within the campaign and, if the campaign is part of an integrated marketing campaign, the other forms of marketing communications that will be used. You also need to make some basic decisions if you want consistency across your campaign. Will it be headline-driven? A headline is a phrase or word that intrigues the audience and is the focus of the advert. Will it be visually led? This means that the visual must work hard, as it needs to intrigue the audience, explain the idea and answer the endline or brand.

Often each ad focuses on a slightly different aspect of the campaign thought. For example, Tesco's endline 'Every little helps' can encompass two-for-one offers, locally sourced apples and baby changing-rooms. Certainly executions need to reinterpret the thought each time. Executions might be all in one media, such as a press campaign, or they may be in a variety of media, and each media choice may require a different approach.

The rule of thumb for creating executions is that you need to think of at least three to make a campaign, even if you are only asked for one. The third execution, as any creative will tell you, is always the most difficult as the first two can just be the polar opposites of each other – such as running towards a great-smelling guy and running away from a terrible-smelling guy. If clients have asked for a campaign they often want to see more than three executions in order to understand the scope of the campaign. This can be the case in a pitch meeting, either when the agency is competing against other agencies to win new business, or when presenting a new campaign thought to an existing client. Many of the executions presented in these meetings will not ever get made, but they show a client what the idea means.

TASK
Find an existing campaign in which you can see at least three executions and think up a new one. Make sure you follow all of the existing rules evident in those ads.

'We presented ten or twelve "finished" commercials to Comcast in the initial pitch. We took all kinds of different content you find on TV and "comcasticized" it.'

JAMIE BARRETT, EXECUTIVE CREATIVE DIRECTOR, GOODBY SILVERSTEIN & PARTNERS, SAN FRANCISCO

THE ENDLINE

The idea itself is usually summed up in an endline (also known as a tagline or slogan). This is the line that completes the advert. At the early developmental stage, some creative directors are happy with a 'working endline', which does the job of explaining the idea but is not interesting enough to be the final endline; others want to see the final endline so that interesting twists on it can be explored. Many teams develop their campaign executions while using a working endline, then try to crack the endline a little later when they believe they have good executions. In some teams this is done together, in others the art director trawls through reference material to craft the visual look and feel that expresses the idea while the copywriter (see Chapter 7) tries to turn the working endline into a proper endline.

'I often find a good endline the hardest thing to write for that reason, because it's the full stop on the end of everything and makes sense of everything that's gone before. It boils down to being the most important thing, no matter how good the previous 28 seconds have been, or the rest of the poster. One of the frustrations of copywriters, if you work in a traditional team, is that you have your art director looking at you saying "what's the endline?" and you reply "I'm just working on it, it's going to work, it's going to be brilliant".'

BRENDAN WILKINS, CREATIVE DIRECTOR, EURO RSCG LONDON

TASK
Take the endline of an existing campaign and see if you can write another one that expresses the same idea.

THE CAMPAIGN THOUGHT

A campaign thought is simply an idea big enough to stretch over a number of executions. Some ideas can maintain only one or two executions; some, such as Nike's 'Just Do It' or Tesco's 'Every little helps', are flexible enough to be expressed in a number of ways. Communicating the campaign thought through multiple media channels does not necessarily make it a big idea, though, time permitting, it is always worth exploring how an idea can be executed in more than just one medium as it may present an opportunity for you.

'A big idea should be measured by how many people it influences, not by how many media channels it's in. It could be in only one media channel but it could change the world.'

JUSTIN TINDALL, GROUP EXECUTIVE CREATIVE DIRECTOR, LEO BURNETT LONDON

Nike's 'Just Do It' has supported women's campaigns, kids' campaigns, illustrated executions and photographed executions worldwide. Once campaigns become this big then new campaign thoughts are developed that can fit under the tonal umbrella of the overall campaign idea and strategy.

THE SINGLE ADVERT

Sometimes single advert briefs are given for a brand without a campaign, in which case you need to deliver the single execution as requested, but it is still in your interests to show where else the campaign thought could go now or in the future.

If you are given a brief in which you have to deliver a single advert to an existing campaign then more often than not you will start directly on the execution. You will need to do some research to answer such questions as what is the existing tone of voice? What have the previous ads been like? What have you not seen before? You will probably be working for a creative director who is responsible for that piece of business and is possibly the creative who conceived the entire campaign thought. Find out if this is the case before going in and claiming you have a much better campaign idea.

COMING UP WITH AN IDEA

There is no single way to generate ideas. Some people only draw, others only write, still others only talk. One creative may work by writing down everything they think of on a pad, another by systems of Post-it notes on the wall, and yet another by going for a walk to think. Some creative teams work separately for a day and then come together and discuss their thinking; others start by talking together and then work separately. While some teams always work together and everything comes out of discussion, other teams will work separately, then choose the best idea and develop it. Often it is a mixture of all of the above. There is no right way; there is only the way that works for you.

You may find that the best creative process for you is letting your mind wander when you are on a bus. If it is then you need to factor this in to your day, but in a way that does not completely disrupt your work with your creative partner or creative services. Whatever other people may think in an agency, creatives are hired on the quality of their ideas delivered on time, not for their physical presence in a particular chair.

'If I work alone I have to ride my bike or go for a walk for at least 30 minutes. I don't think I ever had a unique idea at the office. I guess it has to do with relaxing your brain or something.'

MIA ROBERTSSON, COPYWRITER, FAMILJENPANGEA, STOCKHOLM

'If there was one particularly successful formula I'd do it every time. It does make sense to think about it in several different ways. But if you just applied that one special technique every time you'd get the same kind of advertising every time. Quite often I just find myself, as I am now, staring at a pad writing down random words and hoping something will stick, but really it's just using ink.'

BRENDAN WILKINS, CREATIVE DIRECTOR, EURO RSCG LONDON

'The idea process is somewhat chaotic and insecure. In general I would say that we don't apply a technique, at least not consciously. Maybe when the process comes to the end we can analyse which techniques were used. But they are not applied as a formula when thinking up ideas.'

MARIO CRUDELE, SENIOR COPYWRITER, PONCE BUENOS AIRES

A variety of starting points are available to you that may stop your brain freezing under the pressure and allow you to start making some marks on your pad so that you are not just facing a blank sheet of paper.

HELP KEEP JAMES READY A BUCK.

SHARE OUR BILLBOARD.

MAKE US AN OFFER AT JAMESREADY.COM

THANKS CORY FOR KEEPING J.R. A BUCK.

The 'Share our Billboard' campaign for James Ready beer encouraged local people to share their adspace to keep the beer cheap.

'WORKING ON SEVERAL PROJECTS AT THE SAME TIME.'
ERGIN BINYILDIZ, GREY ISTANBUL

'If I am on my own, I put on my music, find a large paper mat, divide it into four parts and start working on several projects at the same time. I like jumping from one to the other and then back.'

ERGIN BINYILDIZ, EXECUTIVE CREATIVE DIRECTOR, GREY ISTANBUL

Many creatives find that they are at their most creative when they have a number of projects on the go at once. If they are stuck they move from one to another. In this way the brain does not actually stop working on the issue; it carries on in the background while the conscious mind is focused on another problem. Ideas often strike after the brief has been left alone for a day or so. Michael Michalko suggests in *Cracking Creativity* (2001) that you post a letter to yourself with the problem written succinctly inside it. I like the surrealism of this suggestion; it possibly reinforces the process. If you have a few days to spare and you are stuck it may be worth trying. Certainly hopping from project to project is one approach worth having a go at.

'THINK ABOUT THE WEIRDEST, CRAZIEST, CRAPPIEST THING YOU COULD EVER MAKE ON THAT PRODUCT, AND PUT IT ON THE WALL.'
SABINA HESSE, HEIMAT, BERLIN

One of the most fun bits of advice, which can be particularly useful if you are really stuck and you want to start the ball rolling again, is to deliberately think up bad ideas. You never know – a good idea can always be inspired by a bad one. A bad idea can also be used to kick start the creative process.

'It relaxes and opens your mind.'

SABINA HESSE, COPYWRITER, HEIMAT BERLIN

'FIRST I WRITE DOWN KEY WORDS.'
ALBERT S. CHAN, OGILVY & MATHER FRANKFURT

Write lists and find images of everything that you can think of that is associated with your product, the product category, the emotion you are trying to get across, and the benefit. Instead of stifling your brain by trying to think of a 'big' idea you simply think of words and images that connect with your product.

'IN MY HEAD THE KEY WORDS CONNECT TO FUNNY THOUGHTS AND PICTURES.'
ALBERT S. CHAN, ART DIRECTOR, OGILVY & MATHER FRANKFURT

This technique can be helped by giving yourself strict time limits. When I work with students I usually have them close their eyes and not write anything for five minutes but simply think about the subject area, and then they are given a five-minute frenzy of writing. However, closing your eyes and timing yourself isn't compulsory.

'IT'S HELPFUL TO TRY AND DEFINE WHAT THE BUSINESS PROBLEM/OPPORTUNITY IS.'
SHANE BRADNICK, BMF, AUSTRALIA

Sometimes the business problem is explained in the brief; sometimes it is not there at all. It can help to think about what the business or client is trying to achieve and whether there are obstacles in the way. With the TED 696 work (see Chapter 3) Shane Bradnick and his partner thought about the problem that all longneck beers have in Australia – that at purchase the bottles are put in a paper bag and, essentially, de-branded. This presented a path to an idea: they could do something with the bag, make the bag belong to TED 696 – but at no point did they simply slap the logo

on the paper bag. That would not be exploring the possibilities of the idea but simply stopping at the root idea.

Ask yourself: what is the client trying to achieve? Why did they generate this brief? Sometimes thinking in those terms can trigger inventive solutions. You will still have to deliver the three ads as briefed, but perhaps they will form part of a much bigger campaign thought that could help the client's business.

'BILL BERNBACH ALWAYS SPOKE ABOUT THE IMPORTANCE OF LOOKING DEEPLY INTO A PRODUCT, AS THE ANSWER TO YOUR PROBLEM LIES WITHIN THE PRODUCT.'
SIMON HIGBY, DDB STOLKHOLM

There are many famous ads that have started with the product itself, and this is most successful when it is done visually. However, in terms of generating ideas, this is one of the hardest routes to follow and does not always lead to engaging results. You may produce a clever visual but does it actually speak to the target market or simply to other advertisers? The trick is to look at the packaging and think about what it reveals about the product, or to look at the product itself and think about what that

reveals. For example, a fry with spicy sauce on the end can look like a match; and the reflective, slightly rippled surface of a tin of tuna can look like a peaceful lake perfect for fishing. Bernbach's advice however was broader than simply trying to create striking visuals; it is to look more deeply into the truth of the product to see what it offers. For Volkswagen it was, famously, 'size' (see chapter 2).

FIND OUT ABOUT THE PRODUCT'S HISTORY
Sometimes your research can reveal that the product is made in an interesting way or has a heritage of a significant number of years or an association with a particular place. A whisky manufacturer should know how to make good whisky if they have been doing it for more than 100 years; an airline may have the highest safety record; a car manufacturer may consistently be the first to bring innovations to market. The product manufacturer may be from a particular part of the country and perhaps this influences their outlook. Research is the key to this technique. Speak in depth to the planner: what do they know about the brand? Are there any company films you can watch? Can you speak to people that work there? What can you find out on the Internet?

Global downturn.
What's the first mistake
businesses make?
www.ft.com/budgets
We live in FINANCIAL TIMES

LEFT
This 2007 ad by Berlin
agency Scholz & Friends
for Weru is part of a
long-running campaign
that uses humour to
highlight the product's
benefits – in this case
reducing the noise of a
passing fire engine.

ABOVE
This DDB London
campaign for the
Financial Times in 2008
uses the product's well-
respected historical
position of financial
knowledge to question
the sense in cutting ad
spend in a recession.

'I JUST THINK ABOUT WHY PEOPLE MADE IT.'
ADAM TUCKER, LEO BURNETT LONDON

'What's the one thing that they think it's better at than its competition? Even if we think something is a "me too" product, the people who manufacture it probably don't. They believe their beer is more "nutty", or their phone has buttons that are easier to use, or their washing powder leaves a nicer smell. Sometimes you just have to ask them.'

ADAM TUCKER, CREATIVE DIRECTOR,
LEO BURNETT LONDON

Find out what the manufacturer is passionate about, and consider how you can deliver this within the proposition. Sitting with the engineers who design Volkswagens in Sweden, listening to them explain the technology and the thinking behind the cars, led the Tribal DDB team to develop the multi-award-winning 'Fun Theory' campaign, creating experiences and advertising that demonstrate how people will willingly help the environment, provided it is fun to do so.

'Volkswagen began the Fun Theory project over two years ago now. They simply believe that the easiest way to change human behaviour for the better is by making it fun to do. This is the thinking behind their environmental innovations, BlueMotion Technologies.'

SIMON HIGBY, CREATIVE DIRECTOR,
TRIBAL DDB STOCKHOLM

'I TRY AND THINK OF THE CONSEQUENCES OF USING THE PRODUCT.'
JUSTIN TINDALL, LEO BURNETT, LONDON

'If the Volkswagen Touareg can go to a wading depth of 4 feet [1.2 metres], what might be the consequences of that? Well, one might be that it gets a great big fish caught in the grille. The client gets what they want — a lovely shot of the car — and I've got my bit — the idea of a salmon caught in a grille — and it obeys the laws of normal disrupted, which attracts the passer-by.'

JUSTIN TINDALL, GROUP EXECUTIVE CREATIVE
DIRECTOR, LEO BURNETT LONDON

Think about what it means to have the product, to use it, to aspire to owning it. What might be the consequences of not owning it? The consequences can be as personal, as extreme or as surreal as you like, but they need to follow a logical path stemming from the product's benefits.

'Showing what the product can do for the consumer is definitely one of the things I keep in mind while thinking of an ad. Throw yourself this question while answering a brief — "It's as if..." And you'll think of crazy ways to answer the problem.'

RAYLIN VALLES, CREATIVE DIRECTOR,
MUDRA DELHI

'OBSERVE HOW PEOPLE BEHAVE. WHAT DO THEY DO AND HOW CAN YOU BUILD ON THAT.'
MADELEINE MORRIS, GREY LONDON

'We were looking for absolutely irresistible things for women. We realized that chocolate is one of them. Women all have different tastes but it's very difficult to find a woman who doesn't like chocolate.'

MARIO CRUDELE, SENIOR COPYWRITER, PONCE
BUENOS AIRES

In answering a brief for Lynx (known as Axe in many markets) Mario Crudele and his partner came up with the idea that women behave in a certain way around chocolate and then exaggerated it. A young man sprays himself with Lynx/Axe in his bathroom and he turns into a man made of chocolate. Every woman that he interacts with from then on finds him irresistible, answering the brand campaign thought that this product is irresistible to women.

Much car advertising uses obsessional behaviour as a starting point; for example the designer/scientist is so obsessed with how a windscreen wiper wipes that they can't sleep, so the car buyer can be assured that the rest of the car will be of the same high quality. The reason this works is because it rests on the believable observation that people can stay awake worrying over a problem and that at work a certain type of worker will strive for perfection.

"I never read The Economist."

Management trainee. Aged 42.

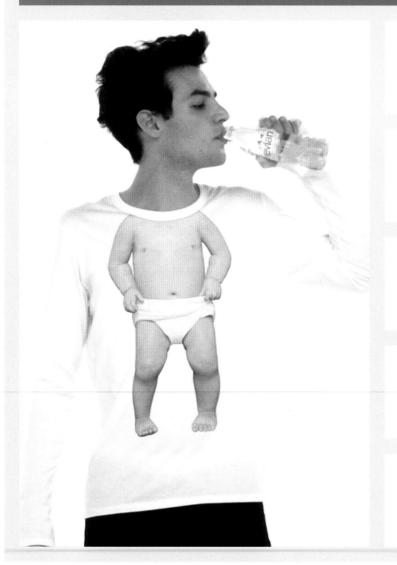

ABOVE
This famous 1989 AMV BBDO London poster for *The Economist* shows the consequences of not purchasing the product.

LEFT
BETC Euro RSCG's hugely successful campaign for Evian takes the thought that drinking water keeps you young to its extreme. In this 2011 TV execution, 'Baby Inside', the youth-giving consequences of using the product are evident without descending into exaggeration (people literally turning into babies).

'JUXTAPOSITION'

JON DANIEL, EBB & FLOW LONDON

Juxtaposition works by putting two things in the same advert that are so diametrically opposed that they each enhance the meaning of the other. You cannot always apply juxtaposition as it is not always right for the target market or brand.

'What I love about juxtaposition is that it nearly always results in something different or unique, depending on the elements you juxtapose. I have found it's an extremely powerful tool to help tackle difficult briefs in particular.'

JON DANIEL, EXECUTIVE CREATIVE DIRECTOR, EBB&FLOW, LONDON

For their award-winning 2002 UK NHS recruitment campaign Jon Daniel and his creative partner were able to contrast a moment in a person's life – a woman smiling, a child playing, a man falling – with the busy sounds of the ambulance crew, nurses, doctors, specialists, physiotherapists that had to help put these people together again.

Juxtaposing the poem 'I Have a Rendezvous with Death' with game animation from *Gears of War* allowed John Patroulis and Scott Duchon to evoke the sense of camaraderie and human spirit that this game touches on.

'We didn't change the world, but turning a video game into a legitimate entertainment property full of depth, story and emotion validates why a lot of people choose to invest so much of their time into these experiences.'

JOHN PATROULIS AND SCOTT DUCHON, EXECUTIVE CREATIVE DIRECTORS, AGENCY215, SAN FRANCISCO

T.A.G. juxtaposed Alan Seeger's moving poem 'I Have a Rendezvous with Death' with simulated violent gameplay on the Xbox console. Seeger (1888–1916) was killed in action in World War I.

I HAVE a rendezvous with Death
At some disputed barricade,...

...It may be he shall take my hand
And lead me into his dark land
And close my eyes and quench my breath...

...I have a rendezvous with Death...

...And I to my pledged word am true,
I shall not fail that rendezvous...

WHO OR WHAT IS AGAINST US?

Often ideas come if you spend a while thinking about who does not want to use this product, or wishes it did not exist. Sometimes this is a competitor product manufacturer; sometimes this is another person with a vested interest. Who might not want you to look radiant on your wedding day? An ex-girlfriend. Who might not want a new car to be cheap? A used car salesman. A lot of fun can be had following this technique.

This 2011 campaign for Biothymus F anti-hair-loss scalp serum by NudeJEH Bangkok shows hair's daily enemy – the hair brush.

CHANGE THE MEDIUM

'Sometimes one of the most refreshing ways to crack a brief when you're struggling is to change the nature of it. So if you're working on a TV brief, try thinking what you would do if it was a poster or a radio brief or a product.'

JON DANIEL, EXECUTIVE CREATIVE DIRECTOR, EBB&FLOW, LONDON

This can help you simplify, deliver interesting situations in which you might encounter the brand, or change how the ad could be experienced.

SPOOF

Spoofing is simply imitating or parodying something else. In advertising, spoof is really an executional style and many ideas generated by other techniques can be brought to life by spoofing another genre, whether it be another advertising genre or another art/media genre.

An excellent example is the 2000 Andy award–winning advert 'Lawyer' for *The X Show*, a 'guy-themed' variety show that ran from 1999 to 2001 in the United States on the Fox network. Created by Jamie Barrett's team while he still worked at Fallon McElligott, it quickly went viral before anyone really understood how to give awards for 'viral' advertising. It can still be found on the internet after a bit of searching.

'Lawyer' appears to be a typical advert for a personal injury lawyer, set in a typical lawyer's office. His tone and delivery are exactly those of a lawyer but the words he is saying are incongruous, such as 'we don't football sex bowling till you pizza'. The reveal is in the endline – 'We know what guys are really thinking', with the logo for *The X Show*. The advert 'spoofs' the personal injury genre.

'The idea was simply to find different situations where men speak, and have them speak the thoughts that are really in their head, versus the words the world expects to hear.'

JAMIE BARRETT, EXECUTIVE CREATIVE DIRECTOR, GOODBY SILVERSTEIN & PARTNERS, SAN FRANCISCO

More recently the Old Spice campaign from Wieden+Kennedy Portland (see Chapter 6) cleverly spoofs men's aftershave advertising from the 1970s and 1980s. In fact the Old Spice YouTube channel has been so successful that it has had more than 55 million views so far. The first advert, 'The Man Your Man Could Smell Like', has itself had more than 12 million views.

Thinking in terms of ambient advertising allowed Saatchi & Saatchi Los Angeles to come up with this dramatic poster campaign for the Surfrider Foundation in 2008.

ANALOGIES, METAPHORS AND SIMILES

Analogies, metaphors and similes are figures of speech, which are commonly used in advertising when it is difficult or impossible to show product benefits literally. Sometimes it can be more emotive to show a different object from the product being advertised, or it can make a complex subject more readily understood, for example a car engine pumping fuel like a heart. They can be used visually or verbally, as follows.

- Analogy is when a similarity can be found between two completely different things and portrayed so that the meaning is instantly clear. Words and images are not used literally: riding a motorbike on country roads might be compared with riding a rollercoaster, while squeezing a fruit might be used to imply pain.

- A metaphor is an object, word or image that is symbolic of something else and is reliant on the fact that we will not interpret it literally: love is a rose, the world is a stage, he was blown away by the quality of sound.

- A simile is similar to a metaphor but the words or images are used to say that something is 'like' something else rather than that it 'is' something else: he is as white as a ghost, a peppery beef burger looks like the top of a pepper grinder.

ABOVE
The simile at work in this 2012 ad by Brazil's Z+ Comunicação for Baruel foot deodorant is that without this product the shoe smells of fish.

RIGHT
This ad for the Italian luxury brand E. Marinella is part of a campaign by Foolbite where the product is associated through visual analogy with the culinary delicacies of a series of European cities and, therefore, with inherent good taste.

LUGANO

E. MARINELLA
NAPOLI
Since 1914, the taste of elegance.

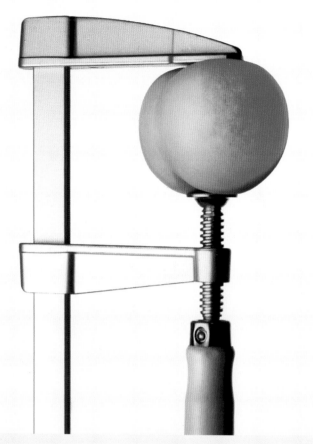

During your period the muscles in your womb may tighten up making you feel rather

tender

Try stroking your tummy, the rhythmic movement will relax and warm your muscles. Also, avoid unnecessary stresses by wearing comfortable reliable protection like Always pads. Unfortunately that won't stop other stuff irritating you like that unidentifiable smell in your fridge, the spot on your chin, and pens that run out mid sign ...

" always "

Talking your body's language

ABOVE
This press ad for Always used the visual of a peach held in a clamp as a sophisticated analogy for pain. It is more than a simple simile and needs a little explanation, hence we should call it an extended simile or analogy. The image translated well and the ad was used across Europe.

RIGHT
The 2007 Pepsi Light truck wrap by BBDO Dusseldorf uses a metaphor: Pepsi Light is lighter than air.

TAP INTO POPULAR CULTURE

Sometimes advertising campaigns come out that perfectly capture the interests and mood in a country at that moment. In this case a whole country can get behind the campaign, as happened with the Brazillian ads for Bombril described in Chapter 2. In the UK in 2011, anticipating and capturing interest in the Royal Wedding created good opportunities. Sometimes, as in the case of the 2010 Smirnoff Nightlife Exchange, in which clubbers from around the world experienced a club night from a different city, utilizing popular culture can create a global phenomenon that people identify with, want to share and be part of.

'The idea of the countries exchanging nightlife was a really simple one. It started from a little question of what if — what if Manhattan nightlife swapped with Brooklyn? — and we just kind of evolved it from there.'

MATT MACDONALD, EXECUTIVE CREATIVE DIRECTOR, JWT NEW YORK

In order to tap into popular culture in this way a creative must be an avid consumer of all sorts of culture. Challenge yourself and do not stay in your safety zone. If you only ever look at, listen to and read things that you have liked from childhood you will not have the breadth of knowledge needed to tap into a wider cultural experience.

Mother New York tapped into the public's desire to be involved in stunning must-see events with their 'Kaleidoscopic Fashion Spectacular' for Target. Collaborating with Daft Punk's lighting designer and using 170 rooms of New York's Standard Hotel and over 60 dancers, they created a visual experience showcasing the 2010 Fall collection. It can still be viewed on YouTube.

SOCIAL COMMENTARY

A number of creatives look at the culture that they are in, and if criticizing the culture rather than celebrating it is a better expression of the brand's intentions and personality, then they will approach the brief from a critical viewpoint.

In 2006 Ogilvy & Mather Toronto, as part of the Unilever Dove 'Campaign for Real Beauty', launched the online advert 'Evolution', which showed how an ordinary young woman could, through the power of the beauty advertising machine – hair, make-up, lighting, retouching – end up looking like a supermodel. The advert and campaign managed to enhance the brand's appeal to real women by being honest about the industry. While this may appear to be altogether too altruistic, the exposure for the brand generated by this advert has been estimated to be worth over $150 million.

The 2009 TBWA 'Trillion Dollar' campaign for *The Zimbabwean* newspaper won worldwide recognition and awards. *The Zimbabwean* was the only newspaper still free to give a different opinion from that of President Robert Mugabe's ZANU PF government in Zimbabwe, though the government tried a number of heavy-handed ways of shutting it down. When those activities drew negative global attention, the government levied 'a luxury import tax' on the newspaper, aiming to price it out of ordinary people's hands. This meant that the newspaper had to encourage South Africans with ties to Zimbabwe to buy it in order to subsidize sales across the border. The TBWA/ Hunt/Lascaris Johannesburg creative team had an idea that would increase sales of the newspaper while making the kind of political statement for which *The Zimbabwean* was known. South Africans had seen the rate at which the value of Zimbabwean bank notes was plummeting but they had not quite grasped what the denominations were, escalating as they were from millions to billions to trillions. The 'Trillion Dollar' campaign created handouts, billboards and posters printed on thousands of worthless hundred trillion dollar Zimbabwean

Ogilvy & Mather Toronto didn't realize they were going to start a global campaign when they made Dove 'Evolution'. They had made a comment on society that people were willing to hear.

banknotes, and the advert also featured on hundreds of international websites and blogs.

'The concept actually was that the money became the medium; there was no symbol that was a better shorthand for what was going on in Zimbabwe than this worthless banknote. You could print on it – the fact that it was as cheap as paper almost made the news real for people. All advertising needs to be a kind of shorthand where you need to get a point across very quickly. I think when people saw the message on the banknote, that it was cheaper to print on money than paper, they got the whole story about how a whole country has been reduced to economic ruin and most importantly that *The Zimbabwean* was the kind of paper that wasn't afraid to challenge it.'

RAPHAEL BASCKIN, SENIOR COPYWRITER, TBWA/HUNT/LASCARIS JOHANNESBURG

'WHAT WOULD INTEREST ME?'
MATT MACDONALD, JWT NEW YORK

Matt Macdonald, Executive Creative Director, JWT New York suggests another way of gaining inspiration:

'One thing I do a lot is think what would I want to do or what would I want to see? Just as a person who consumes a lot of media. What would be the movie I would want to watch? Or what would be the thing that I'd want to do on a Saturday? If I start to think like that it starts guiding me down the path of what other people might want to see or do.'

This can also lead you to think about what you have not seen yet that you would like to see, both in terms of idea and execution.

The TBWA/Hunt/
Lascaris Johannesburg
2009 campaign for *The
Zimbabwean* newspaper
took a social stand.
The newspaper wasn't
pretending to be a
charity; it was perfectly
clear that it was a
business that wanted
people to buy its product.
This was the only way
that it could pay its
reporters and continue
to stand up to the
Zimbabwean regime.

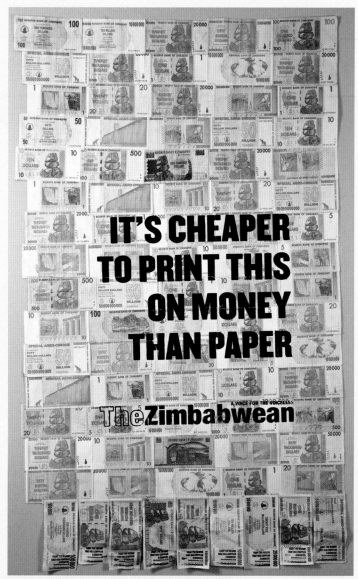

ONCE YOU HAVE YOUR CORE IDEA

There are a few things that are worth doing once you have an idea that you love – just to check it.

'Ask yourself: "Is my ad relevant for these people? Is it touching them in any way?"'

SABINA HESSE, COPYWRITER, HEIMAT BERLIN

'We always ask ourselves, if our dad had given us this money to try and change this behaviour would we really do this nonsense thing with rabbits or would we say "actually that's not really going achieve it"?'

ANGUS MACADAM, EXECUTIVE CREATIVE DIRECTOR, DENTSU LONDON

It is also worth leaving it overnight. When you have been working really intensely on something you can sometimes be too close to judge it. Put your favourite initial scamps on the wall. Leave them. In the morning that idea might still seem great and you might see another way of pushing it, or that idea might not seem so insightful any more, but another idea that you had previously discarded may seem full of possibilities.

'There's something I ask my teams to do, which is write it in a sentence because that forces them to clarify their thinking, to get to the simplest expression of their ideas.'

MATT MACDONALD, EXECUTIVE CREATIVE DIRECTOR, JWT, NEW YORK

'A technique that Crispin Porter & Bogusky used to judge work, and it was actually on their briefs, is "what will the press write about this idea when it gets into the world?" That's how I judge a lot of the work – if people are able to give you what the press headline is going to be that goes with the work.'

ROCKY NOVAK, DIRECTOR OF DIGITAL DEVELOPMENT, FALLON MINNEAPOLIS

SCAMP IT UP

'Scamp' is a term referring to a roughly drawn-up version of the execution. Scamps are usually created on an A3 (B size) pad with a black permanent marker – though some creatives prefer to use pencil, some prefer to collage up an idea and some prefer to quickly knock it together in Photoshop. With every stage of scamp the communication of the idea is the most important thing and not design details: that all comes later.

Initial scamps, which tend to be no more than enlarged thumbnails, are usually for the benefit of yourself and your partner to see if an image can be created for your idea, or whether the headline works, or whether the idea itself is even understandable.

The next level of scamp is something drawn up a little better with some hierarchy of information in place so that whoever you are showing it to knows where they are supposed to look first. In this version if you are drawing an elephant it will usually look like an elephant (rather than a large dog or suitcase as in your initial scamp) and if you are thinking of using large lettering as an essential part of the advert you will have included it as part of the execution. This can be shown to your creative director and reference material may accompany it, showing the style of photography/illustration you had in mind. Presentation scamps for meetings with clients are usually drawn up to a better standard.

Scamps also give you an opportunity to think about the media in which you have been briefed. You might have a great idea for a poster campaign, but could you do something with that media that would make it sensational? Seeing it drawn up in that format helps. These first scamps are unlikely to be the final scamps on your campaign. You may come up with entirely different executions once you have seen them drawn up, or after a conversation with your creative director. You will certainly push them further once you start thinking about media and craft.

It is important to bear in mind that more complex interactive ideas move past scamps and into demonstrations very quickly.

'Clients sometimes can't understand early or pitch versions of interactive ideas without experiencing them directly, either by real interactive demonstration or by video/animation demonstration. Even if a client can understand the scamp or pitch version, he or she can't share the idea internally within their company without a more final version.'

HIROKI NAKAMURA, HAJIME YAKUSHIJI, SHINSAKU OGAWA, HIROSHI KOIKE, TSUBASA KAYASUGA, CREATIVE TEAM MEMBERS, DENTSU TOKYO

A WOMAN ENTERS A LIVING ROOM CARRYING A LARGE TRAY OF DRINKS

SFX: LAUGHTER

WE SEE A BANANA SKIN IN THE MIDDLE OF THE FLOOR

SFX: WE HEAR A LOUD CRASH

CUT TO THE PRODUCT SHOT SUPER:
YOU CAN RELY ON BRAND X
FVO: YOU CAN RELY ON BRAND X

A detailed scamp and
one of the resulting final
ads for the 'Bullywatch'
campaign by Ebb&Flow.

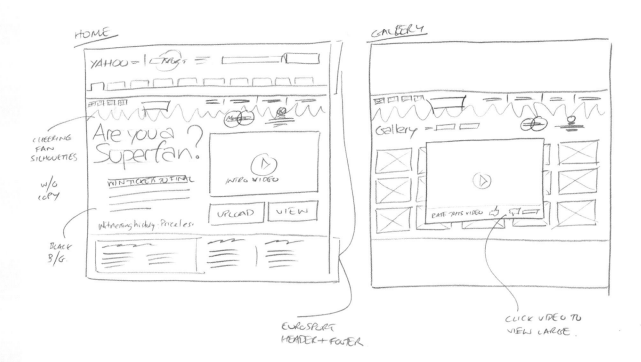

Kodu Digital London produced scamps for this microsite for Mastercard in 2010 before creating it digitally.

HOW WILL YOU SAY IT?

6

MEDIA

Within an agency there are a variety of different media specialisms. The more integrated the agency, the more likely that any team will be able to work in any media. In the traditional agency model there would be 'above-the-line' teams working in television, print and radio and 'below-the-line' teams focusing on direct mail, in-store activity and brand activation. Then, in the 1980s, came 'through-the-line' agencies and teams, which could deliver in any media, from television to point of sale.

Printed media have been around for hundreds of years, and painted media for even longer (see Chapter 2), but, while consumers will continue to use traditional media as a reliable source of information, there has been a major shift to the Internet over the last decade as our most accessible source of news and information. Digital agencies sprang up when this trend was first perceived, specializing in what was called 'new media'. New media differs from traditional media in that it involves the digitizing of content, which is available via the Internet. The power of digital content is that it can now be produced in real time.

While at first sceptical, the advertising industry has now wholeheartedly embraced digital media, and digital advertising has become part of the traditional agency offering. It is worth bearing in mind that as technology changes our lives many media definitions are becoming quite arbitrary; television is sometimes Web content, direct mail is sometimes digital, posters are sometimes ambient, social media becomes Web content becomes television. Always try to keep your ideas about media fluid, tied to your campaign thought and open to all possibilities.

'Already by now advertising is using so much more than just classic media. Today everything can be advertising – a stunt, a song, a picture, a word, a poem, a dance, a colour. The medium will more and more follow the thought.'

SABINA HESSE, COPYWRITER,
HEIMAT BERLIN

Nowadays all agencies strive to be integrated, offering any media choice internally or through partnerships with sister agencies. That does not mean that all briefs will require an integrated solution. Often all that is required is one specific medium done well.

On an industry brief, you will be given descriptions of the format for delivering your campaign: the size of poster (such as 96 sheet), length of television or radio ad (such as 30 seconds), description of your interactive space (such as a standard banner), description of your press ad (such as quarter page), and a general description of ambient or experiential activity that may simply include those words. A creative rarely needs to know the exact sizes, simply the format. The format changes the execution. If a television script is written that lasts 27 seconds it can be edited or shot to be 30 seconds: what matters is if the overall format is wrong and it has been conceived as a 60-second ad. The exact size or length is technical information that designers and editors need to be aware of.

Scamps are drawn and ideas are conceived to rough format shapes and time lengths so it is worth knowing what they are. The industry convention is that initial scamps for traditional and digital media take up an entire A3 page no matter what the proper format size actually is. If you want to be clever with your use of media it is worth thinking of your A3 (B size) page as a canvas on which you draw your media shape, because then you can show how you plan to build out from a billboard or plan to extend the activity beyond your banner ad.

Standard Formats
(exact sizes and names change from country to country)

LEFT
These print formats will help you visualize your ads, though they are by no means all that is available.

Poster Formats

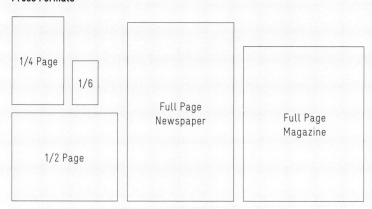

48 Sheet

6 Sheet

96 Sheet

Press Formats

1/4 Page

1/6

1/2 Page

Full Page Newspaper

Full Page Magazine

Web Formats

LEFT
These Web formats will help you visualize your digital ads.

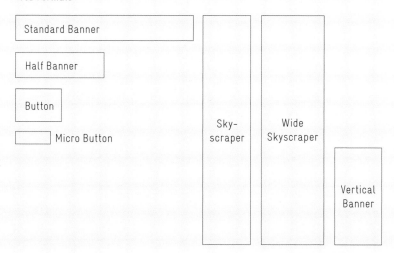

Standard Banner

Half Banner

Button

Micro Button

Sky-scraper

Wide Skyscraper

Vertical Banner

INTEGRATED CAMPAIGNS

Integrated media campaigns coordinate the use of a variety of media channels to communicate one succinct brand message. They can be part of an integrated marketing communication (IMC) client policy, which seeks to align all promotional activity – advertising, sales promotion, public relations and direct marketing – under one brand message. Not all integrated advertising campaigns are part of an IMC push from the client organization; sometimes they are just an acknowledgment that a big networked agency can deliver many parts of the promotional activity or that the agency in question is not traditional and is able to work through multiple media. This, however, does not mean that the PR company or sponsorship division of the client organization may not be doing something completely separate from the advertising company. This diversity between messages, and the resulting consumer confusion about the brand message, is what has led to the push for more integrated and single-minded communication.

Integrated media campaigns are arguably one of the most effective ways of getting a message across, and for a creative can be one of the most liberating. You can see your campaign idea realized in many different media. In fact the aim is for media neutrality, where the idea comes first. In the past this used to mean integrated campaigns that used traditional and ambient media, and then it came to mean campaigns embracing traditional, ambient and digital media. Now it appears to mean just about everything – product innovation, experiential, digital, social media, traditional and ambient, reminiscent of Mary Wells' and David Ogilvy's early integrated approach to advertising in the 1950s and 1960s.

A classic integrated campaign is the 1998 FCA!, Welsh Tourist Board campaign, in which all possible media were pursued to show how much cleaner, fresher and more pleasant it is to unwind in the Welsh countryside than in a polluted city: television, posters, press, leaflet mailings, inserts, PR and ambient media such as air fresheners and clear acetates on car windscreens. The Welsh Tourist Board generated an additional £60 tourism spend for every pound spent on the campaign.

'The line "Two hours and a million miles away" has two elements that we used to make the idea work across various media – time and the visualization of a place very different from where you are right now. The print work and television had to create a contrast between the beauty and tranquillity in the main picture and the crappy experience in the smaller picture. The headline then linked the two. In all other media we either played on the time factor, such as in van and tree, or the visual contrast, as with the window sticker. As long as we stuck to these rules, the campaign could work anywhere.'

ADAM TUCKER, CREATIVE DIRECTOR,
LEO BURNETT LONDON

These multi-award-winning ads from 1998 by FCA! London for the Welsh Tourist Board made the industry aware of the possibilities of truly integrated campaigns.

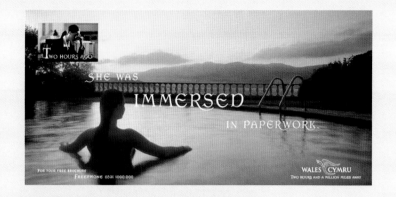

In 2008, Macy's and JWT New York created the 'Believe' campaign, taking inspiration from an editorial published in the *New York Sun* in 1897 answering a little girl called Virginia O'Hanlon who had written a letter asking if Santa Claus really existed. The editor published an unequivocal 'yes'. The campaign launched with a reprint of this editorial as a press ad with the facing page an open letter to Santa, inviting people to write to Santa and mail it in Macy's special Believe letterboxes. For every letter mailed, Macy's donated a dollar to Make-A-Wish, giving up to $1 million for the campaign. A large 'Believe Meter' was erected to keep track of the responses. There was a television ad and a Believe website that featured a playful app to let viewers transform themselves into Santa and share the image using social media. This website received 10 million views. The team continued the campaign in 2009, pushing the boundaries of traditional advertising by developing a 30-minute animated Christmas special for CBS based on the story of Virginia O'Hanlon, centred around the 'Believe' campaign message and featuring the Believe meter. The show drew more than 3.7 million viewers and was well received in reviews. It was also turned into a book and a DVD and featured as a parade balloon.

Integrated campaigns require familiarity with a number of media channels. You need to be sure of your idea and to be able to simplify it to one sentence, as each medium may require an entirely different approach. Your television ad may have people dancing in it but your press ad may work better with an analogy. Your campaign cannot be reliant on a single executional technique, and the various executions in your campaign must have a unifying theme and a strong, recognizable idea, as individual executions may be very different.

JWT New York and Macy's created this integrated campaign for ©Macy's. The animated Christmas television special *Yes, Virginia* drew over 3.7 million viewers. Objects that appeared in the show, such as the Believe meter and the mailbox, could also be found in stores.

TRANSMEDIA CAMPAIGNS

In a transmedia campaign each part of the story unfolds in different media, transferring from one medium to another, and this progression is integral to the idea.

'Integrated just says we have all these different media executions working together. Transmedia is essentially each one tells a little bit of a different story, all working together to make a larger whole.'

AARON SEYMOUR-ANDERSON,
ART DIRECTOR, FALLON MINNEAPOLIS

A great example of transmedia at work is the 2009 Fallon Minneapolis, Syfy Channel 'Alice – Follow the White Rabbit' campaign.

'This is almost more like staging as you would a play, your idea enters stage left, which is social media, and then exits stage right, which is on the streets of Manhattan.'

ROCKY NOVAK, DIRECTOR OF DIGITAL
DEVELOPMENT, FALLON MINNEAPOLIS

Fallon were briefed to advertise a new show, a modern-day reinterpretation of Lewis Carroll's *Alice's Adventures in Wonderland*, in which an assassin with the head of a giant white rabbit is hired by the Queen of Hearts. The character of the rabbit assassin so intrigued the team at Fallon that they developed 'White Rabbit Inc.', a secretive society of rabbit-headed assassins that the audience could contact on Twitter. In fact, all media pointed to a specially created Twitter account. Rich media (digital interactive media) allowed the rabbit to jump out of his web banners and run across website content. The rabbit then hopped off the Web and was projected on to New York building facades. This was followed by a 50-strong team of rabbit-headed assassins invading the city and taking rides on the subway. Hundreds of tweets, photos and videos were uploaded by consumers who spotted the rabbits in New York City, and 1.4 million clicks were driven to syfy.com, the science fiction cable channel. The campaign won bronze for Best Use of Integrated Media at Cannes 2010.

Once you have a strong idea, if you want to think in terms of a transmedia campaign, try to think of a narrative: ask yourself, how can the story unfold? As a cultural reference it is worth considering how experimental theatre puts on great shows, or think of dance performances or art performances, which often mix media to explore multilayered and rich content.

TASK
Visit three experimental live art forms that take you out of your comfort zone. Evaluate how they use media to explore different ideas and themes.

The 2009 transmedia campaign for the Syfy channel created by Fallon Minneapolis used Twitter, microsites, projection, public stunts and direct mail to bring an idea to life.

Follow me

DIGITAL

The interactive space is an intimate and playful medium, somewhere in between television, social media and print, and anyone working in it needs to think of the possibilities in those terms. For a client it allows effective targeting, and effectiveness can be monitored in terms of click-through. Interactive is often part of a more integrated campaign that drives people to the interactive component.

In 2011 Grabarz & Partner Hamburg created the Side Assist Office, an idea that worked with the psychology of the target market – 25-year-old male office workers. Making use of the office workers' own webcams alongside a banner ad integrated into those sites an office worker might like to visit but not get caught on, Side Assist Office scanned the area behind him as he surfed the net. If somebody suddenly showed up over his shoulder, a business chart popped up on the screen, making the worker look busy. This idea creatively demonstrated the properties of the new assistance system by Volkswagen, Side Assist, which warns drivers if any vehicles are approaching from behind. Over 8 per cent of visitors to these various websites activated Side Assist Office, and out of those, 40 per cent of them wanted to know more about the assistance system, Side Assist.

You need to think dynamically when you develop interactive advertising. In the digital advertising industry you will usually be part of a team of developers, information architects, experience architects, designers, copywriters, art directors, creative technologists, social seeders and producers, and you will need to think not only about the things you can do but the things other people could do: working with other disciplines opens up new possibilities.

'The techniques for interactive advertising are progressing every day. Therefore we share seeds of an idea with Web productions and do some brainstorming together. Actually the idea of the Lucky Switch came from that process.'

HIROKI NAKAMURA, HAJIME YAKUSHIJI, SHINSAKU OGAWA, HIROSHI KOIKE, TSUBASA KAYASUGA, CREATIVE TEAM MEMBERS, DENTSU TOKYO

Consider the software applications that can or will be used. Banner ads, and skyscrapers (ads that appear as a column along the side of a website) as they usually have a requirement for limited file size such as 30kB, are often conceived as moving press adverts. In other words, only a small element is animated – perhaps the words – and everything else remains the same. Therefore the relationship between headline and visual will play a large part, rather than the development of a story, as with larger file sizes that can show filmed content. Like television, interactive can allow for build-up of drama or humour when more memory is allocated, though it is arguably most effective when the full interactivity of the media is utilized and consumers can play.

Dentsu Tokyo's 2009 digital application 'Lucky Switch' for UNIQLO is one in a long line of thoughtful and inventive ideas that the creative team have developed for this innovative client. The Lucky Switch allows the consumer to change all the images on a blog site into lottery tickets. If a ticket wins, both the player and the blog owner win UNIQLO tote bags.

'One of UNIQLO's advertising philosophies is to create something awesome that has never been seen before. We wanted to make something beyond the banner ad, so we presented the Lucky Switch.'

HIROKI NAKAMURA, HAJIME YAKUSHIJI, SHINSAKU OGAWA, HIROSHI KOIKE, TSUBASA KAYASUGA, CREATIVE TEAM MEMBERS, DENTSU TOKYO

TASK
'Create a campaign only using 30kB leaderboards (a banner ad treated as a small press ad), perhaps using techniques like four animations of copy coming in, but then also stretch the campaign to a 500kB ad where you can scroll over and it drops down and a video plays, or something like that. Basically this is like executing your idea as a small press campaign and then thinking how you would do it on telly.'

PAUL HARRISON, CREATIVE DIRECTOR, KODU LONDON

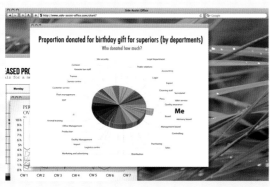

BELOW
Dentsu Tokyo's 2009
Lucky Switch widget
for UNIQLO allowed the
user to change all the
images on a blog into
lottery tickets for
a UNIQLO prize.

ABOVE
The 2011 Grabarz &
Partner 'Side Assist
Office', which allows
bored office workers to
visit sites like Facebook
but instantly bring up
'Office'-style documents
if it detects another
person near
the computer.

ウェブサイトの画像がオンラインくじに！

UNIQLO LUCKY SWITCH

「UNIQLO LUCKY SWITCH」は、
ウェブサイトの画像をオンラインくじに変換する
ファーストリテイリング創業60周年記念特別ブログパーツです。
オンラインくじをクリックしてアタリがでたら、
ユニクロオリジナルバッグをプレゼント。
（12月1日〜12月31日 総計1000名）

▶ 設置事例（FFFFOUND!）

▶ 利用規約　▶ プライバシーポリシー

PUSH

スイッチを押して、めくってみてください。

■ ブログの中にLUCKY SWITCHを

ラッキースイッチを押すと、ブログの画像がオンラインくじに瞬時に変わります。

ブログパーツ使用法

1 下の「ENTER MAIL ADDRESS」欄にメールアドレスを入力し、OKボタンをクリックします。
2 タグが発行されるので、コピーボタンをクリックし、ご利用中のブログサービスヘルプを参考に、指定の場所に貼り付けてください。
3 ブログに出現する「UNIQLO LUCKY SWITCH」を押すと、画像がオンラインくじに変換されます。
4 変換された画像をクリックし、アタリがでればオリジナルバッグの応募フォームに進めます。

▶ 各ブログサービスの設置ガイドはこちら

| ENTER MAIL ADDRESS | OK |

【ブログオーナーにも特典が！】
当選者がでれば、ブログパーツを設置したオーナーにもオリジナルバッグをプレゼント。

■ お気に入りの中にLUCKY SWITCHを

ブックマークを押すと、表示されているページの画像がオンラインくじに瞬時に変わります。

ブックマークレット使用法（Internet Explolerの方）

▶ ADD LUCKY SWITCH TO BOOKMARK

SOCIAL MEDIA

Social media have become a force to be reckoned with. They have turned consumers of content into generators and publishers of content. Consider Facebook, Twitter, YouTube, blogs, Wikipedia, LinkedIn and Flickr; they are all interactive, user-generated and accessible, and are unified in blending technology and social interaction. The enormity of this cannot be underestimated, as this is content that other people, other consumers, want to read and search out. Reviews are written by ordinary people, whom other ordinary people trust precisely because they are not paid by corporations to have an opinion: yet they can sway purchasing decisions in the same way that adverts do. Blogging has opened up new opportunities for advertisers. Successful bloggers can establish their own deals to have selected advertising featured on their websites and blogs or woven into the copy.

Used in the right way, the social media technologies can be an extraordinary tool for brand interaction. They can be fun, playful, engaging and informative and are definitely a media channel to consider. Social media were an essential element of the global Smirnoff Nightlife Exchange experience (see p150) and 'Follow the White Rabbit'.

The 2009 SapientNitro Australia's Tourism Queensland 'Best Job in the World' campaign made dramatic use of social media and showed just how powerful they can be. They were tasked to make people aware of the islands in the Great Barrier Reef. Rather than just running a typical 'come to our sunny islands' tourism campaign they developed the idea that people could apply for a job as 'caretaker of the islands'. The campaign started with a simple classified ad and drove people to Tourism Queensland's website, asking for one-minute video applications for the job of caretaker, based on Hamilton Island. The successful applicant would blog and film their experiences and earn US $100,000 for a six-month contract. Within 30 hours the site had 400,000 new visitors, a million visitors by the end of day two, and 336,000 Facebook-referred website visits

overall. It reached a global audience of three billion. Nearly 35,000 people from more than 200 countries applied for the job, uploading content on social media. The campaign went on to become the world's most awarded campaign, taking three Grand Prix and five Lions at the Cannes Lions International Festival of Creativity. You can see a case study on adforum.com.

The 2010 Wieden+Kennedy Portland, Old Spice 'Responses' campaign was an evolution of the hugely popular 'The Man Your Man Could Smell Like' campaign that propelled athlete and actor Isaiah Mustafa into the spotlight. The original television commercial premiered during the Superbowl 2010 and was a huge success. Spoofing men's aftershave ads from the 1970s, Wieden+Kennedy managed perfectly to capture the zeitgeist and create a tone of voice that everyone responded to, creating a cultural phenomenon. For 'Responses', an online campaign was created that allowed the actor featured in the ads to respond in this tone of voice to genuine questions from members of the public that had been put to him via personalized online videos, 186 in total, and via Twitter over the course of three days. The Old Spice YouTube channel is YouTube's most-viewed sponsored channel of all time and total campaign impressions since February 2010 have come close to 1.2 billion. The 'Responses' campaign picked up the top Grandy prize at the 2011 Andy Awards.

Write a Twitter feed for one of your campaigns; stay on tone throughout.

TASK

'You have 140 characters, which is all you can write on Twitter, and this is how a lot of younger people are consuming media these days. Learn how to write really concisely yet interestingly.'

AARON SEYMOUR-ANDERSON, ART DIRECTOR, FALLON MINNEAPOLIS

RIGHT

The 2010 TBWA Skittles
'Update the Rainbow'
campaign on Facebook
allowed Facebook fans
of Skittles to post their
current status update
to a special call-centre
operator. The operators
then created a little film
that rainbowfied the post
before sending it back to
the user's Facebook wall.
Skittles 'Update' winners
can still be seen
on YouTube.

ABOVE

Fallon's 'Follow the White
Rabbit' campaign made
full use of Twitter.

LEFT

This campaign by BETC
Euro RSCG for the Syfy
channel centred around
ten alien 'children' toys
that were placed in cities
across France. The public
were encouraged to find
the toys through posters
and a dedicated website.
Later in the campaign a
Facebook page was set up
where users could 'meet'
one of the aliens.

EXPERIENTIAL

Experiential or relationship campaigns used to mean direct response marketing, in-store activity and brand activation. They emphasized customer retention and satisfaction and clients loved them, as it was usually more straightforward to measure their effectiveness. Today's experiential campaigns still put the customer/brand relationship at the heart of their thinking but offer a more holistic approach to the use of media. The campaigns are often integrated or transmedia in approach and tend to make good use of social media. They are a public, playful and immersive media experience, targeting consumers unexpectedly and able to communicate a campaign thought rather than simply, for example, a price promotion two-for-one offer.

The 2010 JWT New York Smirnoff Nightlife Exchange project was a global experiential campaign that continued Smirnoff's 'Be There' campaign. Fourteen cities across the world took part and were partnered up with each other, Toronto with Dehli, London with Miami and so on. On 27 November 2010 clubbers from these cities took part in a club night that reflected the culture, music and nightlife of their partnered city. Through the involvement of the Smirnoff audience on Facebook, Nightlife Exchange curators from each country collated the best local nightlife and artefacts from their city, ranging from musical choices to phoneboxes to food. These cultural ingredients were crated up and flown over to the sister city somewhere else in the world.

'I went to cover the London event and what was most fun for me was that I was not just seeing what was happening in my immediate surroundings but actually seeing all the tweets rolling in from around the world. I got to see how the whole thing unfolded, one after the next as we crossed from time zone to time zone.'

MATT MACDONALD, EXECUTIVE CREATIVE DIRECTOR, JWT NEW YORK

A helpful way to think about experiential campaigns is to think about how you can encourage consumer interaction rather than creating a brand monologue. Matt Macdonald's comments about the Smirnoff campaign hold true for all experiential campaigns. Think about the best live events and performances you have been to. What did they do? How did that engage you?

'Where a lot of brands go on the wrong path is that they want people to take action, where they're doing something for the brand, or they're asking the consumers to do the advertising for them. I don't think that's right. I think consumers want to do something where they feel they can do some good in the world or they can have a great experience.'

MATT MACDONALD, EXECUTIVE CREATIVE DIRECTOR, JWT NEW YORK

So if you are thinking experientially ask yourself what you are offering to your audience rather than asking them to give back to you.

This JWT New York experiential campaign for Smirnoff culminated in a worldwide party. Partygoers then posted their pictures and shared their experiences with their friends creating a user-controlled ongoing campaign.

Coca-Cola commissioned a group of designers, led by architects Asif Khan and Pernilla Ohrstedt, to create the 'Coca-Cola Beatbox' pavilion for the 2012 Olympic Park in London. Designed as a multi-sensory experience, visitors could trigger extracts from a specially created recording by producer Mark Ronson by touching parts of the building, while the pavilion's lighting responded whenever it 'heard' the clink of visitors' Coca-Cola bottles.

TELEVISION AND CINEMA

Television is a time-based medium in which events unfold to reveal the link between the product and the story. The creative is in control of when the reveal is delivered. The nature and type of reveal can add humour, drama and impact. The reveal often twists the story, so that the viewer has thought it was about one thing but it turns out to be about something else; or the reveal makes sense of a story where the viewer had no idea what it was all about until that moment.

The 1963 DDB New York Volkswagen Beetle 'Snowplow' television ad shows a small VW Beetle car driving through very snowy, hazardous conditions early in the morning. We are at least halfway through the ad before the question 'Ever wondered how the man that drives the snowplow gets to the snowplow?' is asked. It is a surprise to discover that what we have been watching all along is in fact the product, and this clever trick is what creates the twist in the story. The ad has demonstrated the benefits without creating a product demonstration advert.

Clients are often very wary of using a reveal as they believe that the target market will not remember the product and brand if it only takes up a small amount of screen time, and prefer to reveal the product from the very beginning, thereby removing one of the major dramatic tricks open to creatives. If you have been asked to deliver a product demonstration or comparative ad in which, for example, one detergent is compared to another, then the dramatic reveal possibilities are limited. The trick is then to ask yourself what you can do or what character you can create that will help you tell this story in a unique way. Perhaps it could be a superhero that needs to get their clothes super clean.

There are many ways in which a television ad can be conceived. It can be a narrative made up of characters, a demonstration of product benefits, a series of vignettes with or without the product, an extended analogy or metaphor such as the 'Hutch becomes' Vodafone ad (see Chapter 3); it can be surreal like a pop video, such as the 2011 ad for Hornbach by Heimat Berlin, in which a whole village of people have forgotten how to use their arms, and it takes the arrival of a giant walnut to remind them of the purpose of these appendages. It can be a fictitious event or a documentary. It is important to think about what can disrupt the usual flow of adverts: what would make your ad stand out?

Grey Melbourne's 2010 'The Ripple Effect' ad for the Transport Accident Commission is a powerful series of stories, building out of the feelings of the people at the scene of a car crash, through everyone that is affected, until we reach the family. The story was based on real events and the actual people were filmed. There are no clever gimmicks; it is a simple story sensitively explored in a documentary style.

You also need to be aware that adverts are seen multiple times by viewers, who may or may not be part of the target market. Many clients act as though the television audience will only see the ad once and so think that the brand name needs repeating over and over again. They worry that consumers with a remote control can skip through numerous satellite and cable TV channels, ignoring their adverts. How well the ad has been branded will form a fairly consistent part of your conversations with clients, particularly as television is such an expensive media channel compared with other media, such as radio or press.

A related media channel is cinema. Cinema ads and television ads are often the same, usually filmed for cinema and then transferred for television. If you are thinking of a cinema-specific ad then you should consider your environment. The audience is in a public space, the screen is enormous and the sound is epic. How can you push these aspects? Perhaps your ad will have no visual, leaving the audience sitting in the dark; perhaps it will use the surround-sound of the auditorium to make viewers think footsteps are behind them or a door is opening to the left. Though you may be able to conceive of your cinema execution in the same way that you did a television ad, it is a good challenge to push this media channel as far as the client will let you.

Television-style content specifically developed for the Web is another related media channel. The 2010 Agency215 San Francisco 'Bright Falls' campaign for the Xbox game *Alan Wake* used a key consumer insight – that these gamers were big fans of American television series such as *Heroes* and *24* – to push the boundaries of television-style advertising. Agency215 developed a prequel series about the mysterious town of Bright Falls, the town in which *Alan Wake* is set, and showed the episodes online in the weeks preceding the game launch. The final film finishes at the starting point of the game.

The *Alan Wake* game had to be bought in order to find out what happens next.

'When we all realized that *Alan Wake* was a new game designed more like a psychological TV show we had the idea of letting the marketing reflect this unique game. So creating Season 1 in the form of content that resembles an episodic show and then the game would turn into Season 2, created something that blurs the lines of marketing and content.'

JOHN PATROULIS AND SCOTT DUCHON, EXECUTIVE CREATIVE DIRECTORS, AGENCY215, SAN FRANCISCO

TASK
'Don't write a TV script. Write about something else, something you care about. The time your dog died. How you felt when your team won the World Series. What you want your life to be like in five years. And then, once you've got something, try to edit it down to 30 seconds. It ain't easy.'

JAMIE BARRETT, EXECUTIVE CREATIVE DIRECTOR, GOODBY SILVERSTON & PARTNERS, SAN FRANCISCO

RIGHT
The 2011 TV ad 'Every Change Needs a Beginning' by Heimat Berlin for Hornbach, at the moment when the giant walnut lands.

ABOVE AND RIGHT
San Francisco's Agency215 created an entire series of webisodes in 2010, starring Christopher Forsyth, as a prequel to the Xbox game *Alan Wake*.

RADIO

Although it is a public media channel, radio feels very intimate, perhaps because of the fact that you have to imagine the scene within your own mind. This ability to have the audience feel that they are being spoken to personally can be very powerful. Every sound, every pause, is significant and adds to the experience.

Many radio scripts are written as television scripts simply without the visuals, so a story is developed with characters, a plot, a tone of voice and perhaps a reveal linking it all back to the product. As with television, in radio ads sometimes there is no reveal because the product is mentioned all the way through the advert. Mandatory statements expressing limitations and constraints on offers are squeezed on to the ends of radio ads and on occasion creatives play with these conventions also.

However, other scripts are written that push the possibilities of the medium further. In the 2002 AMV BBDO, COI DTLR Mobiles 'Two Things at Once' spot we can hear two warnings delivered by the same female voiceover at the same time and we are unable to understand either of them properly. The idea is simply that it is hard to concentrate on two things at the same time and so we should not drive while speaking on our mobile phone.

The 2008 Grey Istanbul 'Google Search Tips' spot started with all the noise of a busy port town and slowly removed one by one as instructed by an almost godlike voice until, at last, the only sound that could be heard was the cheep of a little zebra finch, the bird that was being searched for.

'It's simple. Impactful. Fun to listen to. But I think what it does really, is actually set the whole scene in your mind visually. I think that is the most crucial asset.'

ERGIN BINYILDIZ, EXECUTIVE CREATIVE DIRECTOR, GREY ISTANBUL

When writing radio ads think about how you can deliver the unexpected in this medium. A starting point could be the context that people are in when they listen to the ad, perhaps in the car, or the content that surrounds the ad, such as music, talk radio or drama. Listen to experimental musicians and artists and think about how they manipulate sound to create impact. Take it in turns with your partner to listen to the script with your eyes closed – what else could you do?

BELOW
Grey Istanbul's radio ad for 'Google Search Tips'.

OPPOSITE TOP
This 2009 South African radio ad for Toyota by DraftFCB dramatizes what happens when you replace Toyota car parts with foreign parts.

OPPOSITE BOTTOM
This government-sponsored radio ad by AMV BBDO appeared in 2002.

Man
Silence the horn.
The jackhammer.
The alarm.
The pounding.
And that mobile.

Welder, peddler,
milling machines.
The noisy toddlers,
the loudmouth teens.

Stop the bike, the motorbike
And the honking, this instant!
The automobiles
And that little van still
driving in the distance.

Turn off the music.

Guys?

Wind... Aeroplane.

Shut up Spot!

The humming.

The clinking.

Sshhh. Sparrows, quiet please.
And seagulls. Speak no more.

There you are zebra finch...
You are the bird I've been
looking for.

Use Google Search Tips.
Reduce the whole world
to a single result.

Radio
El Loco

MVO   The parts in a new Toyota are all original,
genuine Toyota parts. There's a good reason
to keep them this way. Because if you start
introducing foreign parts, things quickly start
going muy malo. As you continue driving
your car, more stukkies start wearing out, so
you replace them with icheapele piesa. After
a while nad habariako partes original any
vladivosok. Nothing seems to graft so je
t'aime any kosher babushka and the whole
garankwa starts to no hable el loco. La luna
yokosuma el nino original in vitro del fume
nostrovia. No perestroika. Au revoir.

VO   Use only genuine parts on your Toyota.
Toyota. Lead the way.

V/O: (Both at same time)   You're four times more likely to have
a crash when you're on a mobile
phone. It's hard to concentrate on
two things at the same time.

V/O: (Both at same time)   You're four times more likely to have
a crash when you're on a mobile
phone. It's hard to concentrate on
two things at the same time.

V/O: (Single Voice)   You're four times more likely to have
a crash when you're on a mobile
phone.

V/O: (Single Voice)   It's hard to concentrate on two
things at the same time.

V/O: From 1st December, it will be illegal
to drive while using a hand-held
mobile phone. Think. Switch it off.

PRESS

Press advertising involves creating an ad to promote a product or service in printed publications. It could take the form of a double-page spread in a Sunday newspaper supplement or a small advert in a trade magazine. Traditionally, press ads have relied heavily on the skills of the copywriter to win the attention of the audience but this changed with the rise of visual advertising (see Chapter 2).

In a similar way to radio campaigns, press can also take the viewer into a personal space as it is primarily a private media channel, though visual rather than auditory. Teams working in this medium often use juxtaposition, humour and exaggeration to make their point. As with any good joke, there is a set-up and a punchline: one thing to bear in mind is that you should let either your visual or your headline have fun, and make the other do the explanatory work – they cannot both be wild.

'A great press ad should be direct and inform the consumer about the benefits of using the product. It should stand out from the surrounding work and so should look visually appealing. And it should always, always be very simple.'

RAYLIN VALLES, CREATIVE DIRECTOR, MUDRA DELHI

The award-winning ad by SRA Rushmore Madrid for Renfe, the railway company owned by the Spanish government, utilized the design-aware context of photography, architecture, cinema and art magazines for its 'Pantone' campaign. Four ads were created as spoof Pantone colour charts in yellow, blue, green and grey and were aimed at a creative and professional target market. The endline was: 'High-speed rail. Over 300 landscapes per hour.'

In the past copywriters would be expected to convince a person of the benefits of using a product over the course of a page and the art director's job was to make all that long copy look as appealing as possible. Paul Rand changed that way of thinking in the late 1940s and early 1950s, and a more visually led advertising style became possible. For a while the ads that won awards were the ones with little or no copy on them. More recently there has been a return to copy, but not long copy. It is perhaps easier to think of it as an extended headline, or a headline written in a more conversational way.

'I think it's just the reality of the market place really. It comes from an understanding that consumers aren't waiting there to read your long copy press ad, there's so much going on now – that cliché about how many ads we're exposed to – it's a bit more of a smash and grab now.'

PAUL JORDAN, EXECUTIVE CREATIVE DIRECTOR, DENTSU LONDON

OPPOSITE
This 2012 Pereira & O'Dell press ad – 'Green Brick' – followed Lego's accepted product benefit of letting kids use their imaginations, and is a great example of the return of copy. It isn't 'selling copy', it tells a story and engages the viewer quickly. Even though there is a lot of copy, it is still far from the word count of the pre-1950s ads that relied on copy for their sale.

BELOW
SRA Rushmore press ad for Renfe from 2010, promoting high-speed rail travel.

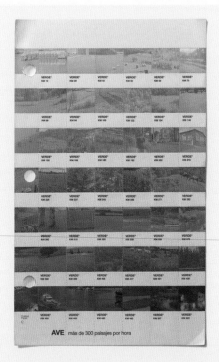

A little green dinosaur escaped from Alcatraz to catch a train to the Ninjago Temple, but he jumped off at a station of firefighters looking for the pyramid beside the Leaning Tower of Pisa, and was so worried to find a rocket full of robots that he called the ambulance and asked why the gas station was over the igloo, so he stopped, looked around and saw The Evil Dwarf, two Statues of Liberty and a giant snow ball coming in his direction, and he had no doubt, so he caught his light saber and defended himself, sticking an Eiffel Tower right in the ship of the evil pirate.

Every LEGO brick tells a story. Build yours.

There's always
a stain waiting
to happen

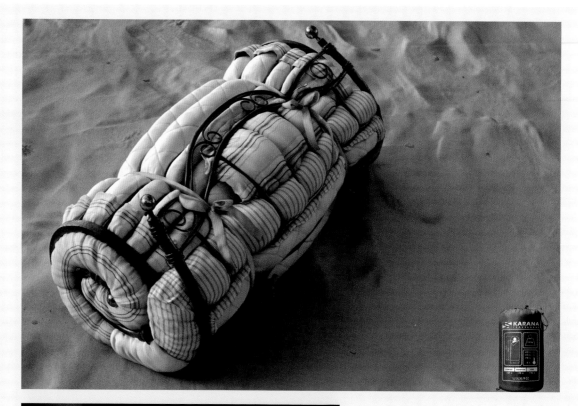

ONE OF THE SEVEN SEEDS.

OUTDOOR

Many of the distinctions between media channels in this area have become blurred; posters, ambient and digital ambient can often exist in all three categories. A number of agencies have taken to calling it 'out-of-home advertising', referring to encountering advertising in public spaces. Most poster executions tend to be in paid-for and expected locations such as at bus stops or on billboards, but there are other posters that perhaps require a special build (extensions to or cut-outs from billboards) or digital technology that work precisely because they are where people do not expect to see a brand message. What unifies such activities is that they are primarily visual and very public media channels, having little or no room for copy (a few specific poster exceptions include trains and stations, where people have time to read and are generally pretty bored and looking around for something to do).

'Outdoor is a tough medium. You have three seconds to raise people's interest for your poster, to make them stop on their way, to fascinate them and make them get your point. That's a lot you ask from them. Therefore you have to make the idea big and quick. Or you make the logo bigger. Just kidding.'

SABINA HESSE, COPYWRITER, HEIMAT BERLIN

POSTERS

Like press, posters can use juxtaposition, humour and exaggeration freely. There is often, but not always, a headline, and usually the hard work is done by the visual. This is where lateral thinking is employed. There are key things that you can think about when you have a poster brief. Jon Daniel, executive creative director at Ebb&Flow, London, suggests asking yourself the following questions:

1. What's the single most powerful statement I can make on this blank rectangular shape?

2. Can I make that statement without words?

3. How can I use the space for dramatic effect?

4. Where can it be hung or placed for dramatic effect?

The award-winning 2011 Mudra Delhi Philips 'Flipped City' poster campaign showed an illustration of someone walking through the noisiest cities in the world, oblivious to all the noise because they were wearing Philips headphones. The visual twist was delivered by the idea that, in the creative director's words, 'it's as if…' the city has been flipped under the headphone wearer and they are walking on in empty space.

While a poster requires a simple and direct message, that does not mean you need to think like a graphic designer or the king of one-liners; you can think more like an installation artist if you choose to do so. Posters are outside, which allows for creative play with scale, interaction, location, materials – but remember that special builds or any changes to surface are going to be a harder sell to clients, and therefore account teams, because they move out of known, safe territory. Although the poster is a traditional media channel, it can take a much more ambient approach and the lines are often a little blurred between these two definitions in awards.

'One of the comments at Cannes, for example, was that it might be the last time that a traditional billboard wins a grand prix but for us it wasn't a "traditional" billboard, it was just a billboard, so the idea of traditional or not is quite subjective, as it's not what you would classify as new media.'

RAPHAEL BASCKIN, SENIOR COPYWRITER
TBWA/HUNT/LASCARIS JOHANNESBURG

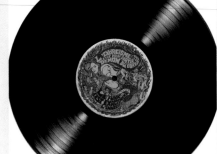

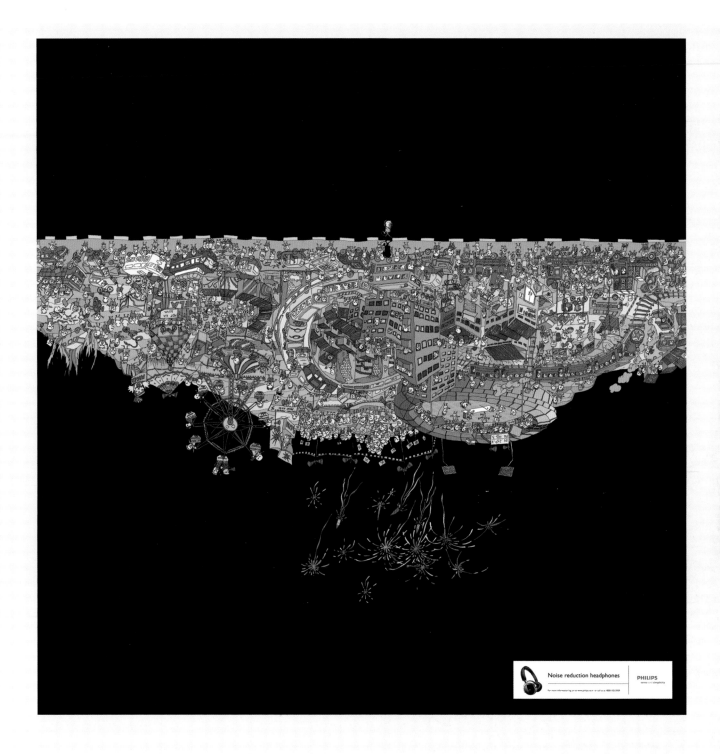

OPPOSITE
These posters from the
2008 Young & Rubicam
campaign for France's
Nova Radio use beautiful,
but not simple, imagery
to bring the variety of
music that Nova plays
to life.

ABOVE
Mudra Delhi 2011 press
ad for Philips noise-
cancelling headphones.

AMBIENT

The outdoor space can target consumers unexpectedly: any surface is fair game, but it still needs to communicate a campaign thought. Ambient advertising refers to any marketing using non-traditional spaces such as trees or pavements. However, the days of simply stickering a surface with a logo are over, as people are not sufficiently intrigued any more.

The 2009 Ogilvy Frankfurt 'Contemporary Beauty Ideals' campaign for ANAD, a German anorexia support organization, reinterpreted a selection of famous paintings and then hung them in a gallery setting. The concept was to contrast today's potentially dangerous beauty ideals (such as excessive thinness) with beauty ideals from the past. It was essential to bring the work to where the target market – potential donors – would be: within a cultural space.

'The artist Remus Grecu created perfect, breathtaking reproductions of the originals. The disruption between the beautiful painting and the terrifying subject is unbelievably moving. If you stand in front of the imposing *Olympia* for example, which is around 2 metres [6 ft 6 in.] in length, you inevitably get goosebumps. In one second the whole scenery and all the details get a completely new denotation: the maid doesn't bring flowers to a graceful lady any more, but to a dying woman on a sickbed.'

SABINA HESSE, COPYWRITER, HEIMAT BERLIN

DIGITAL AMBIENT

The outdoor space can also be very playful, and digital interactive executions make the most of this. The opportunity to have fun with media found the perfect client with Volkswagen and the perfect campaign in 'the Fun Theory' from Tribal DDB Stockholm.

'In the first phases of the project we launched the theory on a philosophical basis, beginning a conversation with the consumer on the role of fun in behaviour change for good — first by proving it through the piano staircase, the deepest bin and the bottle bank arcade. After that we asked the public to think about and apply it through the fun theory award. The result of which were hundreds of ideas from across the globe. The best of which — the speed camera lottery — we executed in Stockholm, Sweden.'

SIMON HIGBY, CREATIVE DIRECTOR, TRIBAL DDB STOCKHOLM

The public's imagination was captured when Tribal DDB launched the campaign, overlaying an interactive touch-sensitive staircase, in which each step played as a piano key, over an existing staircase in a Swedish subway. The idea was to see if people would change behaviour to something more environmentally responsible if it was fun to do. It worked. More than 66 per cent of people now chose the steps rather than the escalator. This execution was followed up by the other digital ambient executions mentioned by Simon above – the World's Deepest Bin and the Bottle Bank Arcade, which also made it fun to change behaviour. The short films that were made about each became the world's most watched virals at the time. The fun theory worked.

Tribal DDB Stockholm created fun digital pieces for Volkswagen. This piano staircase encouraged people to walk up the stairs at a metro station instead of using the escalators.

This impactful 2009 campaign by Ogilvy Frankfurt for the eating disorder charity ANAD used illustrator Remus Grecu to recreate well-known masterpieces, which the team then displayed in a gallery context.

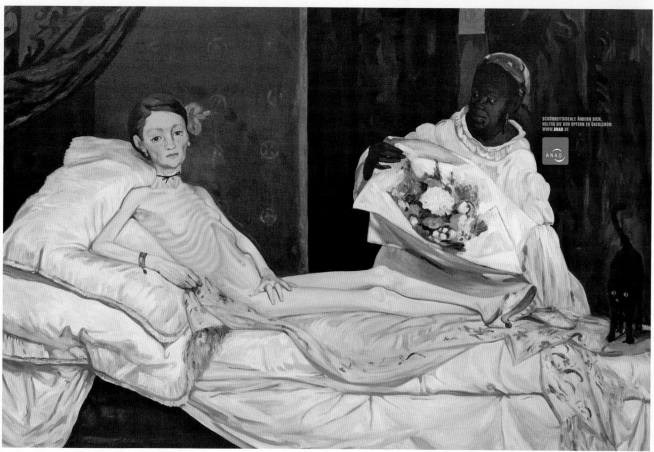

DIRECT ADVERTISING

Direct advertising can be thought of as either targeted or blanket media: targeted because people can request information, or they are known to be interested in this product area, or blanket when the promotional activity is unsolicited and enters the consumer's personal space – their home, mobile phone or email inbox. Of all the promotional activities it is this potentially unsolicited aspect that draws the most criticism. If you work in direct advertising you are usually required to solicit some kind of action. Clients love this because the response is measurable, even if consumers are more irritated by junk mail and spam emails than by any other kind of advertising.

Direct advertising is usually asked to deliver a specific direct mail message rather than a branding campaign. Examples of direct mail messaging include money off – 'you can save this much if you do this activity' and 'contact this retailer/website to get your free trial'. Getting people to take action in a way that has thoughtfully engaged them is the challenge.

At its best, however, direct can either continue a branding campaign or sustain a campaign thought on its own. The 2008 Syrup Stockholm *Fria Tidningen* newspaper 'Hello Fra' direct digital campaign is a good example of this. FRA stands for FRA-lagen or FRA law – *Fria Tidningen*, a small independent newspaper, was worried about its right to protect its sources when the Swedish parliament wanted to introduce this law, which would have made it possible for them to monitor electronic traffic such as email and text messages. This threatened to change constitutional rights protecting the anonymity of anyone who contacts a journalist, as well as wider rights, as FRA law would allow the Swedish state to wiretap without a warrant all telephone and Internet traffic that crosses Sweden's borders. *Fria Tidningen* wanted to take action rather than just complain. Syrup created a simple campaign that anyone could participate in just by adding a simple signature to their emails. The text in the signature contained randomly changing trigger words that forced the FRA to check every single email personally. A case study is still available on YouTube.

'For a tiny budget, we wanted to create something that would get a life of its own. Also, it had to be easy for everyone to use. We kept the tone of voice civil but with a twist of sarcasm since there were enough angry voices out there. So the concept turned out to be: a polite resistance.'

MATTIAS CEDERFELDT, ART DIRECTOR, POND, STOCKHOLM, AND MIA ROBERTSSON, COPYWRITER, FAMILJENPANGEA, STOCKHOLM

This award-winning mailer by The Bridge for the Scottish National Blood Transfusion Service is a brilliant example of a simple but immediately engaging direct mail message.

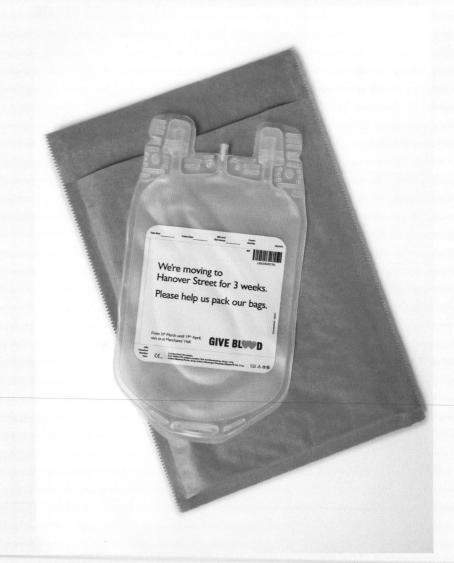

LEFT
This idea from Denvir for a stripclub in Moscow won a Best Direct Mail award at the Chip Shop Awards.

BELOW
Syrup Stockholm's 2008 digital direct piece for *Fria Tidningen* newspaper allowed people to participate in direct political action without having to leave their living rooms.

MAKE A POLITE RESISTANCE

FRA (Swedish National Defense Radio Establishment) will start to scan all internet- and mobile phone traffic that passes the Swedish border next year. E-mail and SMS that contains certain words will alert the FRA-system and they will then be controlled manually. The goal is to discover external threat to Sweden's security

We don't believe that the new law will stop any terrorist attacks. The attacks won't likely be planed by unencrypted e-mail. On the other hand the new law will be a threat to right for journalists to protect their sources. A right protected by the Swedish constitution that shall guarantee anonymity to anyone that contact a journalist. With beginning next year no contact with any journalist via e-mail or SMS can be anonymous. And that's a bigger threat to our society.

Sabotage!
Force FRA to read all your ordinary e-mail by adding the .sigfile, with "dangerous" trigger words, to your e-mail.
Make a polite resistance

FRIA**TIDNINGEN**

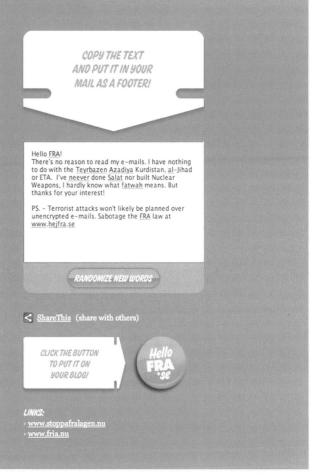

SERVICE DESIGN AND PRODUCT IDEAS

'The communication overdose that we live in, which includes advertising, means that it's not easy to capture our audiences' attention. They have no desire to be convinced whatsoever, but they do want to be swept off their feet, to be fascinated, and above all, to enjoy themselves. As Bill Bernbach wisely said: "The truth isn't the truth until people believe you, and they can't believe you if they don't know what you're saying, and they can't know what you're saying if they don't listen to you, and they won't listen to you if you're not interesting, and you won't be interesting unless you say things imaginatively, originally, freshly."'

LUCA D'ALESIO, CREATIVE DIRECTOR, TOUCHÉ ADVERTISING, BOLOGNA

As advertisers, to get people's attention in today's society, we need to do things differently than in the past. Service and product design is an area of opportunity, and clients are becoming more open to this type of relationship with their advertising agency.

'Basically it's being useful to people. Don't try and get in their way to get your message across, give them something. Create services that are inventive and fun, not just ads.'

PAUL JORDAN, EXECUTIVE CREATIVE DIRECTOR, DENTSU LONDON

Crispin Porter and Bogusky created a service for Domino's Pizza in 2008 known as the Pizza Tracker. You can order a pizza online and build your pizza and then follow your pizza through the process; you know when it goes to the oven, you know when it is on the bike. You can track it. It created a fun experience that helped Domino's business.

Another great example of service and product design is the Nike+ application, developed with Apple. Having looked at what the brand Nike offers – access to sport – a service project was developed to see how Nike could actually go about delivering it. A chip inside select running shoes transmits details of the user's run to their iPod. The app then allows runners to track their

runs and become part of an online community of like-minded people. Nike+ provides a great service, bringing both Apple and Nike to the heart of that experience.

An important part of the course I have developed is getting students to develop new products or services for existing brands, because this is developing into an important part of a modern ad agency's offering. Target markets are not behaving in the way that they traditionally behaved. People tend not to stick with one brand all their lives: they are more marketing-aware, and they have multiple media and entertainments vying for their attention. In order for a consumer to pick your brand's offering from all the other messages it must really stand out. It must give them something that they need or that will help them. This is where product design and service design fit in to the promotional picture – what better way of re-engaging a brand's audience then a great new product or service?

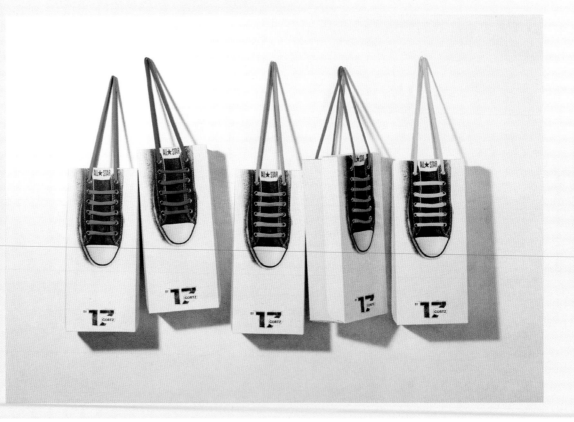

Kempertrautmann created packaging design as a point-of-sale brand communication for Görtz 17's Converse Collection, to focus on the brand's attributes of design and functionality. During the campaign, sales increased by 15 per cent.

Clemenger BBDO created
a direct campaign for
Guide Dogs Australia,
in which you showed
support by purchasing a
scented item, allowing
those who are blind or
visually impaired to know
that you supported them.

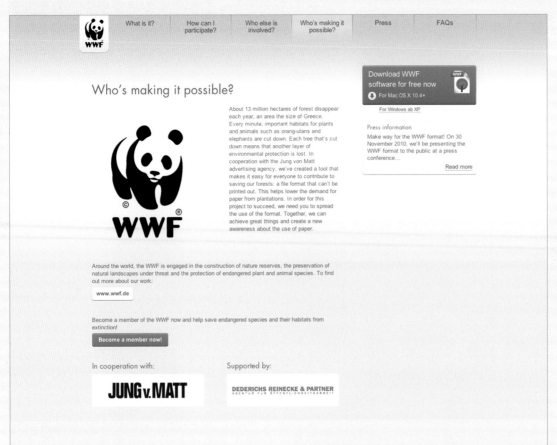

Who's making it possible?

About 13 million hectares of forest disappear each year, an area the size of Greece. Every minute, important habitats for plants and animals such as orang-utans and elephants are cut down. Each tree that's cut down means that another layer of environmental protection is lost. In cooperation with the Jung von Matt advertising agency, we've created a tool that makes it easy for everyone to contribute to saving our forests: a file format that can't be printed out. This helps lower the demand for paper from plantations. In order for this project to succeed, we need you to spread the use of the format. Together, we can achieve great things and create a new awareness about the use of paper.

Around the world, the WWF is engaged in the construction of nature reserves, the preservation of natural landscapes under threat and the protection of endangered plant and animal species. To find out more about our work:

www.wwf.de

Become a member of the WWF now and help save endangered species and their habitats from extinction!

Become a member now!

In cooperation with:

Supported by:

In 2011 Jung von Matt released the WWF format for saving files on behalf of the World Wide Fund for Nature. The idea is that the user chooses which documents don't need printing and then saves them as a WWF. The WWF is simply a PDF that cannot be printed, so it avoids unnecessary printing. In order to use it, the user needs to download free software that can support the WWF format. Four weeks after launch the website had received 200,000 visitors from 183 countries and had 30,000 software downloads. This was not just clever advertising, it was product creation for the client – in other words, the product is the message.

SAVE AS WWF,
SAVE A TREE

CRAFTING YOUR IDEAS

7

7 CRAFTING YOUR IDEAS

'Probably the most practical thing is to concentrate on your craft. Knowing your voice as a writer, your point of view as a designer, and continually working to make that part of your skill-set better is the single most important thing you can do.'

JOHN PATROULIS AND SCOTT DUCHON,
EXECUTIVE CREATIVE DIRECTORS, AGENCY215, SAN FRANCISCO

There are a number of different skills that a creative needs: business skills, teamwork skills, the ability to generate strong ideas and the technical know-how to be able to develop and craft work. Working in today's multimedia world also calls for distinct skills such as media fluency and cultural awareness. Being a good ideas person does not necessarily mean that you will be a good crafts person or vice versa, but the creative muscle needs to be developed on both sides. The crafts of writing and art directing are the creative's responsibility.

As you develop your skills and become more senior in the industry you are likely to craft aspects of your work at the same time as you develop your initial executions. You will know how your headline will look, what it will say, how you will crop your image, whether you will use illustration or photography. But when you start either as a student or as a new team, crafting your ideas usually comes after someone else has agreed the idea in the first place.

CULTURAL CAPITAL

'I want people who consume a lot, who are big readers, who have a wide swap of interests, because of the theory "garbage in garbage out". The better taste you have in what you consume, like the movies you watch, the books you read, the music you listen to, the more likely you are to create things that stand up to that.'

MATT MACDONALD, EXECUTIVE CREATIVE DIRECTOR, JWT NEW YORK

Awareness of culture is called our 'cultural capital' and it is what creatives use all the time as references. Cultural capital is essential for advertising because it is the way in which we link to our target market. Referencing is not the same as spoofing. Referencing is to be informed by other people's work, not to recreate it. It can help you choose interesting or impactful typefaces or intriguing layouts. It can give the flow of your words on paper a pleasing rhythm, for example, by referencing the style of a well-known poem. It can help you envisage interesting scenes and how they unfold. It is the political stance a brand can safely take and it is how we play with our media.

Creatives cannot choose to remain ignorant of the culture that surrounds them and new creatives will not be employed unless they can show cultural awareness. You need to get into the habit of keeping a scrapbook. In it you need to collect images from magazines, jokes that you like, notes on films or scenes, leaflets from art exhibitions, innovations of interest, photos you have taken, and anything else that you can think of that could inspire you.

'I always think it's interesting to look at other industries and sectors, and apply their thinking in different ways to different projects.'

JON DANIEL, EXECUTIVE CREATIVE DIRECTOR, EBB&FLOW, LONDON

'Check out different cultures, and always stay focused and observe: you never know where you can get ideas from.'

RAYLIN VALLES, CREATIVE DIRECTOR, MUDRA DELHI

You need to consume vast amounts of information and cultural events just to remain on a par with other creatives. This must not only be the music you like, the films you like, the books you like. You need to broaden your cultural appetite.

'Every day I try to invest at least 45 minutes in the Web to get innovations and news.'

ALBERT S. CHAN, ART DIRECTOR, OGILVY & MATHER FRANKFURT

COPYWRITING

In many of the more visual markets long copy has almost disappeared and the longest sentence will be in the endline. That is not to say that there is no need for copywriters. Ideas are conceived in teams, executions are expanded upon in teams and television and radio scripts will always need to be written.

'Copy in Argentina has fallen into disuse. It's hard to find good copy in print ads in this country.'

MARIO CRUDELE, SENIOR COPYWRITER, PONCE BUENOS AIRES

In the global context of the World Wide Web, text has returned in a big way: in social media and digital content, good writing is key. A copywriter needs to develop an interesting style and manner of writing, one that is attractive, engaging and likeable – in other words, charming – as well as be able to write in many tones of voice. It is essential that you hone these skills by practising your writing.

'Copy should provoke emotion. It should move people. It should break forms so that you ring something other than the routine in people's minds.'

ERGIN BINYILDIZ, EXECUTIVE CREATIVE DIRECTOR, GREY ISTANBUL

> **TASK**
> 'Anyone can start a blog. It helps you hone your writing skills. A person can look for things they find interesting, they can collect good ads on it, they can do bits of writing. Just doing that makes you engage with technology and after a while your personality will emerge. We all look at amazing blogs every day. And every time you go to see a team you can say "here's my blog".'
>
> PAUL JORDAN, EXECUTIVE CREATIVE DIRECTOR, DENTSU LONDON

ENDLINES

'A good endline is simply a summation of your idea. It's the full stop to your thinking. Don't try to write something that sounds clever if it doesn't explain your ad. Write what you want to say in longhand. Then edit it down. Keep going until it is as succinct as possible. People think endlines are all about wordplay; they aren't. "If only everything in life was as reliable as a Volkswagen" was one of the most famous endlines of all time. There are no puns, or trickery. It's just a simple, powerful and thought-provoking statement.'

ADAM TUCKER, CREATIVE DIRECTOR, LEO BURNETT LONDON

For most creatives writing an endline is hard work. We write pages and pages of lines and listen to pages and pages of our partner's lines. Writing good endlines takes practice, and familiarity with good lines written by other creatives helps. Pick 20 adverts that you like and look at their endlines: do they seem to sum up or add to your understanding of the advert? Some of them will be witty and some of them very straightforward but they will all generally be charming and eloquent. For example, for Saatchi & Saatchi New York's 2008 ad for Cheerios you could write a number of lines but are they all as interesting as the original?

- Example 1: *Cholesterol blocks your arteries* – literal and boring.

- Example 2: *Protect all that you are by looking after your heart* – far too worthy.

- Example 3: *Love and life flow better without cholesterol* – better but perhaps too explanatory.

- Saatchi & Saatchi's endline: *What runs through your veins runs better without cholesterol* – its nuances imply the richness and uniqueness of the life that you lead.

When searching for a good endline there will be times when you are swayed by a clever-sounding set of words. One of you puts five words together and you are so relieved that you do not notice it's a red herring. We have all been seduced by an inappropriate endline and wasted lots of time trying to get it to fit our idea or trying to change our idea to fit it. Sometimes we do not even notice that it is an endline to a completely different idea. This is a common experience and you are not a bad creative if you find writing endlines difficult; everyone does. But then you will write one that you hardly even notice because it feels so natural, it is the 'summation of your idea' written simply and with some charm. When you are re-reading, either you or your partner will pick it up – this is one of the advantages of working with someone else.

To do this you need to find out about the brand and the campaign and then, like a detective, try and work out what was being said.

> **TASK**
> '"Just do it", "Think different", "It is, are you?". What do you think the longhand versions of these were? What is the argument for the brand being presented? For example, "The future's bright, the future's Orange" could be the endline for "Orange is a telecoms company that is developing technology that will help to shape a better future".'
>
> ADAM TUCKER, CREATIVE DIRECTOR, LEO BURNETT LONDON

Touché Advertising's endline manages to balance the lengths people will go to to get something they truly desire with the obvious freshness of the fish suggested by the images. It also implies that this is food you won't have to wait for.

HEADLINES

A headline is a writer's opportunity to flex their craft muscle. Headlines are supposed to grab people's attention and you need to think laterally rather than literally. The strengths of headlines are in how they capture your attention and intrigue you.

Headlines also work best in contrast or in juxtaposition with the image. There is no point in having a headline that simply repeats what the image is – or, as I was told when I first started in the industry, why draw a dog and then write dog underneath it? If we look at BBH London's 2000 campaign for the children's charity Barnardo's this becomes clear. The campaign is powerful because although the image seems to be showing a moment of total despair in a young boy's life, this is juxtaposed with the headline 'Martin Ward: Age 29'. It makes you ask yourself 'How did he (or will he) get to this point?' in a way that simply showing a 29-year-old man about to commit suicide would not have done.

A clever headline can allow the agency and client to use a stock shot, which is substantially cheaper than organizing a shoot.

While traditionally headlines were only eight or so words long, if not shorter, a new hybrid headline/body copy form has emerged. It is based on an art-directional understanding that typographic design is in itself an image.

Sometimes the headline plays straight man to the visual. This 2011 Sosushi ad campaign from Touché Advertising, Bologna, works in this way – the visual is already surreal so the line must be straight in order for the ad to make sense. It is best not to have two lateral thoughts fighting with each other, one in the headline and one in the visual, because something does need to explain what is going on.

craving sushi? sosushi.it

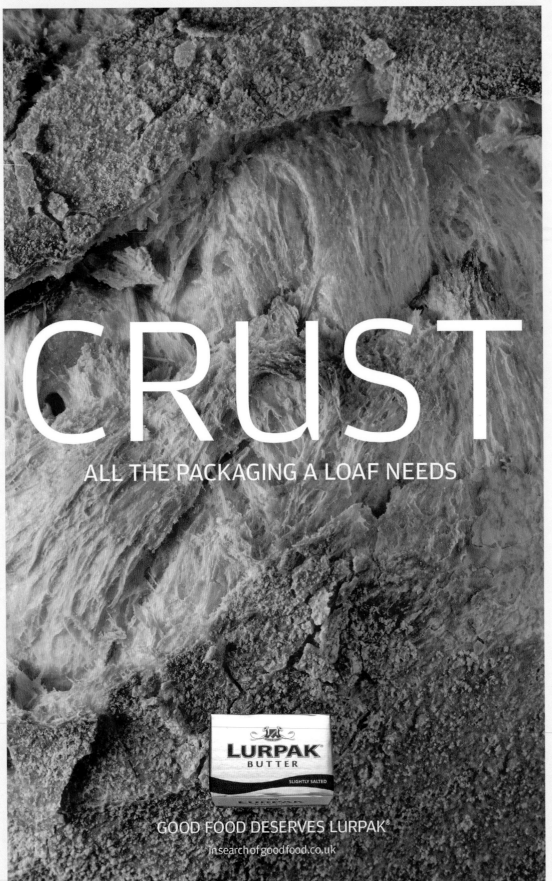

CRUST

ALL THE PACKAGING A LOAF NEEDS

LURPAK®
BUTTER

SLIGHTLY SALTED

GOOD FOOD DESERVES LURPAK®

insearchofgoodfood.co.uk

This headline-driven ad by Wieden+Kennedy for Lurpak makes you think about how delicious the food pictured can be with the brand's butter.

OPPOSITE
The use of juxtaposition of headline to image by BBH London in 2010 for Barnardo's makes its point so much more strongly.

Barnardo's
GIVING CHILDREN
BACK THEIR FUTURE

Martin Ward | AGE 29

Made to feel worthless as
a child, it was hardly
surprising that Martin could
see no other way out.

With Barnardo's help, an
unhappy childhood need not
mean a hopeless future.

Although we no longer run
orphanages, we continue to help
thousands of children and
their families at home, school
and in the local community.

To make a donation or
for more information
please call 0845 844 01 80.

www.barnardos.org.uk

Child depicted is a model

Is your train of thought subject to delays?

The Economist

LABOUR ISN'T WORKING.

UNEMPLOYMENT OFFICE

BRITAIN'S BETTER OFF WITH THE CONSERVATIVES.

Get off at Knightsbridge, visit the discerning shopper's fave department store, ascend the exotic staircase and let Piers in the pinstripe suit demonstrate the magic of the latest high-definition flatscreen then go to dixons.co.uk and buy it.

Dixons.co.uk
The last place you want to go

Audi
Vorsprung durch Technik

THE NEW MORE FUEL EFFICIENT AUDIS

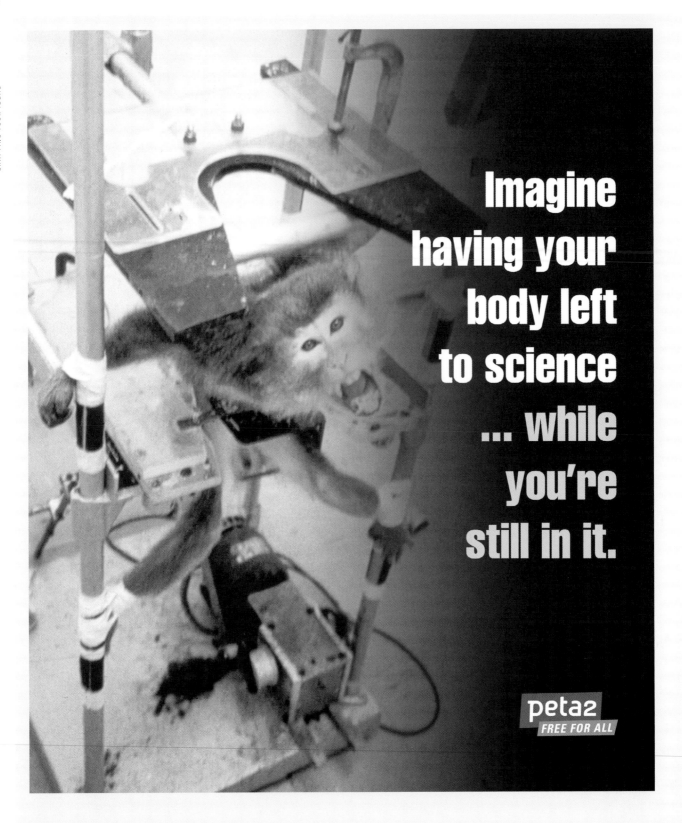

Imagine having your body left to science ... while you're still in it.

peta2
FREE FOR ALL

Thought-provoking headlines can become shocking when juxtaposed with the right image, such as in this 1988 ad for PETA by the Martin Agency.

BODY COPY

Body copy houses the product information. Sometimes it is a paragraph, sometimes it is just a line. As with every aspect of the advert you need to consider what you want to say overall. There will be a tone of voice that you will need to maintain, a campaign thought and a theme running through that particular execution. An invisible thread links the headline to the body copy. In some adverts the headline will appear as though it is the first sentence of the copy; in other ads it will not flow so obviously but it will be part of the same conversation.

'You need to make sure there are no clichés in your writing. You make sure there's no puns in it. You make sure there are no unnecessary words in it. You make sure it's everyday language. And you write it loads and loads of different ways until you find a way that feels a bit sticky.'

ANGUS MACADAM, EXECUTIVE CREATIVE DIRECTOR, DENTSU LONDON

You also have to give yourself a bit of distance from what you have written. Write down first drafts and then walk away from them. Read them again and find the one that offers the best starting point. Now start to edit it, avoid repetition and try to keep it as simple and concise as possible.

And learn to write it as a list of benefits as well: this will help.

TASK

Take an existing text such as an opinion piece and write it as a press release, editorial or copy for an ad, a blog post, a tweet, etc.'

MIA ROBERTSSON, COPYWRITER, FAMILJENPANGEA, STOCKHOLM

CONTENT WRITING – WRITING FOR THE WEB

Content for the Web is a form of body copy and writing it is similar to writing articles for magazines or a letter to someone. It has to be interesting, it has to have a point, but you often have considerably more words to play with to make your argument. You also have to have a real feel of whom you are writing for.

'There was no copywriter on "Follow the White Rabbit" because it was more content writing, which is the term people use when referring to writing for the Web or longer-form stuff. It's conversational and community management. You really need to know more about the people that are following you.'

ROCKY NOVAK, DIRECTOR OF DIGITAL DEVELOPMENT, FALLON MINNEAPOLIS

'It didn't need to be eloquent, snappy writing. It's someone that can talk in the voice, understand the feel and be more long-form, conversational and empathetic to the target market.'

AARON SEYMOUR-ANDERSON, ART DIRECTOR, FALLON MINNEAPOLIS

SCRIPTWRITING

Writing for television, cinema and radio requires you not only to envisage an interesting scenario but also to create characters that speak in believable ways. Listen to real conversations. It is important that there is a fair balance between believable conversation and product information. Often clients simply want the characters to mention the product over and over again, which can weaken the message being communicated. In those circumstances it is advisable to try and get the scenario to support the product message more effectively rather than relying on speech alone. It is often easier to see if the speech is working in a script when the actors and director come on board. Sometimes it becomes necessary to tweak the wording but this always needs agreement from the client and can prove very difficult once the internal approval procedure has already been completed in the client organization.

'A lot of scripts were written, a lot of combinations of words were tried. Where it all really came together was in the auditions, when you could see which words and which rhythms were working the best.'

JAMIE BARRETT, EXECUTIVE CREATIVE DIRECTOR, GOODBY SILVERSTEIN & PARTNERS, SAN FRANCISCO

It is also important to know when to enter and leave a scene. What most of us do when we first write a spot is to spend too much time setting it up. As with every kind of writing: edit. Do you really need to see a man walking up to his house or just him coming through the door? The same is true at the end of the ad – do we really need to see a man slip on a banana skin or does the presence of the banana skin and his diverted attention tell the joke?

ART DIRECTING

There is a difference between being an art director and being a designer and it is one of the most difficult things for new creative teams to understand. It is very common to want to create every aspect of how something looks if you are supposed to be the art director, or to feel like you should create it. This is a misunderstanding of the role.

'I want someone who knows the difference between art direction and design. Art direction is just the visual expression of a creative idea, where the idea and visual are inseparable.'

JUSTIN TINDALL, GROUP EXECUTIVE CREATIVE DIRECTOR, LEO BURNETT LONDON

Designers can spend time with the interplay of colours and textures; art directors must concentrate on the communication.

The job that art direction has to do is to enhance the meaning in an advert. The visual will have been decided within the creative team in the same way that what

must be said in a headline will have been decided. The image itself is not in question at this stage, rather the crafting element of the art direction: what can be done to make this ad better? There are three main places to start:

• Reduction – removing all extraneous information; think 'how many visual elements can I remove while allowing the ad to say the same thing?'

• Exaggeration – magnifying the most important part of the image; think 'how can I highlight the aspect that I want people to focus on?'

• Design principles – organizing the various visual elements to best tell the story; think 'how can I direct people's attention through this advert?'

Art direction, if you have a particularly straightforward idea, is to communicate that idea so simply that it almost art directs itself. But what happens if you have to do a really

boring ad where the image will be a pack shot with a mundane headline? The art director's job in this case is to make the whole thing look considerably better than it actually is. While art directors are not designers, it doesn't mean that they shouldn't have design knowledge and be able to use it when necessary. If you are creating the designs yourself, which you will be for your portfolio, you need to know some design basics.

'I studied graphic design before I got into art direction, which kind of gave me a really good understanding of how design works within advertising; a lot of art directors don't have that classical training in design which is quite useful. It's important to know the balance and structure of ads. It's not just about photography or illustration, you still have to have a certain sense of aesthetic, so I would say practising design disciplines is quite important.'

SHELLEY SMOLER, CREATIVE GROUP HEAD, TBWA/HUNT/LASCARIS JOHANNESBURG

1. This image lacks focus and direction. It is difficult to know what I want the viewer to look at...

2. ...so I remove as many of the unnecessary elements as possible to focus their attention.

Through the placement of typography I can help draw the viewer's attention where I want it. Imagine what fun can be had once you start to play with typeface choices and colour.

3. I then try and exaggerate the important areas through colour, composition or, in this case, crop.

4. The final advert

REDUCTION

The amount of design that a creative will need to be capable of varies from agency to agency. If you work with designers your responsibility is to keep your art direction as simple as possible so that they have some room for the input of creative ideas: reduce, reduce, reduce. Reduction is essential. If the purpose of the ad is to promote a sauce, then perhaps you do not need all the details of the room, what the other person is eating, your actors' entire wardrobe, the beautiful garden in the background.

'To learn to art direct an editing task is good. Take an ad in its current form and start removing things until you get to the critical point whereby everything superfluous has been taken away and if you take away one more thing it won't make sense.'

JUSTIN TINDALL, GROUP EXECUTIVE CREATIVE DIRECTOR, LEO BURNETT LONDON

EXAGGERATION

You can exaggerate your point through the use of colour and image composition. This is not the same as conceiving an idea – for example, your idea may be exaggerated (a man carrying an enormous bottle of sauce on holiday) – but exaggerating in the crafting sense would be highlighting that sauce bottle within the scenario that you have established. The most direct ways of doing this are through colour, lighting and composition.

COLOUR THEORY

We usually create colours in three different ways: the primary colours in paint, yellow/red/blue (YRB); the ink colours used by printers, cyan/magenta/yellow/black (CMYK); the colours used in light technology such as televisions or computers, red/blue/green (RGB). A separate subsection of ink colours is the Pantone Matching System (PMS), which allows you to specify colours with a code from a book to a printer – this is usually done for branding books and special print runs rather than advertising.

The colour wheel can be split into two parts, warm and cold. Warm colours are lively and tend to come to the foreground. Cool colours are calming and tend to create background. From the colour wheel there are a variety of tints (adding white), shades (adding black) and tones (adding grey).

Simply changing the saturation or tint of a colour can change the feel of an image completely. Culturally, the meanings of certain colours as signs varies (see Chapter 2).

IMAGE CHOICE AND COMPOSITION

How you will execute your images is an important part of the art director's job. As a creative team you will decide on a visual approach, and you will look through numerous portfolios to get the person whose work you like. But how do you choose between illustration and photography, animation and film?

'We chose an illustration style to bring out the madness in the city, illustrations rather than realistic so we could go a little crazy and exaggerate. With illustration we would have control and wouldn't be restricted.'

RAYLIN VALLES, CREATIVE DIRECTOR, MUDRA DELHI

Drawn or composited imagery gives you greater flexibility and can create a surreal feel more than a real image captured on camera or film. It can be as extreme as you like, though that is also its downfall – to many it does not feel real enough. This feeling of reality within a photograph can also be played with. Consider how you can shoot something in a way that makes it look as if it has never been seen before – the very fact that it is 'for real' lends extra impact.

How images communicate meanings and whether you want to use film, photography or illustration is for you, the creative, to consider, not for the director, illustrator or photographer to stipulate. You can use your choice of elements within your images to exaggerate meaning:

- The main character – age, gender, race or nationality, body shape, height and presence, attractiveness, facial expression, clothing, pose
- Relationships – eye contact with viewer or others within the image
- Focus – literally what is in focus, close-up, cropping, camera angle
- Performance – staged, naturalistic, documentary, surreal, humorous

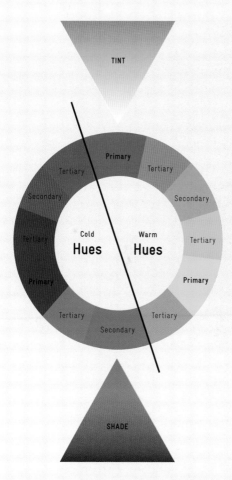

The colour wheel showing primary, secondary and tertiary hues.

This 2011 campaign by
Creative Juice Bangkok
for M Wrap uses digital
techniques to create a
surreal image.

This 2009
Wieden+Kennedy ad
for Honda's Insight
Hybrid uses traditional
photography techniques
for a surreal image.

INSIGHT HYBRID | HOLY ISLAND

HONDA
The Power of Dreams

DESIGN PRINCIPLES

There are some basic design principles that it is a good idea to be aware of. Of course all rules are there to be pushed and broken, so have fun, but make sure you are communicating the idea.

TYPOGRAPHY

Typography is a highly specialized field covering the arrangement of type. Art directors need to know about how type can be arranged to promote a product effectively. Considerable sums of money are spent on branding because how words are visualized instantly creates a brand identity. At the very least we should know if a word is **bold**, *italic*, *script*, serif or sans serif.

It is tempting to art direct an ad with the latest fashionable typeface; however, a better place to start is the typeface used by the brand. The client chose it for a reason, for a certain tone of voice. You can choose to maintain this tone of voice by finding another typeface that has a similar feel, or perhaps is also an elegant font or a bold newspaper font. You can also choose to contrast with or complement this typeface by looking within the extended family range of the logotype or outside of it, for example using a light sans serif next to an ornate script font. It is considered good practice to use a serif in contrast to a sans serif. But as with anything else, you do not have to follow the rules. As you try things out, just like crafting and re-crafting words, the end product should feel right in tone but may be different from what you had originally discussed.

'The typography started off very different from the outcome; it was blue to begin with because that was the colour of their original masthead. It also took up the whole poster. But then we realized that the type had to be smaller so that the money could shine through as much as possible. We needed a font that was really bold that would really stand out when it wasn't huge on the poster and it needed to be instantly recognizable and with no cultural attachments. Just simple and to the point like the posters themselves were.'

SHELLEY SMOLER, CREATIVE GROUP HEAD, TBWA/HUNT/LASCARIS JOHANNESBURG

Think about what you are stressing when you create typography as it can change the meaning of a sentence, as follows:

- **Advertising** is fun.
- Advertising **is** fun.
- Advertising is **fun**.

While you are unlikely to be expected to kern your letters personally (change the space in between the letters) or alter the leading (the space in between the lines) you certainly need to know if what you are presented with is the look that you are after and to direct the designer to alter anything that may need changing.

Sometimes typography itself can be the image, and many teams conceive an idea typographically and then find the best way to execute it with a specialist typographer, designer, illustrator or photographer.

LAYOUT

A layout is the arrangement of visual elements on a page or screen. The following are some basic layout points.

- Balance – a feel to the whole layout achieved through either symmetry or asymmetry.
- Tension – unlike balance, tension creates interest by giving one particular element more emphasis than the others.
- Contrast – the difference between visual elements is exaggerated through juxtaposition; this can be between light weight and heavy weight or colours, for example.
- Positive and negative space – positive space is the object on the page, negative space is all the space around it. Playing with positive and negative space by making the background a more dramatic colour than the object or giving it a texture allows the environment to be foregrounded and the object or letter form to recede.
- Alignment – using one edge of an element or text as a guide for other elements, so that things visually line up.
- Texture – the use of a variety of textures and surfaces within a layout adds interest and focuses attention.

An example of the creative use of texture is the 2009 TBWA 'Trillion Dollar' campaign (see Chapter 5), which created flyers, inserts, posters and murals using Zimbabwean trillion dollar notes as the base paper. The headlines and the logo of *The Zimbabwean* were literally printed on to real notes that had been individually glued down within the agency and then pressed and screen-printed by a printer.

'We did get the best silk-screener here to do the posters for us, who'd studied in Japan, and she recommended the best paint to use and inks. We had bags of money! We actually started sticking them together here with the help of our studio and then we sent them through to her and she pressed them and silk-screened them and went through that process. There were hundreds of posters so there were hours and hours of work and quite a few people had many sleepless nights over this.'

SHELLEY SMOLER, CREATIVE GROUP HEAD, TBWA/HUNT/LASCARIS JOHANNESBURG

USING A GRID

A grid is more commonly used in magazine and newspaper layout and is now being used in Web layouts. One has been used for this book. It is less usual to use it for adverts as they usually have fewer elements to place on a page. A grid is simply a series of margins and rulers that provide a template and therefore order and consistency across all your executions in a campaign, which helps to create a more visually pleasing advert.

HIERARCHY OF INFORMATION

This means arranging the text and elements of ad content in logical groups in order to pass on information to the viewer in the right order. This can be achieved through weight, alignment and placement. In any advert there will be an order in which you will want people to look at things; picture, then headline, then endline; headline, then picture, then endline; picture, then endline. If people do not follow the right order then the joke will be spoiled, the poignant impact lessened, the drama diminished.

> **TASK**
> Find a campaign that you like with three print executions. Using a ruler, draw guiding lines along the edge of the images, text and headlines. See where all the elements align and if there are similarities across the ads in the campaign.

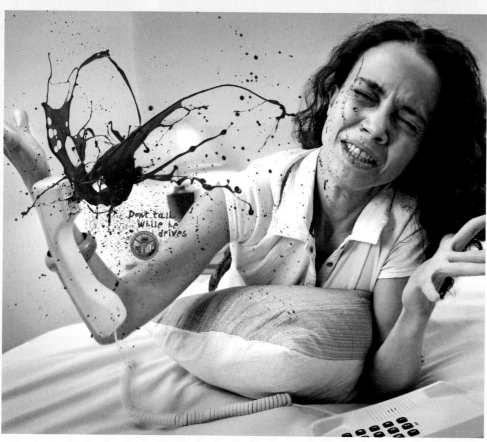

LEFT
Australian agency Rare uses a serif font to imply tradition in this direct mail piece for the Perth Advertising & Design Club.

BELOW
Jung von Matt Hamburg created this typographic ad in 2007 for the Young Global Leaders Earth Love Movement Foundation, creating the words from the environment.

ABOVE AND RIGHT
The 'Talk Them Dead' campaign by Mudra Mumbai of 2009 uses typography expressively. The endline is literally written in the victim's blood, which explodes from the end of the phone.

BELOW
Anomaly UK's 2010 ad for Diesel uses tension to add drama. The ad is weighted on one side with heavy typography and a bold use of red, leading your eye to the endline. The majority of the page, however, is left dark with little going on.

RIGHT
'Whale Cow', created in 2009 by Ogilvy Singapore for Unilever, creates a typographic sculpture.

Now food can tell you how fresh it is.

With over 25% of the world's food lost to spoilage, IBM is helping retailers in Canada and Norway track food from farm to fork.
ibm.com/smarterplanet

IBM

LEFT
Positive and negative space is played with in this 2010 Ogilvy & Mather Paris press ad for IBM. At first the face reveals itself, and then the chicken in the negative space of the background.

BELOW LEFT
This design uses blank space to graphically separate the *Financial Times* into a direct, rational and informed section of the ad, implying that the newspaper is based upon similiar brand principles.

BELOW
This DLKW press ad for Marston's sponsorship of English cricket during the 2009 Ashes uses texture to add interest: the mirror in contrast to the wood in contrast to the typography.

Unlike millions of other websites, we know exactly what you are looking for.
Find expert analysis of global business at **ft.com**

We live in FINANCIAL TIMES®

baby bond | Search

Pedigree
England has it

WE HAVE BEER IN OUR BLOOD

AUSTRALIANS HAVE LEMON JUICE IN THEIR HAIR

drinkaware.co.uk

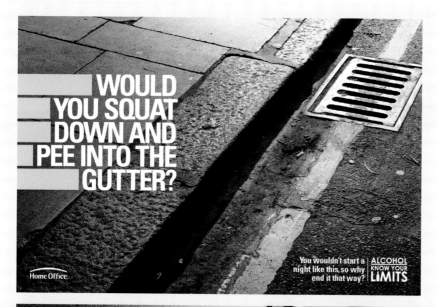

WOULD YOU SQUAT DOWN AND PEE INTO THE GUTTER?

You wouldn't start a night like this, so why end it that way? | **ALCOHOL** KNOW YOUR **LIMITS**

Home Office

WOULD YOU SMASH THIS IN SOMEONE'S FACE?

You wouldn't start a night like this, so why end it that way? | **ALCOHOL** KNOW YOUR **LIMITS**

Home Office

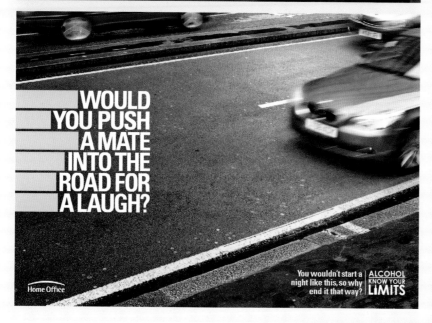

WOULD YOU PUSH A MATE INTO THE ROAD FOR A LAUGH?

You wouldn't start a night like this, so why end it that way? | **ALCOHOL** KNOW YOUR **LIMITS**

Home Office

The ads in this series from the VCCP London campaign for the UK Home Office all use the same grid. Their elements are placed according to particular rules, which gives the campaign consistency.

VISUALIZING

There are various ways of visualizing, through using scamps to presentation visuals to creating the final pieces yourself. With some ideas the way it will be visualized is so integral to the concept you have to take the executions to a fairly finished state in order to sell the idea.

'Before presenting the executions we first roughly laid out the images in Photoshop. Only that had an immediate effect on the viewer. The clients felt that this could get much bigger than a simple anti-anorexia ad.'

SABINA HESSE, COPYWRITER, HEIMAT BERLIN

TAKING A PHOTO

Unless you are someone with a passion for photography and habitually walk around with a digital SLR camera, then you are most probably like the majority of people in this industry – you own a digital compact camera. While the digital compact camera is great for taking snaps and instantly capturing information, it may not give you the look and feel that you want. Everything in an image can be read as a sign, so if you are trying to get a particular look then you may find it difficult with a compact or snaps camera – this is why we employ professional photographers. If you are taking a photo yourself, either for your portfolio or for a mock-up for presentation, then you need to know a few photography basics.

• The shot – try to find a location that is close to what you had in mind so you only have to make minimal changes (for example, use your friend's mum's kitchen rather than your shared accommodation flat). Follow your scamp for composition, take wider shots as back-up, shoot with a lot of daylight available (this may mean setting up your pack shot outside in front of white card). Beg or borrow some lighting equipment and keep the background simple.

• Resolution – a 10 megapixel camera can take a photo with 10,036,224 pixels, that is 3872 mm x 2592 mm at 72 dpi (dots per inch). Bear in mind what media your photo is for: the Web only needs 72 dpi, whereas print needs 300 dpi. In this example you can convert your photo in Photoshop to a 300 dpi image that is 328 mm x 220 mm. The image will simply pixellate if you resize the proportions but have not changed the dpi to 300 before enlarging it, and even then you can scale it up only a little before it will start to pixellate.

USING SOFTWARE

Some people believe that focusing too much on finish will come at the expense of strength of ideas. While this can be true, it can also help you to be able to think about how you could take your ideas further, and many new hires at agencies have an ability in production (the creation of the images themselves). Find out which media your course has specialist lecturers in and try to develop your skills in those areas.

'Our diverse staff of academics, researchers and industry specialists work together as a team, each delivering their specialist skill and knowledge, so students graduate with a holistic understanding of media and its communication potential.'

NICKIE HIRST, DESIGN FUTURES PROGRAMME
LEADER, UNIVERSITY OF GREENWICH, LONDON

PHOTOSHOP

Adobe Photoshop is a computer program designed to manipulate and retouch photographs, though it can be used to create many types of illustration, short animations and design work for websites. It creates raster images (a grid of pixels known as a bitmap), which, while allowing for realistic-looking alterations, pixellate when enlarged.

Pierre Berthuel-Bonnes, a student at the University of Greenwich, London, answered a hypothetical D&AD brief for McDonald's. His campaign, which won a D&AD Yellow Pencil, was based on people's individual eating habits, acknowledging that these habits reflect our personality. For Pierre there is a McDonald's for everyone because the brand embraces these habits and differences.

Pierre used Photoshop to hone his campaign:

'As a graphic designer looking to expand my creative possibilities in the digital arena Adobe Photoshop CS5 is the ideal software for me. I have been practising with this software for the last three years, and I can now create any kind of creative ideas, use different effects, photographs and composite images and even create animations. To enhance this campaign I was able to cut, paste and retouch the light to make the visual sharper.'

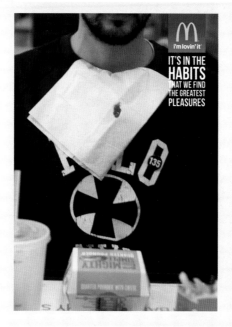

Greenwich student Pierre Berthuel-Bonnes used Adobe Photoshop to create an integrated campaign for McDonald's using posters, press ads and ambient media, such as straws and stamps.

ILLUSTRATOR

Adobe Illustrator is a vector-based computer program designed for illustration and typography, although it is often used to create page layouts. It uses vector graphics, which allow the enlargement of images without loss of quality.

University of Greenwich student Dimitra Papastathi answered a D&AD brief for Oxfam and was included 'in book' 2011, meaning that although her campaign did not win a pencil it was included in the D&AD annual. The campaign asked people to 'spare more than a thought' for others. Focusing on the transience of a thought as opposed to the permanence of action she created visuals that, through the use of optical illusion, would literally fade away as a person walked past the posters.

'In order to bring my ideas to life I had to work a lot in Adobe Illustrator,' says Dimitra. 'Illustrator is a program that gives a designer flexibility on screen. Vectors allow me to sketch my ideas from nothing. I created patterns that I could easily resize, cut, mask, overlay ... Typography can also be treated as letters or as objects that I can re-adjust. Illustrator is a large digital canvas, where I can spread all my graphic elements around and tidy them up for a final result. It feels like a digital sketchbook where ideas can take form more quickly and precisely.'

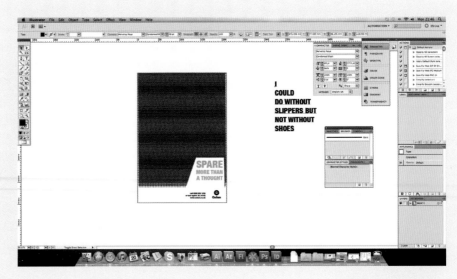

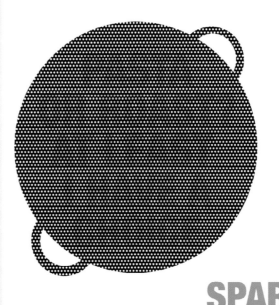

Greenwich student Dimitra Papastathi used Adobe Illustrator to create an integrated campaign for Oxfam using posters and ambient media, such as conveyor belts and scratch cards.

SPARE MORE THAN A THOUGHT

call 0300 200 1292
or text 'spare' at: 34345
www.oxfam.co.uk

Oxfam

INDESIGN

Adobe InDesign is a desktop publishing program and is primarily used for multi-page layouts. It allows you to precisely control the size of placed images and text blocks, and to create templates to be used through multiple pages.

University of Greenwich students Anna Barisani and Frazer Shaw developed a campaign for another D&AD brief – the release of a refreshed edition of *The Copybook*, a D&AD publication on the subject of writing great copy, primarily targeting designers. The campaign thought that they developed was to identify the sins that we all commit against good writing, portraying *The Copybook* as an almost holy book that can give guidance. Anna and Frazer started the work in Illustrator and then moved on to InDesign.

'We used both Illustrator and InDesign to create this project; we used Illustrator to create the initial roughs and to build the vector backgrounds from scratch. We did this instead of building it all in InDesign because we felt that Illustrator offers a much faster way of testing different layouts. Once we had decided on a style and layout we wanted to use we exported the background as a high-resolution image and placed it in to InDesign. This was then used to finalize the text positioning, kerning and spacing. This is a far slower but much more accurate than trying to create everything in Illustrator.'

When they entered the competition the endline was not as helpful as it could have been ('Absolve your sins'), nor the campaign as polished. They then took stock, worked on it some more, and have turned it into a very good campaign for their portfolios.

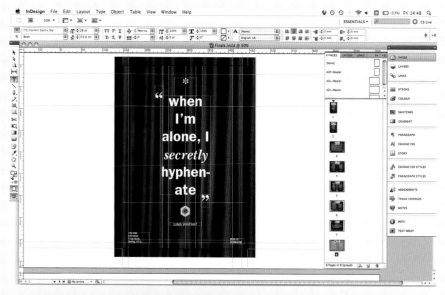

Greenwich students Anna Barisani and Frazer Shaw used Adobe InDesign to created an integrated campaign using posters, press and Twitter.

AFTER EFFECTS

Adobe After Effects is a digital motion graphics software package allowing complex animations and titles to be created. It works in a series of layers that anyone familiar with the Adobe suite would recognize and is often used in conjunction with Photoshop.

University of Greenwich student Anton Burmistrov answered a brief to create an ident for Channel 4, a UK television channel. An ident falls between branding and advertising, and advertises a television channel during the programming schedule. The brief was to publicize Channel 4 during a series of medical documentaries. Within the scene we see a beating heart break into millions of figure 4s and then reform into the 4 logo. Anton used After Effects to create his work.

'Through the program I was able to manage individual objects, use a camera and create illusions. The program also allows you to play and experiment with something when you have lots of different ideas for possible executions.'

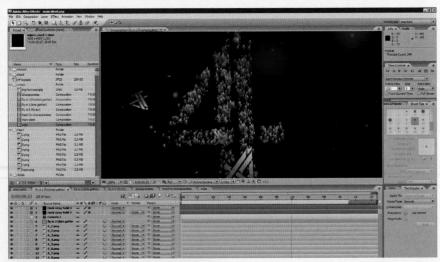

Greenwich student Anton Burmistrov used Adobe After Effects to create a TV ident for Channel 4.

INTERNET APPLICATIONS

It is worth mentioning Adobe Flash Professional at this stage. Using the familiar elements of imaging programs such as Photoshop or Illustrator, Flash allows the creation of animations, websites, games and other interactive elements on a Web page. Complex imagery can also be created in Flash using drawing tools that are similar to those in Photoshop. All computers and smartphones, except the iPhone and iPad, can utilize Flash (Apple has famously refused to allow Flash on its mobile devices). Flash is, however, in many cases being superseded by HTML5, the upgraded Internet language.

HTML is the language that runs across the whole Internet; without it you would not be able to see anything. HTML uses tags to indicate what various sections of your Web page are to the browser. In order to publish on the Internet you need these tags, from the simple body tag, ‹body›, which is the body of your Web page, to the image tag, ‹img›, and everything in between. HTML5, among other improvements, has new tags; one of these is ‹canvas›, which enables you to create dynamic scriptable bitmap images. Video and audio tags help make HTML5 less reliant on plug-ins (such as the Flash video player plug-in). Currently Flash has no problem with cross-browser compatibility as long as users have the Flash plug-in, which is free and already on most computers worldwide.

Adobe has already withdrawn support for Flash on mobile platforms and is concentrating on HTML5 for browser content. It is possible that Flash will become obsolete in the future, but at the moment some of the most exciting Web content is created through it.

The Red Bull Flugtag Flight Lab website uses Flash to allow users to build, customize and fly their own aircraft.

EXECUTING THE EXECUTIONS

8

PRODUCTION

Once you have made your choice, you need to share the director's or photographer's treatment with the client for their agreement to proceed. This is only a preliminary agreement, as the client needs to be properly presented with the treatment during a more formal pre-production meeting. During this meeting the director/photographer/illustrator presents their interpretation and you take more of a back seat, though you are on hand to explain how this enhances the idea. During these pre-production meetings you will work more closely with the art buyer or television producer, who will organize schedules, costs and availabilities and liaise on locations.

YOUR ROLE ON A SHOOT

Once on a shoot your role is to oversee but not interfere. This is harder than it sounds as they may not be shooting it exactly as you had imagined it; actors behave differently in situ than they do in a casting; and the colour palette you had agreed on paper may not seem so obvious in real life. Remember to ask yourself the question: are they getting the meaning across? If they do not meddle, let them create what you had liked about their work in the first place. If they are not getting across the meaning sufficiently then you need to say something, but there is a protocol to follow.

'There is no doubt that Tom Kuntz [the director] understood the main idea very quickly. And he handled the humour in a very interesting way. He also added things to the commercial, resulting in the creation of an excellent piece of work in conjunction with his production staff. Especially with Stan Winston's people, who were in charge of designing the chocolate man costume.'

MARIO CRUDELE, SENIOR COPYWRITER, PONCE BUENOS AIRES

CUT TO LEADING SHOT OF CHOCOLATE FEET WALKING DOWN CITY STREET.

THE SHOT WIDENS TO REVEAL ENTIRE CHOCOLATE MAN.

CUT TO A GIRL READING A BOOK. THE CHOCOLATE MAN WIPES FRAME AND WE SEE HER TAKEN BY HIS CHOCOLATE AROMA.

CUT TO A SHOT PUSHING IN ON TWO GIRLS EATING ICE CREAM IN FRONT OF AN ICE CREAM STORE.

CUT TO A MEDIUM OF THE CHOCOLATE MAN AS HE LIFTS HIS HAND INTO FRAME AND SNAPS A FEW OF HIS CHOCOLATE FINGERS OFF.

CLOSE UP OF FINGERS SNAPPING OFF.

This director's storyboard for the Axe advert shows how the camera will move and where the actors will be looking in minute detail.

EXECUTING
THE
EXECUTIONS

8

8 EXECUTING THE EXECUTIONS

THE PITCH

The realization of your executions always involves teamwork.
Learning to work in a team yet still maintain a unique voice is a skill
that develops over time. Young teams often appear inexperienced
because of their cavalier attitude to other members of the larger team.
Everyone is striving towards a common purpose — to make the ad as
good as it can be. Of course everyone's definition of 'good' will be
different. Managing your own and other people's expectations is an
unwritten part of the creative's job. An ad does not just get thought
up and happen — it has to be bought into by other members of the
team. This all starts with the pitch.

'Pitching' is an industry term for presenting your ideas, but it is actually more than presenting: it is selling. Pitching is possibly the closest that a creative actually gets to the purpose of the job – to sell.

When you pitch your idea in the creative department you are talking to people who believe in the creative process and want to see innovative and exciting ideas realized. Nonetheless, if your idea does not make sense, is boring, has been done before or does not relate to the product, they will tell you. There are many reasons that an ad might die at this stage.

Assuming that all goes well with the creative director and executive creative director, you will need to pitch your idea to the account team and planners. They are familiar with creative work, want to make a sale and want to create work that will get the brand noticed. However, they also represent the client and consumer so they will let you know if the ad is off tone, if it does not involve the product enough or if the client will not like it. The pitch to the account team and planners is important because they have to be sold on the idea or they cannot support it properly.

The part of a pitch that you are in control of can be divided into two parts: the logical part, which can be achieved by following a few simple guidelines, and the inspirational part, in which you bring your idea to life and entertain your audience.

LOGICAL ARGUMENT

Make sure that everything is easily understandable and that the rational reasons for buying your idea – however crazy the execution – are evident. Do this by:

- linking your idea to the advertising strategy – a couple of sentences about why you started thinking in this way;

- summarizing your idea in one line – not an endline, but simply an explanation;

- describing your executions succinctly – each ad in one or two lines.

After the presentation it is often the cold hard rationale that the client falls back on in order to sell your idea internally to their MD.

INSPIRATION

A few pointers for giving an inspiring presentation.

- Develop a comfortable presentation persona: be a bit exciting but also professional; be easy to be around and act naturally. Very few of us are natural performers. Most of us work at it. Simply hiding under the mantle of shyness and letting others take centre stage could be detrimental to your success and will never enable you to develop your presentation skills. On the other hand, doing all the talking can seem egotistical and narcissistic. Aim for a persona that works within your team dynamic, one that is you, not someone new.

- Practise your presentation: who will say what and in what order? Listening to one person can be very dull unless they are a stand-up comedian so add texture by switching between you, altering the pace of your delivery and interspersing visual with spoken.

- Intrigue your audience: think about how you can add drama to the presentation. This can be as simple as posing a question and letting your executions be the answer.

- Excite their imagination: where else could this campaign go? Could they put the endline on T-shirts and sell them, is there a character that can reappear in other ads, can it translate to quirky point-of-sale items? Excite them with the possibilities.

An inspiring presentation gives clients the fire that they need to be able to go back and sell the idea to others within their organization.

THE PITCH AUDIENCE

Unfortunately there is one part of the pitch that you cannot control – the audience. Whether they are the client, creative director, account team or planner they may have had the business objectives changed, had the budget altered, been updated with new mandatories, been given new information about their competitors' activities, or simply be in a bad mood. All of this may make

them unreceptive to even the best pitch. This can happen to anyone and you would not be alone in suffering a non-sale for these reasons.

WHEN TO STAND UP FOR AN IDEA

On occasion you pitch an idea and it will proceed through the ad creation process without a hitch. More usually someone within the team will raise a 'concern' or two. They may feel it could have been better branded or they might not like the scenario and they will ask you to change it. You have to decide which battles are worth fighting and which are not. While you do not want to be known as a disruptive team who are unprofessional, you also do not want to be known as a team that is a pushover and will just do exactly as the client/account team says. If this happens you will only ever be given briefs from conservative clients.

Some ideas are truly great. Without a doubt some of the best ads have been made because people have stood up for what they thought was right; but the agency needs to be behind the idea and the client needs to be brave. And that still does not mean that there have not been amendments.

'You have to realize that your idea is now exposed to a lot of people with different points of view, and everybody's trying to do their best. Sometimes you can feel a little jealous because your idea has been modified by others. At that moment you have to ask yourself if you want to keep the idea as you thought it. Or maybe it's better to accept some changes to make it better.'

MARIO CRUDELE, SENIOR COPYWRITER, PONCE BUENOS AIRES

The trick is in knowing what is an integral part of your idea and what is just an executional detail. Provided the amendments do not change the idea, it may be worth accepting them.

For example, for an imaginary brand of toothpaste for sensitive teeth, 'Toothease', you develop an idea for a television ad, that in a particular part of Iceland there is a man who creates ice sculptures using his teeth. We watch him biting his way through a block of ice to create a naked Aphrodite during an

ice sculpture competition and he reveals at the end that he uses Toothease. The idea in one sentence is: 'The toothpaste is so good at desensitizing that you can bite through ice.'

- **Scenario 1** The planner suggests the target market would respond better if the character was a woman. The client does not want a naked body as it is not in keeping with their family image. Do these changes alter the meaning? Not at all. However, they may make the ad less dramatic and less likely to win awards.

- **Scenario 2** The client takes the view that they like the ad but they do not want the character biting ice, they want him using a chisel like everyone else. Does this alter the meaning? Yes. The planner says that the focus group needs to see the character smiling throughout to show how clean his teeth are. Does this change the meaning? No, but how can he smile if he is biting ice? The creative director thinks the character is too much of a cliché. Does this change the meaning? No, but you would need to create a completely new scenario and character.

Scenario 2 is known as the death by a thousand cuts. This occurs when not everyone has been sold on the idea. When this happens to your idea you need to accept that it is dead and suggest another idea. There is always more than one great creative idea that can be had for most briefs. Sometimes the fear of having to generate another idea will keep teams arguing for and making a million tiny amendments to their creative work. You need to be able to recognize whether your idea will lose its meaning when you make amendments for others.

'Sometimes I find myself defending an idea as if it were a friend or a son of mine. Most of the time I know exactly which are the strong points and which are the weaknesses.'

MARIO CRUDELE, SENIOR COPYWRITER, PONCE BUENOS AIRES

ART BUYERS AND PRODUCERS

Of course it is very difficult to sell something or even properly visualize something without having decided the 'look'. This part of the process involves working with art buyers for still imagery or producers for moving images. When briefing the production department you need to be clear in your mind about what you want, have reference material and show some kind of united front as a creative team, but remain open-minded.

'Be clear and have all the facts. The better the brief, the easier and speedier it is for me to get to work and the better the results for the creative team.'

LEAH MITCHELL, HEAD OF ART BUYING,
LEO BURNETT LONDON

The art buyers will provide you with a targeted range of portfolios and websites that feature the kind of work that you have specified. Similarly, the television producer will supply you with targeted reels or websites that have the look and feel that you have briefed them on.

LOOKING AT FOLIOS, REELS AND WEBSITES

Part of the art director's job is to trawl through all the books and reels and websites that are delivered to your office door. Your job is not to make a decision unilaterally but to show a more limited range of material to your creative partner (who may be working on copy). Do not be distracted by the latest fashionable director/photographer/ illustrator. Make sure that the folio or reel you like conveys the right emotion and meaning for your idea. Together the team will make a shortlist with a particular recommendation and this is shown to the creative director and then accounts and planning. Sometimes the creative director will have a particular person that they want you to try. This could be because they genuinely think it will add to your idea, or it could be because they have always fancied using them themselves and an opportunity has never come up before. Ask yourself if this is the right person for this job. If not, you need to come up with a good reason why not and a good alternative option before you risk saying no to your CD's suggestion.

CHOOSING THE RIGHT DIRECTOR/ PHOTOGRAPHER/ILLUSTRATOR

Choosing the right person to execute your executions is not as simple as just liking their folio or reel. Not only are there issues of cost and availability, but they are about to become part of your extended team and you need to think about personal compatibility and how they will interpret your idea. While art buyers and television producers can check the first two criteria, only a personal meeting can answer the last two.

Looking at folios and showreels is an integral part of both visualizing your campaign and assembling the right creative team.

THE PITCH MEETING

The purpose of the pitch meeting is to get a feel for how other people would bring your idea to life. It is an interesting experience being on the other side of a pitch meeting, and when you are relatively inexperienced it is easy to be seduced by people that 'love' your idea – of course they do, they want the work. Your job is to listen very carefully to what they are saying – is how they are interpreting the idea adding or taking away from the meaning?

Let us take the example of the 'Toothease' commercial again. You have chosen two directors whose reels you love and the CD has agreed them. They present the following:

- **Director 1** A treatment reminiscent of Jacques Tati, the French filmmaker and comedian. The male character has a certain melancholic dignity to him. He unexpectedly starts biting chunks of ice away in what appears to be clown-like disaster, only to reveal a perfect Aphrodite.

- **Director 2** A Lynx/Axe-style treatment. The male character is very modern and sexy, there are lots of knowing winks to the camera, and girls in his audience start swooning when he bites close to supposedly sensitive areas on the Aphrodite.

Both treatments have potential but they bring this story to life in vastly different tones of voice. So how do you choose? You have to take a calculated risk. Which treatment enhances your ideas? Can you work with this person? Will they listen to you? Does this treatment convey what you want to say about this brand? Ask questions. These meetings need to be a two-way conversation in which you find out how your ideas have been understood.

'One of the great lessons I learnt was from Mark Reddy; up to that point I had a very clear idea of how things should be and I'd tell photographers exactly what I wanted. So for Harvey Nicks we went in to meet the photographer with Mark. Mark had a book that he thought we'd like and we did, and I was thinking I'm going to hear from the best what the magic is for getting the best from a photographer. I was getting ready to take notes and Mark just said, "Well we just really like your book and we just want some of that really." It was such a valuable lesson: find the photographer that you like, meet them, check that you like them and can work with them and then give them the freedom to deliver what you liked about their book in the first place.'

JUSTIN TINDALL, GROUP EXECUTIVE CREATIVE DIRECTOR, LEO BURNETT LONDON

I had an experience in which my partner and I had loved a director's reel, but during the pitch he revealed that he was imagining lots of statuesque beauties in sultry light while we were imagining a more comedic execution. When questioned about his vision, his rather annoyed response was that he did not want to put men off watching the ad. His response showed us that he did not understand the meaning of our script and that he was also someone that we would not be able to work with, if he reacted so defensively after just one question. We would not have known this without a proper pitch meeting. Make sure you can work with this person and that you believe in their interpretation.

PRODUCTION

Once you have made your choice, you need to share the director's or photographer's treatment with the client for their agreement to proceed. This is only a preliminary agreement, as the client needs to be properly presented with the treatment during a more formal pre-production meeting. During this meeting the director/photographer/illustrator presents their interpretation and you take more of a back seat, though you are on hand to explain how this enhances the idea. During these pre-production meetings you will work more closely with the art buyer or television producer, who will organize schedules, costs and availabilities and liaise on locations.

YOUR ROLE ON A SHOOT

Once on a shoot your role is to oversee but not interfere. This is harder than it sounds as they may not be shooting it exactly as you had imagined it; actors behave differently in situ than they do in a casting; and the colour palette you had agreed on paper may not seem so obvious in real life. Remember to ask yourself the question: are they getting the meaning across? If they do not meddle, let them create what you had liked about their work in the first place. If they are not getting across the meaning sufficiently then you need to say something, but there is a protocol to follow.

'There is no doubt that Tom Kuntz [the director] understood the main idea very quickly. And he handled the humour in a very interesting way. He also added things to the commercial, resulting in the creation of an excellent piece of work in conjunction with his production staff. Especially with Stan Winston's people, who were in charge of designing the chocolate man costume.'

MARIO CRUDELE, SENIOR COPYWRITER, PONCE BUENOS AIRES

CUT TO LEADING SHOT OF CHOCOLATE FEET WALKING DOWN CITY STREET.

TRACK

THE SHOT WIDENS TO REVEAL ENTIRE CHOCOLATE MAN.

TRACK

CUT TO A GIRL READING A BOOK. THE CHOCOLATE MAN WIPES FRAME AND WE SEE HER TAKEN BY HIS CHOCOLATE AROMA.

wipe

CUT TO A SHOT PUSHING IN ON TWO GIRLS EATING ICE CREAM IN FRONT OF AN ICE CREAM STORE.

CUT TO A MEDIUM OF THE CHOCOLATE MAN AS HE LIFTS HIS HAND INTO FRAME AND SNAPS A FEW OF HIS CHOCOLATE FINGERS OFF.

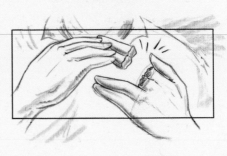

CLOSE UP OF FINGERS SNAPPING OFF.

This director's storyboard for the Axe advert shows how the camera will move and where the actors will be looking in minute detail.

The number of people and the level of complexity involved in getting a shot that would seem as simple as walking down a street is surprisingly huge.

On a stills shoot you should be able to speak to the photographer in between shots or to their assistant if it is too urgent to wait, though things are rarely so urgent they cannot wait a couple of minutes. On a television shoot you need to speak to your producer, who speaks to the director's producer, who then finds an appropriate time to interrupt the director. This may seem very formal but it is for good reason. Television shoots are on a tight schedule and shooting cannot stop every few minutes, while the crew needs to understand who they answer to, so there must not appear to be several bosses. If there is a client on set then they will probably arrive with an account person who will look after their immediate needs, but it is your job to explain what is happening and to allay any fears.

It is always worth ensuring that you have 'safety shots'. These are shots that are very simple but have all the necessary information, such as a wide shot of the action rather than just a close-up, or a straight shot of the pack. It is important to get these shots for a number of reasons: the action may not be as obvious as you thought, the pack may not be clear enough, you may need wider or closer shots to be able to edit with. Directors and photographers are not always happy to deliver safety shots. They tend to believe that clients will push for these less interesting options and they are sometimes right in that assumption. As mentioned earlier, part of the creative's job is managing these different viewpoints within your team.

PHOTOGRAPHER'S 'SELECTS'

You are more directly involved with the final choice in stills photography. The photographer will send you their preferred choices, known as 'selects'. These may be a selection based on technicalities such as focus, colour and clearest facial expression rather than value judgments. You are the person who will choose the most appropriate shot. If you do not believe the shot is there you can ask to see every shot.

ILLUSTRATORS, ANIMATORS AND TYPOGRAPHERS

Working with illustrators, animators and typographers is different from working with live action. It is not feasible for you to sit in on the process as you would with a shoot, so you have ongoing meetings in order to be updated, and are sent drafts to agree. Good communication is key. It is important that the team be briefed thoroughly and correctly to begin with as it is very difficult to change things the further into the process you are. You must inform them at every meeting stage if something is not looking the way that you had hoped. Because you are consulted at every stage it can feel like a more controllable entity than live action.

RETOUCHING

Retouching is a post-production skill for stills. Sometimes the photographer will supply the final shot with the image retouched according to your specifications; at other times you are provided with the raw stills and you will work with retouchers to manipulate anything you may feel needs altering to better fit with your layouts. These might be both small changes and big. You might ask a retoucher, for example, to alter a blue background slightly so that the colour holds better on a magazine page and contrasts more pleasingly with your typography – things that it is not a photographer's job to consider; or you might want a retoucher to cut out an entire object from a shaggy carpet and place it facing in the other direction because it works better in a layout.

LEFT
A safety shot – a shot in which the product is clearly seen in the best lighting. This can apply to a person, action or another object.

LEFT
Mad shot – a more interesting shot of a product that perhaps makes the point rather more dramatically. This can also apply to a person, action or another object.

POST-PRODUCTION

This is a specific term for the technical work done for television and film to edit (cut), grade (colour), dub (edit and mix sound) and add graphics to raw footage. In television post-production you are not there to interfere but to ensure that the meaning of your ad is clear and not lost in the director's interpretation.

THE EDIT – OFFLINE AND ONLINE

Editing cuts sections of moving image on film or tape and assembles them together in an order. The edit can be ordered into a group of sequences that tell a story. Edits have a rhythm that sometimes follows music, but not always. If it is important for edits to fall on the beat this needs to be agreed in pre-production as the timing within each shot needs to take that into account. The edit is in two parts, offline and online. The offline is more of an art as it establishes the order, the rhythm and the pace, and stitches together the best shots to tell a story. Unaltered sound is left in as a guide, and music and rough graphics are added as additional guides.

The online is a far more technical craft and although the online editor does final re-cuts they more usually fix technical problems, add graphics, disguise things that should not be visible (such as logos or faces), add clocks, check the final length and grade to match shots if necessary.

Edit suite in a post-production facility. You will spend a lot of time in rooms like these with an editor or grader sitting at the front and all the agency people sitting away from the desk.

ADDING GRAPHICS

Often computer-animated product demo sequences are created in the graphics departments of the larger post-production houses, though they may be created in specialist graphics companies. Clients often appear to be disproportionately interested in these five seconds out of the 30-second ad because they often believe this is the only part that really speaks about the product's benefits. These sections are also the ones that consumers pay the least attention to, as they disrupt the flow of many commercials. However, they will be an integral part of your job at some point or other. You have to approach it in the same way you approach all graphics – is it as simple as it could be? Does it tell the information clearly with no ambiguity? Is there a clear hierarchy of information? And is the composition as impactful as it should be?

Other graphics devices used are: supers (typography superimposed on top of the image), the endline, graphic elements (such as stripes or floral swirls for ads that have a deliberately graphic look). Many graphic elements can be created in an online suite, an option often favoured by clients and producers for cost-cutting reasons, but this does not create results as good as those from dedicated facilities. The development of digital editing technology affords the opportunity to use an incredible range of electronic tools to enhance and transform the moving image.

This ad for Evian relied almost exclusively on computer-generated imagery to allow its cast of babies to memorably dance across our TV screens on roller skates.

THE DUB

Dubbing mixers (sound engineers) mix and edit sound. They work in sound editing facilities either in a post-production house or in a dedicated facility. Most dubbing studios have a sound booth, which can be for voiceover (vocal track heard with the image), ADR (automatic dialogue replacement: to replace poor production sound or re-voice ads originally recorded in another language), foley (creating sounds such as footsteps) and recording radio ads. Dubbing studios also have extensive sound effects libraries where you can source a wide range of audio tracks from birdsong or busy restaurant atmospheres through to fighter planes. The dubbing mixer will record, add effects and atmospheres, clean up production sound, re-record sound, record voiceovers and make audio levels legal. They then mix the levels of music, dialogue and effects. Sound is an often overlooked aspect of television production but it is an essential part of any ad.

Radio is very much like television in its execution. It can have character dialogue, scenarios, music, an endline, a voiceover and atmosphere, but it does not have any location costs or require a film crew or visual editing. Consequently it incurs only a proportion of the costs spent on television production. For a radio campaign, you can spend your entire time in a dubbing suite. Because of this clients are less concerned with extensive pre-production meetings and generally there is no production company involved. There is also no director, and this puts you in a very different role. You become the director for your actors. If you want them to sound warmer, more sensuous, more enthusiastic, you have to tell them. Directing is all about eliciting the right response from your actors by using a variety of words to explain what you mean. You are also in charge of how much atmosphere or which effects you need in order to create the right mood. Radio is a good introduction to the role of a director, and shows you how easy it is to overcomplicate a scene. If you have recording facilities in your university or college it is worth writing and recording radio ads to practise your skills and to get a better understanding of the director–editor relationship.

'Our sound engineer put a lot of effort and thought into how this ad would sound. We worked on the dub for 12 hours straight. We then loaded it up on our iPods, and for weeks we talked back on forth on how to make the mix even better.'

ERGIN BINYILDIZ, EXECUTIVE CREATIVE DIRECTOR, GREY ISTANBUL

ABOVE
A dubbing suite.

LEFT
The voiceover booth.

WORKING WITH DESIGNERS

Often agencies have dedicated design departments to help art directors lay out their press and poster ads. This can be for standard 'Mac room' work such as placing the logo exactly according to brand book guidelines and formatting each page for specific magazine sizes. Alternatively designers are used to make the layout and typography more dynamic, as they may be more aware of contemporary graphic practice. This has both positives and negatives. Art direction and design are not the same. As with photographers or television directors, in handing over how the ad is visually expressed, art directors risk losing the meaning once more. Provided the designer knows that they are part of your team, they are an invaluable asset, providing a different visual viewpoint. Issues can arise when agencies hire 'star' designers to bring an 'X factor' to print work who then impose their style and agendas over the work of junior teams.

CHECKING COLOUR PROOFS

In print there are colour proofs to check, which are usually brought to you by traffic. This is your ad printed on stock from the magazine or newspaper or printed out as a draft before a poster is created. This is your opportunity to check that the colours are printing the way that you wish, that the blacks are registering properly, that the typography is legible, if the image has been accidentally reversed and if the register is present. If you spot anything, alert traffic and they will resolve the problem.

Checking a physical proof is the only way of knowing for certain how your final ad will look.

THE FINAL VERSION

There should come a point in any medium when you feel an ad is as good as it can be (this is often the exact moment of the deadline.) You have now honed it to perfection, it is your baby and you are happy with it. However, you still have to present it to your creative director and the clients and they get to judge whether they were right to put all that trust in you. It should go fine, as you will have previously agreed every little aspect of the campaign with them.

On occasion you will present 'the final' and it is just that, final, no amendments needed. But more often a number of adjustments will be needed, from relatively small ones (a common request is to make the logo bigger) to much larger ones, such as entire re-edits to make a point more evident. This is where all your skills in managing the team come to the fore. Everyone will have an opinion on your work. The director will not want to hear that the clients want to use all the safety shots or crop out some of their more interesting props. The director will have thought all this was resolved in pre-production. The clients, on the other hand, will feel that they cannot have been expected to visualize everything before the ad was made. Clients also have superiors that they need to sell these ads to and these people may raise concerns at any time. The creative director may feel it is not edgy enough or does not communicate succinctly enough. All these points need to be addressed before everyone can sign off on it. With television you will invariably spend time to-ing and fro-ing between post-production houses. You will need to manage these relationships, make everyone feel that you have heard them and be true to your idea, as you will be working with them all again.

So your work is finally done on this commercial. Everyone is satisfied with a job well done. You have something you can put in your folio and that is part of your ongoing learning experience. Your brain is both exhilarated and exhausted and you feel you should be given a round of applause for managing to execute something in such trying circumstances. You want to know if you can clock off a bit early as your work for the day is done. Then traffic arrives with news of a new briefing in an hour's time. The process begins again.

Presenting your work can be an exhilarating and very satisfying process, but always be at the ready to sort out some final niggles.

CAREER PLANS

9

CAREER PLANS

THE PORTFOLIO

How do you get a career as an advertising creative? There are few conventional routes into finding a job as a creative and they all require hard work and tenacity. Doing your research and planning your approach to an agency is vital and could just give you an edge over other aspiring creatives.

While good qualifications will offer opportunities in account management, planning and production, a good portfolio is the only way into employment in the creative department. Grades are useful in summarizing a general level of education, ability and work ethic but they cannot show a creative director your unique way of thinking. Nothing can compare to actually seeing someone's ideas in a portfolio – it is like an invitation into someone's brain.

'Just try and have yourself in there.'

JUSTIN TINDALL, GROUP EXECUTIVE CREATIVE DIRECTOR, LEO BURNETT LONDON

A portfolio is simply a collection of your best pieces of work. In the past this was quite literally a hard-backed folio that held printed pieces of work; nowadays it is almost certainly a website, whether it be a simple site that works on all digital devices and servers or a more complex Flash site. Online there are numerous sample templates and free 'build your own portfolio' websites, which give you a manageable platform via which to showcase your work. Your folio, online or hard-backed, is often seen without you. A creative director will definitely view your folio before deciding on whether to take up their time meeting you in person.

Many teams meet at university, while others meet while on an advertising short course. When you are first starting out it is easiest to achieve a placement or junior job as a team. If you team up with a creative partner and are creating a portfolio for the first time, spend some time thinking about how best to present your work as a team.

The folio will need to show what your team has to offer that differentiates you from the rest. A girl and boy team will be different from a same-sex team; a team made up of a graffiti artist and a poet will think differently from two marketing people. The unique relationship developed between those two individuals will be expressed in the portfolio.

'It's a team's opportunity to show that they're different from other people, which is what the creative director should really be buying.'

ANGUS MACADAM, EXECUTIVE CREATIVE DIRECTOR, DENTSU LONDON

Creatives traditionally presented their work in physical portfolios but websites are now the norm. Try to imbue a sense of personality into your portfolio website as you won't always be showing it in person.

THE CONTENTS

What should be in a portfolio? What should you consider when selecting what to include? How many and what types of campaigns should feature? Ask yourself what your work says about you and whom you think it will appeal to.

A centrepiece is an idea or campaign that defines you and people know you for; you can create your portfolio around it, surrounding it with contrasting campaigns. It is your strongest and most original idea.

Opinion is divided between countries and creatives about the level of finish that should be evident in a portfolio. For the United States it is particularly important to present finished pieces.

'Their book should be full of good ideas. Now those ideas could be anything; they could be a clothing range, an idea to raise money for charity, it could be a print campaign, it could be an idea for a TV programme.'

PAUL JORDAN, EXECUTIVE CREATIVE DIRECTOR, DENTSU LONDON

'Breadth. Everyone wants to do cool campaigns for space travel, but it is harder to make smart campaigns for boring everyday consumer goods. To have solutions for both is best.'

MATTIAS CEDERFELDT, ART DIRECTOR, POND, STOCKHOLM

'Students have to have more now than ever. The old rule was that you need five campaigns with three ads per campaign. I think now you need a few solid print or out of home (outdoor) campaigns, at least one really good one, to demonstrate that you can do that — because we all still do that; however, I think you need the same amount, if not more, of digital, experiential or even product ideas. People are looking more and more to innovative product ideas because what better marketing tool than a great product? A lot of the forward-thinking modern agencies are all over that.'

AARON SEYMOUR-ANDERSON, ART DIRECTOR, FALLON MINNEAPOLIS

'Sometimes it's good to have a centrepiece to your portfolio, but that will only come over time, when most people agree on the strength of the idea and you build it through multiple media.'

JUSTIN TINDALL, GROUP EXECUTIVE CREATIVE DIRECTOR, LEO BURNETT LONDON

'Ideas that impact human beings. We have a power in our hands to use in some way to influence the world, to change it for the better. Let's use it, make ideas to do it and make the world in some small way a better place to live. It may sound like a big task, but we have to start somewhere, so why not in your book/portfolio.'

SIMON HIGBY, CREATIVE DIRECTOR, TRIBAL DDB STOCKHOLM

'If students are thinking of digital they should make up some interactive tools and put them on their site. Studying PHP [a scripting language] allows you to make some interesting tools using the Facebook API [application programming interface]. It is a lot of fun.'

HIROKI NAKAMURA, HAJIME YAKUSHIJI, SHINSAKU OGAWA, HIROSHI KOIKE, TSUBASA KAYASUGA, CREATIVE TEAM MEMBERS, DENTSU TOKYO

Having a device to present your portfolio on can be handy if you are showing a particularly digitally-focused project.

'Have finished things. I always struggle when students have TV scripts or radio scripts in their book because they're not finished and it's really hard to get a sense of their taste level. I like to see things that are finished, that I could pick that up and run it tomorrow. That's why so many student books start with print because that's something that they could produce on their own. They can make it look finished and they can show off their level of taste and the quality of their ideas. At the same time we're also looking for people that can think in bigger, more 360-degree ideas, which show that from a simple idea there's lots of different things that you can do, and you can think in different mediums other than print. The great thing about the Internet and the democratization of software is that there are people coming out of school who can make television commercials just as beautifully as we can; they may not have the experience but the equipment's certainly there. They should use that; it should show off what their level of taste is. They're saying "This is what I think is good".'

MATT MACDONALD, EXECUTIVE CREATIVE DIRECTOR, JWT NEW YORK

the
TRUTH

HURTS

fur factories exist

the
TRUTH

HURTS

fur factories exist

Anna Barisani's final-year portfolio, using traditional media but a more experimental format.

DESIGN AGAINST FUR
'the truth hurts' campaign

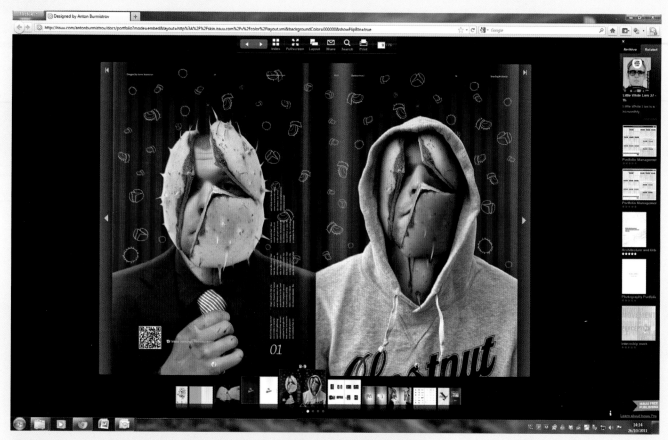

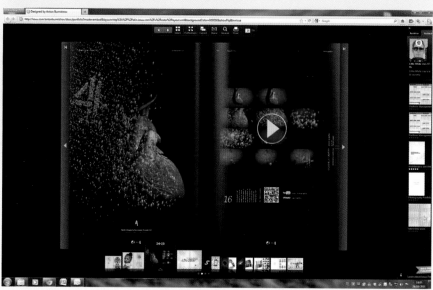

Anton Burmistrov's final-year digital portfolio, using video players, QR codes and interactive elements.

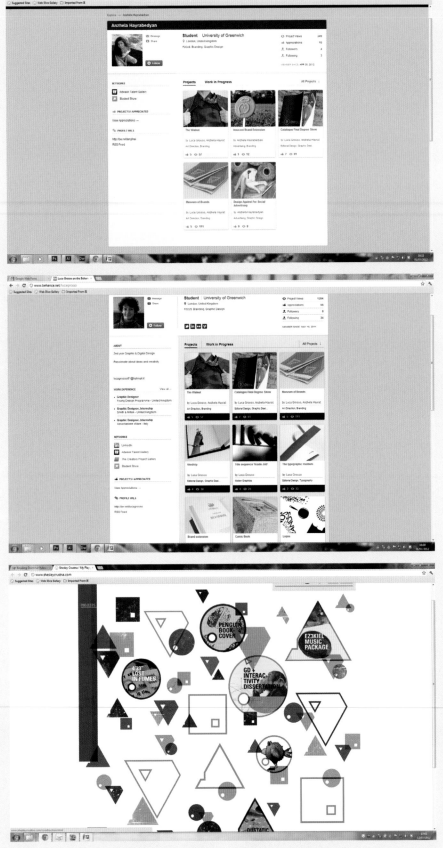

LEFT
Greenwich student
Anzhela Hayrabedyan
developed her online
portfolio on the Behance
Network, one of the
many custom sites that
lets creatives put up
an accessible portfolio
quickly and easily.

LEFT
Greenwich student
Luca Grosso also used
the Behance Network
to showcase his work.

LEFT
Greenwich student
Shesley Crustna
developed his own
website in Dreamweaver.
While not as complex
as Anton Burmistrov's,
because he developed it
himself, the homepage
and subsequent
interactivity is very
personalized.

WHY IDEAS MATTER

'Student portfolios should be all about ideas. Execution can be taught and perfected along the way. But the ability to come up with original and fresh ideas is something that is rare. If a creative director is comparing two portfolios, and say one is full of beautiful executions of average ideas and the other is full of beautiful ideas but averagely executed. The one with the ideas will win every time.'

SHANE BRADNICK, CREATIVE DIRECTOR, BMF, AUSTRALIA

While there is no doubt that ideas rule in the creative department, many creative directors raised the issue of taste time and again in the course of writing this book. Raylin Valles offers a good insight into how you can show your level of taste through craft without spending time polishing advertising ideas that are not necessarily as insightful and original as you might think.

'I think they should have a lot of ideas — you don't necessarily have to have finished ideas — but at the same time you should have a lot of craft work. It could be just designs or something which is beautifully written.'

RAYLIN VALLES, CREATIVE DIRECTOR, MUDRA DELHI

NARRATIVE

Not only should you have unique contents in your folio but you also need to think about the order in which people can experience it. Whether in a traditional folio or on a website, people have the ability to flick from piece to piece, but if you develop a compelling and interesting order the chances are that they will follow it. The order creates a kind of narrative, a little story that reveals either yourself or the team to the creative director. You need to decide whether you have a centrepiece, or whether you put one of your two strongest campaigns at the front of your portfolio, providing a wow factor, and the other at the end, to leave the viewer with a great last impression.

Each campaign needs to be structured so that the ad that is the clearest leads and ads that inspire or are a little more left field follow; any slightly weaker executions should go in the middle. If you have more than one weak ad in a campaign you should remove the campaign.

While a folio needs to speak volumes about you, the time will come when you finally get to meet someone face to face, whom you need to impress, not just by what you say but in how your personality comes across.

DEVELOPING YOUR PERSONAL BRAND

Though it does not seem fair to be judged on who you are as much as what you can create, you can be sure that it happens. This is because advertising is a selling, teamwork and communications profession. If you appear not to have considered how you come across then interviewers will think you have not considered how your work will come across.

There are two parts to presenting yourself; the first is your image and the second is how you sound.

Whether you are in a team or are an individual, 'you' are like a brand. Is your brand casual? Is it smart? Is it sophisticated? Is it edgy? Consider these things and dress accordingly. Think about the basics – are you washed and laundered? Are your teeth clean? It is amazing how many students do not think of these things and are surprised when industry turns them down. Taking care over personal presentation is important when you move from the student world into the world of work.

Before meeting an industry professional, practise what you want to say. While it may be enough to grunt and answer 'don't know' or 'because I liked it' during a critique or tutorial at university, this will not be adequate in industry. You will be required to provide answers because every decision you will make in a campaign has cost implications and repercussions for the client. If you cannot answer a CD how can you answer a client? If you are someone who always rushes what you are saying when you are nervous, learn to speak more slowly. Practise it. If you always ramble on, learn to be more concise. You do not need to change your personality for interviews, but just like for any pitch, you need to be the best version of yourself, and this time what you are selling is you.

GETTING YOUR FOOT IN THE DOOR

'Treat everything as a potential interview.' Is this good advice? No! You hear it often but it is not helpful for those looking for their first opening as a creative.

'Students often act as though every meeting is an interview for a job and it absolutely isn't. It's the start of a relationship which might lead to a placement so keep going back, keep nurturing that relationship.'

PAUL JORDAN, EXECUTIVE CREATIVE DIRECTOR, DENTSU LONDON

Initial meetings with creatives whom you don't know are like the start of any friendship – you need to get to know each other. When you first meet someone you do not expect a marriage proposal; you test each other out. Do you laugh at similar things? Do you see the world in the same way? Do you each contribute something positive? However, you do need to bear in mind that you make an impression with anything you do, and in the same way that you have dismissed people in the past as non-friend material because perhaps they are not fashionable or funny or like-minded enough, so too can you be dismissed.

How do you secure these elusive first meetings when you get to show others how interesting you are?

HEADHUNTERS
Your first port of call should be headhunters. Headhunters actively place industry people in work. They are given briefs by agencies and they look through their client base and put forward folios that they think are appropriate. This is not what they do for students. Headhunters have a huge amount of experience of looking through folios, seeing what does and does not work. They can give you advice and suggest agencies that might like your work. They can also give you the names of middle-weight or junior teams that you can call to ask for advice. These are often teams that the headhunter helped to place so they are predisposed to answering a request for a meeting favourably.

COLD CALLING
Nobody likes cold calling – that is, calling teams that you have never met before and introducing yourself. If you are in a team, don't make it your partner's responsibility to call up teams you don't know to try and arrange meetings because you feel that they are better at it, as this can lead to resentment. It is true that some people are better on the phone than others, but no one really enjoys it – even the confident extrovert in a student team won't like calling strangers and trying to create a rapport. Another thing to bear in mind is that no one knows what personality the person on the other end of the line will respond to. The shy person in the student team may come across as humble and willing to learn, which may be what the creative on the other end of the phone warms to.

'I'm really shy. So it was hard for me to do that. It takes me like a year to finally make the decision. But I did it. The first time wasn't as bad as I'd feared so, I tried again.'

MARIO CRUDELE, SENIOR COPYWRITER, PONCE BUENOS AIRES

'Ask for a meeting and then make sure to give an honest impression. Most advertising people are nice to newbies.'

MIA ROBERTSSON, COPYWRITER, FAMILJENPANGEA, STOCKHOLM

Before calling anyone in an agency look at that agency's work online and, if you can, their creative teams' work. Having shown a proper personal interest rather than just wanting something from them encourages other people to reciprocate the attention.

Aim for middle-weight teams as they are more likely to have the time to see you than senior teams and they will also have sufficient experience to offer advice – not a job, advice. Your folio should only be seen by the CD when it is ready.

'Don't aim too high; try and see junior or middle-weight teams as you're more likely to see them and their advice is probably a bit fresher. They're a bit closer to what's required to get in rather than going straight to creative directors and ECDs.'

PAUL JORDAN, EXECUTIVE CREATIVE DIRECTOR, DENTSU LONDON

EMAIL
Another option to start the conversation is to write a charming email.

'Speak in a chatty way, ask "can I come in for a chat?". Don't try and oversell yourself – anyone that says I'm a digital guru or I was best in my class at advertising I don't even look at. Tell me who inspires you, say "I love Neville Brody stuff, it really inspires me" if it does, because then you'll have got my attention. You'll have told me something interesting about yourself without being conceited.'

PAUL HARRISON, CREATIVE DIRECTOR, KODU, LONDON

Some people suggest sending quirky direct mail pieces or camping outside agency premises but on the whole these tactics do not work unless you have something dramatically different to show. Nonetheless, people respond well to an inventive idea. In 2010 the young copywriter Alec Brownstein bought ads on Google featuring the names of the creative directors he wanted to have an interview with. When these creative directors googled their own names the top result was a message from Brownstein asking for a job – which he was duly offered by one of them. But be aware that turning up unexpectedly and making a pest of yourself can have the opposite consequence.

'There's nothing more annoying than finding someone camped out on the doorstep like a tramp.'

ADAM TUCKER, CREATIVE DIRECTOR, LEO BURNETT LONDON

ABOVE

Cold calling is a tricky process but can lead to meetings. Do your research beforehand and always respect that the person on the other end of the phone is probably very busy.

RIGHT

It's important to hit the right tone when trying to make initial contact. If you do manage to set up a meeting, always show that you're ready to talk about any work you have mentioned liking in your letter or email.

TB

Tim Brown
23 Wells Street
Camberwell
London SE5 8YG

tim@brown.com
timbrownportfolio.com

Fao Joanne Helpful
Made Up
99 Agency Lane
London
W1H 8FG

Hi Joanne,

I hope you are able to spare me a few moments of your time. Joe Pink gave me your number and suggested that I contact you. I very much admire your work, particularly the brand X campaign that you created last year.

My name is Tim Brown and I have just finished a degree in Advertising at University X and I think that it's time to enter the real world of advertising instead of studying it.

I would love to come in and meet you for a chat and for some advice on what I could do next and how I could improve my portfolio whenever you have time.

Best regards,
Tim Brown

PROTECTING YOUR IDEAS

One of the most common questions that students ask with regard to showing their portfolio to others is, 'How can we protect our ideas?'.

First, you should not presume that people want to steal your ideas and it is highly unlikely that anyone would. You will be asking to see teams that have had to work hard on their own portfolios and they are in a job where they have to prove daily that they are able to come up with ideas. Such discipline means that they will not need any of your ideas, as they will have plenty of their own. You have to be capable of revealing your ideas, as they are what will get you a job.

Protecting ideas is a fairly complex area for a number of reasons.

Many people come up with the same idea at the same time without ever seeing each other's work. This is often because there is something within the cultural landscape that is inspiring a number of creatives at the same time. Films, for example, often inspire ads. If a film with superheroes comes out one might reasonably expect to see superheroes in washing powder ads, insurance ads, coffee ads... Similarly, celebrities fall in and out of fashion and once they are in fashion, everyone will want to use them, even if ironically. Because people can come up with similar ideas at the same time independently it is very hard to prove that someone saw your work and then created a campaign based on it.

Not only is it difficult to prove that someone took your idea, it is also difficult to prove that you did not see the ad in their office and copy it yourself. If we take, for example, the rather cheesy execution for the imaginary product Toothease – that speculative (spec) idea is in the unusual position of having been used as an example in a book. All readers can assume that the idea is mine and would find it hard to argue that the idea was theirs first. However the majority of spec ads are held in the privacy of a portfolio so how could anyone be sure who had come up with that thought – the student team or the creative they claim to have shown it to?

While a very small number of people do blatantly steal ideas, the majority of working creatives are concerned to support new talent and would hate to think that an idea of theirs had been inspired from looking at student work, even accidentally. Teams often keep a log of whom they have seen and what was in their portfolio so that they do not even come close to copying. Advice given by a mentoring team may be based on an approach that they are currently taking with one of their own ideas and this may be misinterpreted at a later stage by the student team to mean that the mentor team took inspiration from the student rather than the other way round.

An obvious protection is making it clear that other teams have seen your portfolio, and making sure that you do show a wide scope of teams your portfolio until you discover which teams are the most appropriate mentors for you. While that does not stop an unscrupulous team stealing ideas it would mean that some other members of the industry are aware that they have. Another option is to put your best ideas in an envelope and post it to yourself using registered post; keep the envelope sealed once you have received it back. While this is not the same as copyright, the postal date stamp on the envelope can, if necessary, provide evidence of the date by which you had your ideas.

On a pragmatic level, if you do think one of your ideas has been taken, consider whom you could tell your suspicions to. If you did make a huge fuss then who would want to see you or hire you afterwards? You would be known as a team that claims ideas are taken from them and people would be wary of even looking at your book in case they too were targeted. Telling your headhunter may be a sensible approach so that they do not send any other new teams to that particular prospective mentor and you should avoid that team in the future. Eventually your hard work will pay off and you will be working in the industry and you will know that team for what they are.

LEARNING TO TAKE CRITICISM

When creatives offer advice it is in the form of a critique. A critique is a good thing, it means you have engaged them enough for them to offer opinions on what is or is not working. What a new team actually does not want to hear is 'uh huh, uh huh, uh huh' as a creative goes through their book. This means it is neither good nor interesting enough to elicit comment, it is merely OK. Unfortunately many students or new teams are unable to take criticism in the right way. It is important not to take it personally.

'I was pretty tenacious. I would put my work in front of people and I wasn't afraid to ask questions, ask for advice and follow through on that advice, show people how I'd changed my work based on their feedback. That's really how I got my first job in New York was doing that. You just have to be tenacious and have a thick skin.'

MATT MACDONALD, EXECUTIVE CREATIVE DIRECTOR, JWT NEW YORK

Creatives like to see teams that take feedback seriously and are able to change their work and come back with it even better than the mentors could have imagined.

Aim to get feedback from a number of creative teams and go back to ones that you feel are on the same wavelength as you. These may not be the people who thought the work was great; in fact, it may be the creatives who offered the most criticism whose viewpoint you most stand to benefit from.

Creatives are not going to tell you exactly what you need to do. They have neither the time nor the inclination to sort out five campaigns in a half-hour meeting but like any tutor they will offer pointers to more interesting ways of taking your idea or helping it make sense.

One of the biggest complaints from creatives is that they give up their time to help, but too few students or young teams have the tenacity to come back with changes or new ideas. They think their folio is perfect already and just want someone to tell them that it is and offer them a job.

'But whoever you're seeing, if you think they're talking nonsense don't go back. If you like what they're saying definitely go back. Not enough people go back. You see someone, you like them and then you never see them again. You give them advice and then you don't know if they did it.'

ANGUS MACADAM, EXECUTIVE CREATIVE DIRECTOR, DENTSU LONDON

'Write back and thank people for looking at your book because everyone is so busy these days.'

MATT MACDONALD, EXECUTIVE CREATIVE DIRECTOR, JWT NEW YORK

And make sure you look through award books. Seeing how other creatives have answered similar problems may inspire you. Just do not copy them – most working creatives know what is in the award books and will tell you that your work is very much like so-and-so's work from two years ago.

'I took a night class in New York, learned what an advertising portfolio was, then hustled to put one together. Award show books were incredibly helpful to me at that time, trying to understand what was good, what wasn't.'

JOHN PATROULIS, EXECUTIVE CREATIVE DIRECTOR, AGENCY215, SAN FRANCISCO

Ask the teams that you meet to suggest other names and in this way you will build up a network of creative mentors. Each time try to go more senior in whom you speak to. After you have built up a rapport with a senior team that has a CD's or ECD's ear they may recommend your folio. If they do recommend it then the CD will definitely look at it because these senior teams will recommend only a few new teams. The reason these senior teams need to meet you a few times and see that you have changed your book according to their feedback is to check whether you fulfil the industry standard entry point criteria. These include tenacity, ability to take criticism, responding to feedback, working well in a team, speed of work, communication skills, punctuality and personality, as well as having a portfolio that is worth looking at.

MEETING A CREATIVE DIRECTOR

Your first meeting with a CD is likely to be a nerve-wracking experience, but nearly all CDs want to elicit the best response from a prospective new team or student and they will try to put you at your ease and be friendly rather than overly formal.

There will be moments of awkwardness while they look silently through your work, not asking any questions, and you will be unsure whether to say something or sit in silence. This is normal. Just be ready to answer questions about your work when asked. In a meeting with a CD you will immediately see the industry relevance of cultural capital: being knowledgeable, interested in contemporary graphic practice and design practice, aware of new art or film, reading experimental or historical literature, having seen new theatrical work and being able to talk about their relevance to your work – all will intrigue a CD. This is your chance to show that you are more than meets the eye.

ONLY THE BEGINNING

If you demonstrate some determination and persistence, a CD may offer you a placement, usually two weeks in length. You may have this placement extended or you may need to search out another placement. You must not rest easy and think you are on the way to a job merely because a CD has decided to let you have some industry experience. You have to live up to your promise and work hard, take criticism well and think creatively.

'We worked literally night and day, often sleeping all night at the office. We begged for as many briefs as we could get. We talked to everyone. It's also important to mention that many placements at agencies at that time were unpaid, including ours. So we not only had to try and get to work and subsist for the time we were there, but we also were working 18-hour days unpaid. I only got through it with the support of my girlfriend at the time, who (unsurprisingly) later became my wife!'

JON DANIEL, EXECUTIVE CREATIVE DIRECTOR, EBB&FLOW, LONDON

Even if you are fortunate and achieve some early success, never stop working on your portfolio. Every team should have a 'bottom drawer'. This is simply the place that you store good ideas that you have generated but that were not right for the brief that you were given. These might be right for another client in the future or, with a bit of revision, could make an interesting piece of speculative (personal) work for your folio now. It is easy to stop working on your folio when you are in an agency. You are busy on 'real' briefs and are trying to impress your CD so that you can stay. However, this is an industry where it is common to move on and you need to keep your folio fresh. This then allows you to revisit a CD or team that you have seen before and say that you have new work *and* that you are on placement with another agency. It is certainly true of advertising that if you appear to be in demand you will be in demand.

Some placements do turn into jobs.

'There was a really lucky moment after my internship when they offered a job instead of a further internship.'

ALBERT S. CHAN, ART DIRECTOR, OGILVY & MATHER FRANKFURT

Other placements turn into freelance work. In order to keep you on for a while longer the agency will offer you a better daily rate. This is often the first step from being a placement to being a freelance team. These freelance positions can then in turn become full-time positions.

'Fortunately a first-time creative director named Alex Bogusky saw one campaign in my book that he liked and gave me a two-week freelance gig. It lasted for a year.'

SCOTT DUCHON, EXECUTIVE CREATIVE DIRECTOR, AGENCY215, SAN FRANCISCO

The usual route into an agency job is that a placement or short freelance position will turn into a short-term contract of three months, or a job offer with a three-month probationary period. This gives the agency a chance to find out if you live up to your promise and can work within their team. This enables you to show your skill over a number of briefs for an extended period of time without the agency needing to get involved in the complexities such as pensions, medical and legal cover and redundancy cover that may come with a standard job offer package.

WORKING OUT YOUR RATES

Working out what you can expect to be paid is one of the hardest things to do, no matter where on the ladder you are. The amount people are prepared to pay depends on the economy and on how many other creatives are looking for work. While there are broad salary bands which indicate how much you might get paid, depending on your level of experience, they can vary by tens of thousands of pounds and are different in every country.

Your best bet is to ask a headhunter what the going rate is for your level of experience. Placements often pay nothing or very basic travel expenses; sometimes there is a low pay structure for placement teams, but there really is no industry standard.

Many teams start to freelance after they have been in a job for a number of years, so they base their weekly or daily rate as a proportion of their yearly rate plus own contributions to pensions and 'lean times' accounts. For those junior teams that move from placement to freelance it is much more difficult as you do not really have a wage or much experience to go on. You need to work out what you are comfortable asking for. Total your actual weekly expenses, such as food, travel, rent, utilities and phone. One way of working out the minimum you need to ask for is to divide this figure by five to give you an interim daily rate. Add on an extra day to give you sick days and holiday pay. Add the six days together and divide by five again to give you a new daily rate. This is not a hard and fast rule but will give you somewhere to start from. Unsurprisingly, many people offer new teams a figure that is lower than the one that you just worked out.

There are a number of other factors to bear in mind if you are freelancing. You will be responsible for paying tax, which is usually paid retrospectively on an annual basis. You need to consider pension contributions and accountant fees. An accountant will tell you what you can claim against tax and you will need to keep all work-related receipts safe to give to your accountant at the end of the year. Some agencies have started taking the tax directly from your wages (PAYE in the UK), which is not that helpful if you want to claim against tax. Freelance work offers neither sickness or holiday pay but specifies a completion date. Check any sub clauses to a contract as often no payment will be made if, when freelancing, you were sick or unable to complete the work because of external circumstances. Simply saying that you can do it after the deadline will not be acceptable as you will not have fulfilled the contract.

AWARDS AND COMPETITIONS

Awards and competitions are an important part of the career of any advertising creative. Not everyone can win an award and many good campaigns made for difficult clients never get close to achieving an award. This does not make the work bad, just not award-winning. CDs and clients still value teams that work hard and produce good ads. Every piece of work should not be a race to an award. However, there is no denying that awards help the long-term career of a creative. Your name is known, your work is known. You can move to more creative agencies with braver clients and ask for better wages.

There are also students or young creatives competitions available and these are always worth entering. Look on the Internet: many graphic and design websites and online magazines run competitions to design flyers, posters and logos.

Even if you do not win you will have something else that you can put in your folio. Thinking up briefs for yourself is not always as easy as it seems and neither is working in isolation. A competition has the benefit of showing you what people judge to be a good answer to that brief, even if that answer was not yours. Merely having good practice examples to judge your own work against is a powerful ongoing learning aid. Search out any competition that can help extend your skills and challenge you. It certainly cannot hurt and you might even win. Most of all, never stop learning and never be complacent with your folio.

'One of the things that helped us early on was that we won the Cannes Young Creatives competition with our portfolio, but that was mainly because it was full of ambient stuff and didn't look like any of the advertising courses books, which made it look different. We won that and then we got hired.'

PAUL JORDAN, EXECUTIVE CREATIVE
DIRECTOR, DENTSU LONDON

LEFT
Building on their 'Fun Theory' campaign, DDB Stockholm developed Volkswagen Speed Camera Lottery, an idea suggested by Kevin Richardson in an open competition for creative ideas for VW's Fun Theory Award. The idea was to reward those drivers who obey the speed limit with money raised through fining those drivers who exceed it. The campaign was recognized with a Titanium Award at the 2011 Cannes International Festival of Creativity.

RIGHT
'The Campaign Designed To Drop Sales' by TBWA\Hunt\Lascari Johannesburg in 2010 was created to raise awareness of human trafficking for the International Organization for Migration. It shows how easy it is for people to simply disappear. The agency erected false walls that perfectly mimicked the walls behind them and, as people walked down the pavement, they would seem to disappear from sight.

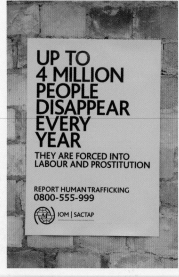

CONCLUSION

CONCLUSION

This book aimed to introduce the subject of creative advertising and show how it is influenced by many factors. It started by showing advertising's place within commerce and some of the criticisms levelled against it. It then looked at how advertising has changed throughout history, how globalization has led to the rise of visual advertising and how the Internet and social media have reinvigorated the use of the written word. This was followed by an introduction to the science of semiotics and semiology — the most straightforward way to analyse the use of signs and symbols, and therefore the creation of meaning, in advertising. It then looked at branding, what makes a powerful brand identity and how a client expects us to build out from this using a tone of voice that resonates authentically with the brand and its audience. This then led into an exploration of target markets, categorization and research methodologies and an examination of how insight into a target market's beliefs and behaviour can develop advertising strategy that answers a client's business objectives. Tips from a number of award-winning creatives from around the world, together with a selection of examples of amazing work, helped to show how to generate ideas and explore media creatively. While quality of ideas is key, many creative directors want to see an ability to craft work in a student portfolio, so this aspect of the job was then explored. This is an ongoing process and a working creative never stops adding to their skills.

The book also made a case for the development of your cultural capital. A great deal of what is taught in schools today is based on what is easy to assess and easily moderated or verified. Politicians, school governors and parents love this system because statistically based charts can be generated showing the number of A grades achieved by a given school in particular subjects, or the improvement in grades a particular educational policy would appear to have generated. Unfortunately this does not take into account the holistic approach to education needed to create culturally aware individuals. Without the ability to reference and understand the meaning and purpose of many cultural events and artefacts a student would not have sufficient cultural capital for proper social mobility into such careers as advertising. A creative needs to be aware of the culture that surrounds them in order to communicate effectively with other members of society. Those with only a limited cultural understanding cannot succeed in this field. It then becomes up to you, the student, to develop and extend your own cultural capital.

The following chapter looked at pitching skills – the act of selling your work to others within the advertising process – and explored how you work within this process when you start making ads for real within an agency. Finally the book concluded with a number of tips given by leading creatives on your portfolio and getting a job in the industry.

While the text could only look briefly into each area, it aimed to link together all the seemingly different disciplines in advertising into a more coherent whole. The further reading section at the end of the book will enable you to take steps to extend your study and knowledge in order to make sensible and informed decisions about entering the marketing and advertising business.

Marketing is all about ideas, but these are ideas with a specific purpose – to increase profit and ultimately the sustainability of any given business. These ideas may start as cold business objectives but they can be transformed through the advertising process into insightful, thought-provoking, culturally aware communications that make a connection with us, members of the public. Advertising is all about communication – communication from a brand to its customers and potential customers about the benefits of using its products.

When, in June 2010,
James Ready realized
that they had sent
out a batch of their
beer bottles without
their usual little
comments printed onto
the underside of the
cap, they asked their
agency Leo Burnett to
communicate the mishap
to their customers.
Leo Burnett used the
camaraderie the brand
had built up with its
customers through great
tone of voice to create
an apology video on its
Facebook page, asking
customers to send
in their blank caps
(or pictures of their
blank caps) in exchange
for a James Ready
mystery gift.

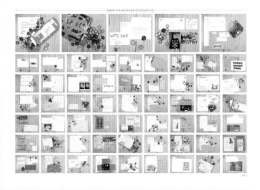

BLANK CAP RECALL

For years, every James Ready Beer came with a message under its cap. These messages are part of the brand and something our drinkers look forward to. But on June 2nd, 2010 the caps went BLANK! It was a big time screw up. Within days, we started getting emails and letters from drinkers. We saw this as an opportunity and launched The James Ready Blank Cap Recall. If you send us back your blank caps, we'll send you "something" from the brewery in return. Over 1,000,000 blank caps kept drinkers and us busy.

2006
YOU DO NOT WIN A BOAT.

KEEPING J.R. CHEAP CAPS.

2007
SHAVE YOUR GIRLFRIEND'S BACK?
HOW CAN JR HELP YOU?

HOW CAN J.R. HELP YOU CAPS.

2008
JAMES READY TO DELIVER — THE — BOARD GAME
IS THAT GIRL TOPLESS!? NO. NO SHE ISN'T.
MOVE BACK 1

J.R. BOARD GAME CAPS.

2009
DECEMBER 27
"READ DIRTY MAGAZINES BY THE FIRE" DAY.

J.R. CALENDER CAPS.

2010

BLANK J.R. CAPS.

CALL FOR BLANK CAPS.

OUR DRINKERS RESPOND.

RECALL LETTER IN EVERY CASE.

ONLINE RECALL VIDEO.

Good ideas and thoughtful communication are your way into this industry. Your portfolio should be full of new and exciting ways to intrigue consumers and to start conversations. However, it is no good to you if no one knows about it: you need to get your website (or hard-backed portfolio) out there for people to see.

In order to succeed in this industry you need perseverance, tenacity, optimism, skills, ideas and an ability to learn from every situation. You need to be a self-motivator. This is probably a phrase that you have heard in your school, college and university classes and it is extremely important for advertising. You need to be able to motivate yourself to learn things, discover things, experiment and develop ideas, particularly after critiques that tell you to start again. You should be constantly asking yourself, how can I make that execution/brand interaction better? Bear these things in mind and with some hard work and the odd inspired moment you could find yourself working in an agency you admire, on brands you find interesting, creating work you can be proud of.

'This quote from the founder of DDB, Bill Bernbach, cited by Bob Scarpelli [DDB chairman] in Cannes in 2011, is perhaps the best advice one can give to young people or the industry as a whole. "Many years ago, a brilliant man, the man who ignited the creative revolution in our industry, Bill Bernbach, said: "The men [and women] who will be in business tomorrow are the men [and women] who understand that the future, as always, belongs to the brave."'

SIMON HIGBY, CREATIVE DIRECTOR,
TRIBAL DDB STOCKHOLM

In 2012 Jung von Matt Hamburg answered a brief by Mercedes-Benz for F-Cell hydrogen fuel technology, which boasts zero emissions, by imagining the car to be invisible to the environment. They created an execution across ambient, experiential, stunt and interactive media. They covered the car with LEDs and positioned a camera on the other side of it so it could transmit what it saw directly to the LEDs, effectively giving it an invisibility cloak. It toured for one week across Germany. It has won many awards, including silver at the One Show Interactive Awards for experiential advertising and installations.

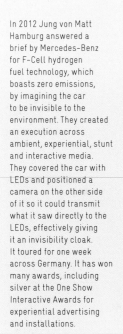

ENDMATTER

above the line: advertising created in television, print and radio media

account handler/manager: the person responsible for a particular client's business within an agency

adcept: a visualization of a strategic concept commonly used for research

advertising agency: a business that provides an advertising service to others

advertising creative: a person responsible for creating advertising ideas

ambient media: out-of-home (outdoor) advertising that does not use traditional media spaces such as bus sides but plays with unexpected places in the environment, such as pavements

art buyer: the link between the art director and illustrators, photographers and typographers

art director: the person in a team responsible for the look of an advert

audience: the people exposed to a particular advert

awareness: a measurement applied to advertisement or brand recall

banner ad: an advert embedded in a website linking the user to the client's website – it is usually rectangular in shape

below the line: direct-to-consumer advertising that specializes in getting a direct response through the use of such elements as promotions, phone lines and coupons

billboard: a large outdoor panel displaying advertising

brand: the core meaning of a distinctive product or service, not the product or service itself

brand identity: how a company wishes their brand to be perceived by an audience, including personality, values, logo and tone of voice

brand image: how the brand is actually perceived by an audience

brand manager: the person in the client organization responsible for making sure the marketing strategy is implemented properly for that particular brand; a business may have more than one brand

brief: the document that specifies what the advertising that will be created is supposed to say

campaign: at least three adverts that explore the same theme, linked by a visual and verbal tone of voice

capitalism: an economic and political system controlling commerce by private owners for profit

CEO (chief executive officer): the highest-ranking executive in a company, with decision-making and management responsibilities and typically reporting to the board of directors

client: a person or company that an advertising agency is delivering a professional service to. Often there are a number of clients representing a variety of interested sectors from within the client organization

client organization: the business that the advertising agency is delivering a professional service to

connotation: a secondary, often more personal meaning or feeling that a sign or word suggests in addition to its primary meaning

consumer group: a group of people that have an interest in a particular product or service and share some of the values expressed by that product

copy-testing: research conducted on advertising before it goes live

copywriter: the person responsible for writing any text in the team

creative director (CD): the person in charge of the creative department or in charge of the creatives working on a particularly large account

cultural capital: a term coined by French sociologist Pierre Bourdieu, referring to the non-financial social assets such as cultural knowledge or education that can allow social mobility by enabling access to a variety of groups and networks

D&AD: one of the many competitions offering awards for excellence in advertising, amongst other categories. It stands for Design and Art Direction and is based in the UK

denotation: primary meaning of a word or sign

digital advertising: previously just at-home Internet-based advertising such as banner ads, now this encompasses moving/digital out-of-home advertising

dubbing/sound edit: the mixing together of sound and vocals in television, film and advertising

edit: the cutting together of moving imagery in television, film and advertising

empathy: the capacity to understand the feelings, motivations and circumstances of others

endline/strapline: the sentence that summarizes the idea behind the advert, often known as a slogan, though this is now often thought of as a rather archaic term, referring to a time when advertising endlines had to rhyme or be instantly catchy

ethnography: the study and interpretation of human cultures

execution: (i) how the core idea is expressed within an advert; (ii) how an advert will actually look or be written

executive creative director (ECD): the person in overall charge of the creative department

experiential advertising: both a marketing strategy and a type of advertising that directly engages with the target market in order for them to become involved in the evolution of a brand rather than buying products per se

focus group: used for qualitative research, this is a small group from a particular target market that are asked for opinions and feelings about products, advertising or strategy. They may or may not use the product

grading: enhancing colour in post-production

guerrilla marketing: a type of marketing that uses unconventional (sometimes barely legal) practices to promote a product, such as fly-posting or actors posing as consumers; often targets hard-to-reach consumer groups

headhunter: a person who finds appropriate candidates for job opportunities, taking a fee from the advertising agency for placing a candidate; they have a large number of people on their books and know current rates of pay

head of art: the person responsible for the quality of print work. If there is a head of art creative teams will need to agree photographer/illustrator choices with this person

hybrid agency: an agency that supplies a number of solutions and specialisms, perhaps branding and advertising or television production and advertising

idea/concept: the single unique thought that an advert will be based on

integrated advertising: advertising that has one message running through a variety of media

IMC/Integrated Marketing Communications: a client-dictated brand-management policy to unite all brand communications to say one message no matter what the media

managing director (MD): the person responsible for the daily running of an organization or business, sometimes equivalent to the CEO (executive head) or sometimes heading an individual part of a company

marketing: the process that identifies who the consumer is and what products and services they may be interested in, and then delivers them to them

marketing mix: commonly explained as price, product, promotion and distribution

media channel: any medium that carries an advertising message, such as television, press, PR

media neutral: an advertising approach that focuses on developing the concept and decides the best media for it afterwards

media planner: the person in charge of deciding which media will be seen by the target market

medium: the material or form in which a piece of work is created. Sometimes used interchangeably with the term 'media', which is a collective noun referring to the main means of mass communication (press, television, radio and increasingly Internet)

Modernism: a cultural movement that rejected traditional ways of creating artworks and literature and chose new ways to express itself. It favoured subjectivity and believed in progress and in striving to reach idealized states

multinational corporation: a business that has facilities in more than one country, with a head office that coordinates global activity.

network agency: an advertising company that owns agencies in a variety of countries

new media: any new technologies that are developed and then utilized for entertainment and advertising, such as websites and text messages

one-off ad: a single execution

pitch: the act of selling a particular idea to an audience

placement team/internship: work experience in an agency; some placements are paid, others are not

planner: the person responsible for the advertising strategy

portfolio: a collection of your best pieces of work. This can be both digital or in traditional book form, although nowadays an online version is essential

positioning: a marketing idea that describes the values attributed to a particular product, such as 'luxury'

Postmodernism: A cultural movement that rejected Modernism, fusing high art with popular culture and everyday life

post-production: work done after filming has finished, commonly editing, grading and dubbing

PR/public relations: the activity of maintaining a flow of communication between an organization and the public. This practice, when it works, can allow access to media that has a huge reach, will not be paid for by the client and does not feel like a sales message

pre-production: any planning activity that takes place before the start of a shoot or a production

product placement: products placed in television shows or films in order to be seen

production department: the department responsible for facilitating the physical production of television and radio ads. Sometimes the art buyer is in the production department

proposition: the single most important thing an advert must get across to the target market

qualitative research: research that asks open-ended questions in order to find out why people do or like things

quantitative research: research that seeks to find out how many people do or like a particular thing

COMPETITIONS

reference: inspiration for advertising or providing an example of a particular style

scamp: usually A3 (B) in size, this is a rough drawing that brings an ad to life

script: a short description and the dialogue for a radio or television ad

semiology: the study of linguistic signs

semiotics: the study of all signs

sign: something that stands for something else, e.g. red for danger

social media: interactive online media whose purpose is audience conversation, comment and content

socio-economic group: a group of people united only by household income or job description

speculative/spec ad: ideas for campaigns that have been created for your portfolio; they may be for real products but you have not been asked, nor paid, to make them

sponsorship: a business relationship between two parties in which one provides funding or resources to another who agrees to be publically associated with them. This can work when both of the 'brands' share a value; for example, the desire for excellence in sport can be shared by a sportsman and a running shoe manufacturer.

storyboard: sequential drawings that visualize a television idea

strategy: an outline of what is the most effective way of targeting a particular group, developed from an insight

Surrealism: an art movement that began in the early 1920s and celebrated the power of the unconscious mind. Imagery was often fantastical and unnatural

targeting: trying to reach a particular group of people through certain messages, tones of voice and media

target market: a group of people that are believed to be a potential market for a particular product or service

through-the-line agency: an agency that is able to create both below the line and above the line advertising

tone of voice: how a brand conveys its values and personality through image and words to its audience

trade ad: advertising that is primarily business to business

traffic department/creative services: the department that manages the work flow

transmedia campaigns: advertising in which different media reveal different elements of the campaign

vector-based graphics: imagery that uses mathematical description for direction and size, consequently is used for creating line drawings (paths). Because the information is stored mathematically rather than as a static image it can be scaled without degrading

viral: an online phenomenon in which people spontaneously pass an advert around friendship groups

word of mouth: people spontaneously sharing product or advertising messages

JANUARY
- Epica Awards
- Prix de la Campagne Citoyenne, Paris, France
- Scandinavian Advertising Awards, Stockholm
- Mobius Advertising Awards, United States
- New York Festivals – the Global Awards, New York, USA
- ADC Schweiz, Zürich, Switzerland
- Effie Slovenia (Effie Slovenija), Ljubljana, Slovenia
- Festival Internacional de Publicidad, Televisión y Cine, Zaragoza, Spain

FEBRUARY
- MENA Cristal Awards, Middle East and North Africa
- New York Festivals – Television & Film Awards, New York, USA
- RAMA Retail Advertising Awards, Washington, DC, USA
- Kuwait Arabic Advertising Awards, Kuwait
- Asia-Pacific Effie Awards, Singapore
- Ramses Funk, Hamburg, Germany
- Red Dot Award, Essen, Germany
- BoB (Best of the Best) Awards, London, UK
- Imagina Awards for Animated Computer Graphics, Bry-sur-Marne, France
- NZ Direct & Interactive Marketing Awards, Auckland
- World Press Photo Awards

MARCH
- Asia Pacific Advertising Festival (ADFEST), Bangkok, Thailand
- CCA-Venus Creativ Club, Vienna, Austria
- Grand Prix Stratégies Marketing des Jeunes, Issy-les-Moulineaux, France
- Caples International Awards, Holtsville, USA
- Advertising Hall of Fame, Washington DC, USA
- Dubai Lynx Awards, Dubai, United Arab Emirates
- MAA Best Awards London, UK
- British Arrows Awards (BTAA), London, UK
- Advertising Creative Circle Awards, London, UK
- Effie Awards Hellas, Greece Athens, Greece
- Premios Best Pack, Madrid, Spain
- Premios AMPE, Madrid, Spain
- Trophée du Média Annuaire, Paris, France
- AIMIA Awards, Sydney, Australia
- Design Week Awards, London, UK
- Australian Creative Hotshop Awards, Sydney
- Australia's Top Emerging Photographers Awards, Sydney.
- Summit Creative Award, USA
- The A-List Awards, Los Angeles, USA
- AWARD (Australian Writers and Art Directors), Sydney, Australia
- Intercontinental Advertising Cup (ICAC), Istanbul, Turkey

APRIL
- International ANDY Awards, New York, USA
- MIPTV, Cannes, France
- FIAP – Ibero-American Advertising Festival (Festival Iberoamericano de la Publicidad), Buenos Aires, Argentina
- CAANZ Media Awards, Auckland, New Zealand
- Premio Folha / M&M, São Paulo, Brazil
- Golden Award of Montreux, Switzerland
- IPM Awards (Institute of Promotion Marketing), London, UK
- SAR – Polish Advertising Festival, Warsaw

(continued)
- Effie – The Best Brand, Moscow, Russia
- Phénix UDA de la Communication, Paris, France
- Soundie Awards, Seattle, USA
- OBIE Awards Washington, DC, USA
- Socially Responsible Communications Award (SRC Award), New York, USA
- Clics d'Or, Boulogne-Billancourt, France
- Media Spikes, Bali, Indonesia
- ASTRA Awards, Sydney, Australia

MAY
- Effie Awards, New York, USA
- FAB Awards, International Food and Beverage Creative Excellence Awards, London, UK
- D&AD Awards (Yellow Pencil), London, UK
- IAB Australia Interactive Advertising Awards, Sydney
- CLIO Awards, New York, USA
- The Laus Awards, Barcelona, Spain
- Astrid Awards, Ossining-on-Hudson, USA
- International Automotive Advertising Awards (IAAA), Macomb, USA
- Commercial Closet Images in Advertising Awards, New York, USA
- New York Festivals, International Advertising Awards in All Media, New York, USA
- Grand Prix Stratégies du Marketing Relationnel & Opérationnel, Issy-les-Moulineaux, France
- Prix Club des Directeurs Artistiques, Paris, France
- El Sol (Festival Iberoamericano de la Communicación Publicitaria), Madrid, Spain
- Australian Catalogue Association, Melbourne
- World Animation Celebration, Agoura Hills, USA
- CAANZ Axis Awards, Auckland, New Zealand
- Melbourne Advertising and Design Club Awards, Australia

JUNE
- AICP, New York, USA
- AdPrint Festival, Bucharest, Romania
- World Advertising Festival of Gramado (Festival Mundial de Publicidade de Gramado), Brazil
- Phoenix Awards, Singapore
- Rainbow Marble (Duhova Kulicka), Zlin, Czech Republic
- Effie Awards Belgium, Brussels
- Grand Prix Stratégies des Média, Issy-les-Moulineaux, France
- Grand Prix Stratégies de la Publicité Issy-les-Moulineaux, France
- Deutscher Multimedia Award (DMMA), Eschborn, Germany
- Cannes Lions, International Festival of Creativity, France
- ADDY Awards, Washington, DC, USA
- Webby Awards, New York, USA
- Chip Shop Awards, London, UK

JULY
- Loerie Awards, Cape Town, South Africa
- 100 Best Posters of the Year (100 besten Plakate des Jahres), Radebeul, Germany
- Effie Awards Netherlands, Amsterdam
- Art Directors Club of Europe Awards (ADC Europe), Barcelona, Spain

AUGUST
- Australian Effie Awards presented by the AFA and the AANA, Sydney.

MORE INFO

SEPTEMBER

- International Advertising Festival Golden Hammer, Riga, Latvia
- Moscow International Advertising and Marketing Festival (Red Apple) (MIAF), Russia
- Euro Effies, Brussels, Belgium
- The APA Show, London, UK
- Effie Awards Austria (Effie Österreich), Vienna
- WebAward, West Simsbury, United States
- AME Awards (Advertising Marketing Effectiveness) – New York Festivals, USA
- Concerned Communicator Award, Jaipur, India
- International AutoVision Automotive Film and Multimedia Festival, Munich, Germany
- POSNA Awards, Essen, Germany
- Die Klappe, Hamburg, Germany
- Brisbane Advertising & Design Club Awards, Australia
- CAANZ NZ Effie Awards, Auckland, New Zealand
- MFA Awards, Sydney, Australia

OCTOBER

- IMC European Awards (Integrated Marketing Communications) Brussels, Belgium
- Caxton Awards, Australia
- Jay Chiat Awards (American Association of Advertising Agencies), USA
- Golden Drum International Advertising Festival, Portoroz, Slovenia
- Premios Eficacia, Madrid, Spain
- International Green Awards, London, UK
- Promax UK Conference & Awards, London, UK
- Effie Awards Germany, Frankfurt am Main
- BAFTA Television Craft Awards, London, UK
- Cresta International Advertising Awards, New York, USA
- WOMCOM Clarion Awards, Alexandria, USA
- AMI National Awards for Marketing Excellence, Melbourne, Australia
- PRIA Golden Target Awards, Australia
- MFA Australian Advertising Media Awards
- Fresh Awards, Manchester, UK
- Radio Mercury Awards, New York, USA

NOVEMBER

- EFFIE Awards France, Paris
- European Car Advertising Film Festival, Paris, France
- World Luxury Award, Cham, Switzerland
- LEAF Lisbon Erotic Advertising Festival, Daventry, UK
- Cream Awards, Birmingham, UK
- London International Awards (LIA), UK
- Eurobest
- APA Customer Magazine Award (APA Awards), London, UK
- IPA Advertising Effectiveness Awards, London, UK
- ADMA Awards, Sydney, Australia
- WIN Awards, Santa Monica, USA

DECEMBER

- YoungGuns International Award, Sydney, Australia
- DMA Awards, London, UK
- Festival de la Publicité de Méribel Suresnes, France
- Grand Prix de la Communication Solidaire, Paris, France
- Cristal Festival Awards, Crans, Switzerland
- Central Europe Cristal Awards Suresnes, France
- B&T Awards, Sydney

CHAPTER 1

Alperstein, N., *Advertising in Everyday Life*, Cresskill, N.J.: Hampton Press, 2003
Bell, D., *The Cultural Contradictions of Capitalism*, New York: Basic Books, 1976
Bircham, E. and Charlton, J. (eds), *Anti-Capitalism: A Guide to the Movement*, London: Bookmarks Publications, 2001
Bond, J. and Kirshenbaum, R., *Under the Radar: Talking to Today's Cynical Consumer*, New York: John Wiley, Adweek Magazine Series, 1998
Carnegie, D., *How to Win Friends and Influence People*, New York: Simon & Schuster, 1937
Chomsky, N., *Rogue States*, London: Pluto Press, 2000
Gladwell, M., *The Tipping Point: How Little Things Can Make a Big Difference*, New York: Little Brown, 2000
Grey, A. and Skildum-Reid, K., *The Sponsor's Toolkit*, London: McGraw-Hill, 2002
Ries, A. and Ries, L., *The Fall of Advertising and the Rise of PR*, London: HarperCollins Business, 2002
Ritzer, G., *The McDonaldization of Society* (5th edn), Thousand Oaks, C.A.: Pine Forge Press, 2008
Schmitt, B., *Customer Experience Management: A Revolutionary Approach to Connecting with Your Customers*, New York: John Wiley, 2003
Smilansky, S., *Experiential Marketing: A Practical Guide to Interactive Brand Experiences*, London: Kogan Page, 2009
Wernick, A. (ed.), *Promotional Culture: Advertising, Ideology and Symbolic Expression*, London: Sage Publications, 1991
Younkins, E., *Capitalism and Commerce: Conceptual Foundations of Free Enterprise*, Lanham, M.A.: Lexington Books, 2002

ARTICLES

Ahuvia, A., 'Social Criticism of Advertising: On the Role of Literary Theory and the Use of Data', *Journal of Advertising*, vol.27, 1998, pp.143–62
Barnes, M., 'Public Attitudes to Advertising', *International Journal of Advertising*, vol.1, 1982, pp.119–28
Bosman, J., 'Stuck at the Edges of the Ad Game', *The New York Times*, 22 November 2005
Brook, S., 'Women Miss Out on Top Advertising Jobs', *The Media Guardian*, 25 January 2006
Cadwalladr, C., 'This Advertising Boss Thinks Women Make "Crap" Executives. It Seems He's Not Alone', *The Observer*, 23 October 2005
Cozens, C., 'Advertisers Fail to Tap Ethnic Minority Markets', *The Guardian*, 3 December 2004
Hodson, V., 'The "Lost" Women of Advertising', *Campaign*, 22 March 1985, pp.77–9
Peacock, L., 'Careers Advice: Battling Ageism in Advertising', *The Daily Telegraph*, 25 February 2011
Surowiecki, J., 'Ageism in Advertising', *The New Yorker*, 1 April 2002
Tylee, J., 'US Ad Agencies Face Legal Action over Racism Claims', *Campaign*, 13 January 2009

CHAPTER 2

Barthes, R., *Mythologies*, New York: Hill & Wang, 1972
Baudrillard, J., *The System of Objects*, London: Verso, 1968
Baudrillard, J., *The Ecstasy of Communication*, New York: Semiotext(e), 1988
Beasley, R and Danesi, M., *Persuasive Signs: The Semiotics of Advertising*, New York: Mouton de Gruyer, 2002
Berger, J., *Ways of Seeing*, London: Pelican, 1973

Berger, W., *Advertising Today*, London: Phaidon, 2001
DeVries, L., *Victorian Advertisements*, London: John Murray, 1968
Dyer, G., *Advertising as Communication*, London: Routledge, 1993
Heller, S., *Paul Rand*, London: Phaidon, 1999
Jameson, F., *Postmodernism, or The Cultural Logic of Late Capitalism*, Durham, N.C.: Duke University Press, 1991
Kilbourne, J., *Can't Buy My Love: How Advertising Changes the Way We Think and Feel*, New York and London: Touchstone, 1999
Ogilvy, D., *Confessions of an Advertising Man*, London: Southbank Publishing, 2004 (first pub. 1964)
Pincas, S. and Loiseau, M., *A History of Advertising*, London: Taschen, 2008
Tickner, L., *The Spectacle of Women: Imagery of the Suffrage Campaign 1907–14*, London: Chatto & Windus, 1987
Tungate, M., *Adland: A Global History of Advertising*, London: Kogan Page, 2007
Twitchell, J., *Twenty Ads that Shook The World*, New York: Three Rivers Press, 2000
Wells Lawrence, M., *A Big Life in Advertising*, London: Touchstone, 2003
Williamson, J., *Decoding Advertsiments: Ideology and Meaning in Advertising*, London: Marion Boyars, 1978

ARTICLES

Boutlis, P., 'A Theory of Postmodern Advertising', *International Journal of Advertising*, vol.19, no.1, 2000, pp.3–23
Costera Meijer, I., 'Advertising Citizenship: An Essay on the Performative Power of Consumer Culture', *Media Culture Society*, vol.20, no.2, April 1998, pp.235–249
Stokoe, C., '100 Years Of Propaganda: The Good, The Bad and The Ugly', *Smashing Magazine*, 13 June 2010

CHAPTER 3

Aaker, D., *Building Strong Brands*, New York: The Free Press, 1996
Adamson, A., *BrandSimple: How the Best Brands Keep it Simple and Succeed*, New York: Palgrave Macmillan, 2006
Airey, D., *Logo Design Love: A Guide to Creating Iconic Brand Identities*, Berkeley, C.A.: New Riders Press, 2009
Hackley, C., *Advertising and Promotion: Communicating Brands*, London: Sage Publications, 2005
Holt, D., *How Brands Become Icons: The Principles of Cultural Branding*, Boston: Harvard Business School Press, 2004
Klein, N., *No Logo*, London: Flamingo, 2000
Lasn, K., *Culture Jam: How to Reverse America's Suicidal Consumer Binge – and Why We Must*, Harper Paperbacks, 2000
Mono, *Branding: From Brief to Finished Solution*, Crans, Switzerland: RotoVision, 2004
Neumeier, M., *The Brand Gap: How to Bridge the Distance Between Business Strategy and Design*, Berkeley, C.A.: Peachpit Press/AIGA Design Press, 2006
Olins, W., *The Brand Handbook*, London: Thames & Hudson, 2010
Pavitt, J. (ed.), *Brand New*, London: V&A Publications, 2000
Perry, A. with Wisnom III, D., *Before the Brand: Creating the Unique DNA of an Enduring Brand Identity*, 2003

Simmons, J., *Brand Stories: Innocent: Building a Brand from Nothing but Fruit*, New York: Cyan Books, 2006

ARTICLES
Arvidsson, A., 'Brands: A Critical Perspective', *Journal of Consumer Culture*, vol.5, no.2, 2005, pp.235–58
Combe, I., Crowther, D. and Greenland, S., 'The Semiology of Changing Brand Image', *Journal of Research in Marketing and Entrepreneurship*, vol.5, no.1, 1999, pp.1–24
Gibson, O., 'Shopper's Eye View of Ads that Pass Us By', *The Guardian*, 19 November 2005
Webber, A., 'What Great Brands Do', *Fast Company*, 31 August 1997

CHAPTER 4
Dibb, S. and Lyndon, S., *The Market Segmentation Workbook: Target Marketing for Marketing Managers*, London: Thompson, 2008
Green, L. (ed.), *Advertising Works and How: Winning Communication Strategies for Business*, Henley, Oxon: World Advertising Research Center, 2005
Hackley, C., *Advertising & Promotion: An Integrated Marketing Communications Approach*, London: Sage Publications, 2010
Hammersley, M. and Atkinson, P., *Ethnography: Principles in Practice*, London: Routledge, 2004
Jones, J. P., *The Advertising Business: Operations, Creativity, Media Planning, Integrated Communications*, London: Sage Publications, 1999
Kent, R., *Measuring Media Audiences*, London: Routledge, 1994
Moores, S., *Interpreting Audiences: The Ethnography of Media Consumption*, London: Sage Publications, 1993
Nava, M. (ed.), *Changing Cultures: Feminism, Youth and Consumerism*, London: Sage Publications, 1992
Schmitt, B., *Big Think Strategy: How to Leverage Bold Ideas and Leave Small Thinking Behind*, Boston, M.A.: Harvard Business School Press, 2007
Yeshin, T., *Advertising*, Hampshire: Cengage Learning EMEA, 2011

ARTICLES
Bech-Larsen, T., 'Model-Based Development and Testing of Advertising Messages: A Comparative Study of Two Campaign Proposals Based on the MECCAs Model and a Conventional Approach', *International Journal of Advertising*, vol.20, no.4, 2001, pp.499–519
Brace, I. and Bond, G., 'Segmenting by Attitudes to TV Advertising – Eye Opener or Blind Alley', *International Journal of Market Research*, vol.39, no.3, 1997, pp.481–508
De-Young, S. and Crane, F., 'Females' Attitudes towards the Portrayal of Women in Advertising: A Canadian Study', *International Journal of Advertising*, vol.11, no.3, 1992, pp.249–55
Fournier, S. and Yao, J., ' Reviving Brand Loyalty: A Reconceptualization within the Framework of Consumer-Brand Relationships', *International Journal of Research in Marketing*, vol.14, no.5, December 1997, pp.451–472
Fournier, S., 'Understanding Consumer-Brand Relationships', Division of Research, Harvard Business School, 1995
McDonald, C., 'Pre-Testing Advertisements', *Admap Monograph* No. 5, 1997

CHAPTER 5
Aitchison, J., *Cutting Edge Advertising*, Singapore: Prentice Hall, 2004
Barry, P., *The Advertising Concept Book: Think Now, Design Later: A Complete Guide to Creative Ideas, Strategies and Campaigns*, London: Thames & Hudson, 2008
Dobrow, L., *When Advertising Tried Harder*, New York: Friendly Press, 1984
Haug, W. F., *Critique of Commodity Aesthetics*, Minneapolis: University of Minnesota Press, 1986
Meyer, J. M. (ed.)/The Art Directors Club, *Mad Ave: Award-Winning Advertising of the 20th Century*, New York: Universe, 2000
Michalko, M., *Cracking Creativity: The Secrets of Creative Genius*, California: Ten Speed Press, 2001
Pricken, M., *Creative Advertising: Ideas and Techniques from the World's Best Campaigns*, London: Thames & Hudson, 2010
Ries, A. and Ries, L., *The Origin of Brands: Discover the Natural Laws of Product Innovation and Business Survival*, New York: HarperCollins, 2005
Sullivan, L., *Hey Whipple, Squeeze This: A Guide to Creating Great Ads*, New Jersey: Adweek Magazine Series, 2003
Webb Young, J., *A Technique for Producing Ideas*, New York: McGraw-Hill, 2003

CHAPTER 6
Ang, I., *Living Room Wars; Rethinking Media Audiences for a Postmodern World*, London: Routledge, 1996
Curran, J., *Media and Power*, London: Routledge, 2002
Himpe, T., *Advertising is Dead: Long Live Advertising*, London: Thames & Hudson, 2006
Key, W., *Subliminal Seduction*, New York: Signet, 1972
Leiss, W., Kline, S. and Jhally, S., *Social Communication in Advertising: Persons, Products, and Images of Well-Being*, New York: Methuen, 1986
Lucas, G. and Michael, D., *Guerrilla Advertising: Unconventional Brand Communication*, Laurence King, 2006
Qualman, E., *Socialnomics: How Social Media Transforms the Way We Live and Do Business*, Hoboken, N.J.: John Wiley, 2011
Scott, D., *The New Rules of Marketing and PR: How to Use Social Media, Online Video, Mobile Applications, Blogs, News Releases, and Viral Marketing to Reach Buyers Directly*, Hoboken, N.J.: John Wiley, 2009
Smit, E., *Mass Media Advertising: Information or Wallpaper?*, Amsterdam: Het Spinhuis, 2000
Stoklossa, U. (ed. Rempen, T.), *Advertising: New Techniques for Visual Seduction*, London: Thames & Hudson, 2007
Williams, K., *Understanding Media Theory*, London: Hodder Arnold, 2003

ARTICLES
Beale, C., 'Why the Academic Take on TV Doesn't Affect Advertisers', *Campaign*, 21 November 2002
Edell, J. A. and Keller, K. L., 'The Information Processing of Co-ordinated Media Campaigns', *Journal of Marketing Research*, vol.26, May 1989, pp.149–63
Moor, E., 'Branded Spaces: The Scope of "New Marketing"', *Journal of Consumer Culture*, vol.3, no.1, 2003, pp.39–60

CHAPTERS 7 & 8
Adorno, T., *The Culture Industry: Selected Essays on Mass Culture*, London: Routledge, 1991

Ambrose, G. and Harris, P., *Layout*, Lausanne: AVA Publishing, 2005
Bourdieu, P. and Passeron, J-C., *Reproduction in Education, Society and Culture*, London: Sage Publications, 2000
Burtenshaw, K., Mahon, N. and Barfoot, C., *The Fundamentals of Creative Advertising*, Lausanne: AVA Academia, 2006
D&AD, *The Copy Book: How 32 of the World's Best Advertising Writers Write their Advertising*, Cologne: Taschen, 2011
D&AD, *The Art Direction Book: How 32 of the World's Best Creatives Art Direct their Advertising*, Hove: Rotovision, 1996
Kress, G. and Van Leeuwaen, T., *Reading Images: The Grammar of Visual Design*, London: Routledge, 1996
Messaris, P., *Visual Persuasion: The Role of Images in Advertising*, London: Sage Publications, 1997
Shaw, M., *Copywriting: Successful Writing for Design, Advertising and Marketing*, London: Laurence King, 2009
Spiekermann, E. and Ginger, E. M., *Stop Stealing Sheep and Find Out How Type Works* (2nd edn), Berkeley, C.A.: Adobe Press, 2003

CHAPTER 9
Baron, C., *Designing a Digital Portfolio*, Berkeley, C.A.: New Riders, 2003
Eisenman, S., *Building Design Portfolios: Innovative Concepts for Presenting your Work*, Gloucester, M.A.: Rockport, 2006
Mandel, S., *Presentation Skills: A Practical Guide to Better Speaking*, Menlo Park, C.A.: Crisp Publications, 1995
Mogel, L., *Making It in Advertising: An Insider's Guide to Career Opportunities*, New York: Macmillan General Reference, 1993
Taylor, F., *How to Create a Portfolio and Get Hired: A Guide for Graphic Designers and Illustrators*, Gloucester, M.A.: Rockport, 2006
Veksner, S., *How to Make It as an Advertising Creative*, London: Laurence King, 2010

PICTURE CREDITS

p10 & p126 t Creative Directors: Alan Strozenberg, Leo Macias; Art Director: Elias Carmo; Copywriter: Leandro Leal; Photographer: Ivan Berger; Agency Producer: Diogo Piccinnio; Art Buyer: Alice Imamura; **p14** Anna Barisani; **p15** Miriam Sorrentino; **p16** tl Jose Fuste Raga/Getty Images; tr Anthony Dickson/AFP/GettyImages; br ©Ian Howard/Alamy; bl Miriam Sorrentino; **p17** t Corbis ©JoAnna Pollonais/Demotix; bl Ross Bartley; br Hoberman Collection/UIG via Getty Images; **p18–19** Adam & Eve: Simon Lloyd (Creative Digital Heads), Christine Turner (Creative Digital Head), Ben Priest (CD), Ben Tollet (CD), Emer Stamp (CD), Nici Hofer (Creative), Jai Tedeschi (Head of Digital Production), Rosy Karula (Account Director), Natasha Lung (Account Manager). Upset Media: Matt Cook (Project Director/Producer), Toby Cook (Executive Producer), Phillipa Culpepper (Production Designer), Will Bex (Director of Photography), Andreas Muller (Music Analyst & Software Developer), Larissa Hadjio (Digital Producer), Daniel Kupfer (Lead Developer), Tommi Eberwein (Lead Designer), Engle Pernaraviciute (Designer); **p20** Photo by Gail Oskin/WireImage for PUMA/Getty Images; **p21** NaohiroTsukada/STASHinc. www.naohirotsukada.com; **p22–26** Leo Burnett; **p31** Corbis; **p32** Jandl Bratislava, Slovakia. Creative Director: Pavel Fuksa, Art Director: Pavel Gajdos, Copywriter: Jan Fajnor, Illustrator: Pavel Gajdos; **p33** t Grey Buenos Aires, Argentina; Creative Director: Daniel Fierro/Gonzalo Ricca, Copywriter: Augusto Herreros Casañé/Leonel Fernandez, Art Director: Martin Bekerman/Cecilia Ognio, Producer: Sergio Bonavia, Photographer: Machado Cicala Morasut; **p33** c & b Longplay 360, Brazil. Creative Director: Fernando Luna, Art Director: Rodrigo Moretto, Copywriter: Francine Bittencourt, Retoucher: Luiz Fazolli, Product: Digital Camera XP10. Client: Fujifilm; **p34** AMV BBDO; **p35** McCann Kenya. Creative Director: Inam Kazimi, Art Director: Martin Mwangi; **p39** tl (C) RMN-Grand Palais (musée du Louvre)/Hervé Lewandowski; **p39** tr Alamy/© The Art Gallery Collection; **p39** b Corbis/©Bettmann; **p40** t & b Image Courtesy of The Advertising Archives; **p41** t Corbis/©Peter Harholdt; **p41** b Image Courtesy of The Advertising Archives; **p42** l Corbis/©Daniel Deme/epa; **p42** r Library of Congress; **p43** Mary Evans Picture Library/The Womens Library; **p44** t Alamy/© Lordprice Collection; **p44** b Akg-images; **p45** t Corbis/© Swim Ink 2, LLC; **p45** b Meltin'Pot 'Start a Revolution' S/S 2010 campaign. Advertising Agency: Armando Testa, Italy. Executive Creative Director: Michele Mariani. Art Directors: Francesco Guerrera, Laura Sironi. Copy Writers: Nicola Lampugnani, Maria Meioli. Photographer: Jean Yves Lemoigne; **p46–47** Yale University Library Manuscripts and Archives/Trustees of the Paul Rand Revocable Trust; **p48** t Image Courtesy of The Advertising Archives; **p48** b Photo Les Arts Décoratifs, Paris/Laurent Sully Jaulmes/Rights Reserved/©ADAGP, Paris and DACS, London 2012; **p49** Volkswagen®, used with permission of Volkswagen Group of America, Inc; **p50** I LOVE NEW YORK is a registered trademark and service mark of the New York State Department of Economic Development; used with permission; **p50** r Wells Rich Greene/Bayer HealthCare; **p51** t Hewitt, Ogilvy, Benson & Mather; client: Hathaway; **p51** bl Wieden+Kennedy; client: Nike; **p51** br AMV BBDO, David Abbott and Ron

Brown, client: The Economist; **p52** t & c Image Courtesy of The Advertising Archives/Dunlop Tyres 1993; **p52** br Image Courtesy of The Advertising Archives; **p53** Armando Testa S.p.A, Italy; **p54** ABSOLUT® VODKA Absolut country of Sweden vodka & logo, Absolut, Absolut bottle design and Absolut calligraphy are trademarks owned by the Absolut company ab; **p55** t Armando Testa S.p.A,, Italy/Lavazza International Campaign, 2010. Photograph Miles Aldridge; **p55** b Washington Olivetto, Creative Directors: Washington Olivetto and Gabriel Zellmeister; Writer: Marcelo Pires; Art Director Itagiba Lages; Photographer: Flavia Assad Calux; Agency: W/Brasil Publicidade; Client: Bombril; **p56** BBH London; client: Boddington's; **p57** Image Courtesy of The Advertising Archives; **p58** Agency: DDB, London. Executive Creative Director: Jeremy Craigen. Copywriter: Jonathan John. Art Director: David Mackersey. Illustrator and Typographer: Pete Mould. Winner of the Cannes Lions International Festival of Creativity 2012, Bronze Press, Art Direction; **p59** Creative Directors: José Bontempo and Diogo Anahory, Art Director: Luis Nora, Copywriter: Marco Pulido, Photo: Heitor Studio, 3D Production: Illusive; **p60** Publicis Conseil (France), Photographer (angels) Dimitri Daniloff, Photographer (car) Anthony Bernier; **p61** tl Sra Rushmore. Account Director; Pablo Irles. Creative Director and copy: Paco Conde. Art Director Elena Delgado and Marta Herradura; **p61** bl Leo Burnett, India. Creative Director: K.V. Sridhar. Copywriter: Agnello Dias. Art Director: K. V. Sridhar. Photographer: D. Radha Krishnan; r Armando Testa S.p.A , Italy/ Cuki Cofrescos S.p.A; **p63** t © Man Ray Trust/ADAGP, Paris and DACS, London 2012; **p63** b Saatchi & Saatchi; client: Silk Cut, Image Courtesy of The Advertising Archives; **p64** l Yale University Library Manuscripts and Archives/Trustees of the Paul Rand Revocable Trust; **p64** r Digital image, The Museum of Modern Art, New York/Scala, Florence/© DACS 2012; **p65** l Euro RSCG 360, France. Executive Creative Directors: Thomas Derouault. Creative Directors: Hugues Pinguet, Stéphane Morel. Art Director: Quentin Delachaux. Copywriter: Stéphane le Frapper. Retoucher: Quentin Delachaux, Adrien Bénard, Jean-Philippe Camus. Art Buyer: Isabelle Baud. Account Supervisor: Arnaud Thizy, Image Credit: Corbis; **p65** r The Bridgeman Art Library/Scottish National Gallery of Modern Art, Edinburgh, UK/©ADAGP, Paris and DACS, London 2012; **p69** Dettol is a brand made by Reckitt Benckiser; **pp70–72** Innocent Drinks Ltd; **p73** D&AD, BBDO New York, HBO; **pp75–76** Wolff Olins, client: Tata DoCoMo; **pp77–79** BMF Advertising. Client Lion Nathan Australia. Client Executives: Dean Grice, Piers Halleen. Executive Creative Director: Warren Brown. Creative Director: Simon Langley. Interactive Creative Director: Chris James. Art Director: Shane Bradnick. Copywriter: Michael Canning. Interactive Art Director: Johnny Brian. Production: Sarah Thompson, Clinton Bell, Sora Nobari. Account Management: Nick Garrett, Fleur Kennedy; **pp83–84** Adam & Eve for John Lewis, Creative Directors: Ben Priest, Ben Tollet, Emer Stamp; **p85** tl MC Saatchi, Australia/Creative Director: Steve Crawford. Writers: Doogie Chapman and Sandra Galiazzo. Art Director: Murray Bransgrove. Retoucher: Ed Croll; **p85** t r & b r Saatchi & Saatchi; **pp86–87** t The Partners. Creative

Director: Greg Quinton. Design Director: Kevin Lan. Design Team: Sophie Hayes, Freya Defoe, Tiffany Hultgren, Jessica Harvey. Client Team: Grace Molenaar, Patrick Ward, Lieke Ypma; **p87** b, **pp88–89** Ogilvy & Mather, India/Vodafone, India; **p93** c Volkswagen®/DDB Helsinki. Art Director: Ripa Hankaniemi. Copywriter: Päivia Topinoja-Aranko. Account Manager: Tuija Airaksinen. © Photographer: Lasse Kärkkäinen. Client: Kirsti Palola. Volkswagen®; **p93** b Heat (previously Black Rocket) Creative Director/Art Director Steve Stone. Creative Director/Writer Bob Kerstetter. Photographer: Stock; **p94** tl CCO: Sebastian Hardieck, Christian Mommerty, Wolfgang Schneider; AD: Achim Metzdorf; Copywriter: Martin Knipprath, Sebastian Steller; Accounts: Sonja Struss, Silke Joosten, Marilen Kurtz; **p101** Alamy/© Pictorial Press Ltd; **pp102, 144–45** Fallon McElligott Minneapolis (chief creative officer: Darren Spiller; creative team: Marques Gartrell, Aaron Seymour-Anderson; creative tech: Kla Haeck; director of digital Development: Rocky Novak; director of digital insight: Aki Spicer; director of digital innovation: Marty Wetherall; producers: Matthew Polski, Kirsten O'Callaghan; media: Amber Paukner, Andrea Brazelton, Brian Olsen; VFX Artist: Matt Craig; Production: Klip Collective, Target Marketing); client: SYFY Channel; **p104** Lowe Howard Spink/with kind permission of Tesco Stores Limited/Image Courtesy of The Advertising Archives; **p106** D'Arcy London; client: NHS; image courtesy of the Advertising Archives; **p107** Leo Burnett for Department of Transport. Creative Team: Paul Jordan and Angus MacAdam. Planner: Becky Barry. Director: Chris Palmer; **p111** DDB London for Harvey Nichols / Photographer: James Day. Art Director Justin Tindall. Copywriter: Adam Tucker; **p113** National Geographic Channel Africa, Thandi Davids. Advertising Agency: Ireland-Davenport, Johannesburg, South Africa; Creative Directors: Phil Ireland, John Davenport, Ross Ventress; Art Director: Bruce Harris; Copywriter: Jason Murison; Photographers: Michael Lewis, Nick van Renen; Client Service: Ryan Livie; Art Buyer: Natalie Andrews; **p116** Leo Burnett, Toronto; **p117** t Tiempo BBDO, Barcelona for Bimbo. Creative General Manager: Siscu Molina. Photographer: Carlos Suárez. Work: Outdoor; **p117** b The H J Heinz Co Ltd Archives at The History of Advertising Trust; **p118** t DDB London for The Financial Times. © Wayne Parker Photography; **p118** b Scholz & Friends for Weru. Photo by Ralph Baiker; **p120** AMB BBDO for The Economist; David Abbot and Ron Brown; **p121** t, **pp202–3** Ponce Buenos Aires for Unilever. Executive Creative Director: Hernan Ponce. Brand Planning Director: Diego Luque. Art Director: Martin Ponce. Copywriter: Mario Crudele. Client Service Director: Vanina Rudaeff. Brand Group Director: Nestor Ferreyro. Brand Executive: Constanza Vanzini. Responsible for client: Pablo Gazzera/Tomas Marcenaro/Hernan de Majo/Fernando Laratro. Head of TV: Roberto Carsillo. Agency Producer: Jose Silva. Production Company: MJZ. Director Tom Kuntz. Executive Producer: Jeff Scruton; Director of Photography: Harry Savides. Editorial House: Final Cut. Editor: Carlos Arias. Postproduction Facility: The Mill LA. Music: Allen Toussaint: A Sweet Touch of Love. Sound: La Casa Post Sound; **p121** b Saatchi & Saatchi Hungary for Proctor and Gamble. Creative Director: János

Debreceni. Copywriter: László: Art Director; Sándor Haszon. Photographer: István Lábady; **p122** Agency: agencytwofifteen, Client: Microsoft, **p123** Creative Chairwoman: Jureeporn Thaidumrong; Creative Director: Adam Siriraka; Art Directors: Matthana Saetiaw, Pattanaporn Kateratorn, Natthapong Sriprasard; Copywriter: Thanapol Jiratadaporn; Published: November 2011; **p124** Saatchi & Saatchi LA on behalf of the Surfrider Foundation. Photograph by Matt Cobleigh; **p125** SRA Rushmore for Africa Directo. Creative Director: Miguel Garcia Vizcaino. Art Director: Marta Rico and Guido Belforte. Copy: German Jimenez. Account Team: Eva Gutierrez and Pablo Irles. Agency Producer: Freelance for Free. Production: Lee Films. Realizador: Nicolas Caicoya. Production Director: Angel Recio. Director of Photography: Paco Femenia; **p125 r** Creative Director: Micky Tudor; Digital Creative: Thiago de Moraes; Porduction Company: The Mill; Director: Jim Gilchrist; **p126 b** Advertising Agency: Foolbite, Monza, Italy; Art Directors: Paolo Guidobono and Michele Sartori; Copywriter: Tiziano Brugnetti; Photographer: Michele Sartori; Retoucher: Paolo Guidobono; Press Agency: D'Angiò Comunicazione; **p127 t** D'Arcy London for Procter and Gamble. Sirma Umur (Femcare CEEMEA General Manager Procter & Gamble); **p127 b** CCO: Sebastian Hardieck, Toygar Bazarkaya; CD: Sebastian Hardieck, Raphael Milczarek; AD: Fabian Kirner, Joerg Sachtleben; Copywriter: Felix Lemcke; Account: Heike Flottmann, Annika Lauhoefer; **p128** Courtesy of Target; **p129** Ogilvy Toronto on behalf of Unilever. O&M: Creative Directors: Janet Kestin/ Nancy Vonk. Art Directors: Tim Piper/Mike Kirkland. Writer: Tim Piper. Broadcast Producer: Brenda Suminiski. Account Director: Aviva Groll. Production House: Reginald Pike. Photographer: Gabor Jurina. Retoucher: Edward Cha: Make-up Diana Carreiro. Editor/Post Production: Paul Gowan (Rogue Editorial). On-line Editor: Kevin Gibson (Soho). Graphics: Eric Makila, Bob Zagorski (Soho). Sound: Technicolour. Sound & Music Vapour. Director of Marketing: Mark Wakefield. Product Manager: Stephanie Hurst; **pp130–31** TBWA Hunt Lascaris Johannesburg for The Zimbabwean; **p134** Ebb&Flow London (executive creative director, Jon Daniel); client: Beatbullying; **p135** Kodu Digital for Mastercard. Creative Director: Paul Harrison. Designer: Alex Mulder; **pp140–41** With the kind permission of Visit Wales Crown Copyright 2011; **pp142–43** © Macy's; **p147 tl, ml, bl** Grabarz und Partner Hamburg; client: Volkswagen; **p147 br** Dentsu Japan (creative director: Hiroki Nakamura; extended creative team; Hajime Yakushiji, Shinsaku Ogawa, Tsubasa Kayasuga, Hiroshi Koike, Qanta Shimizu, Kohei Kawasaki, Ryo Tanizaki, Mayuko Kondo, Teruo Nakanishi, Taku Ichihara, Tatsuhiko Akutsu, Rami Kanno, Koichi Arakawa, Hiroyuki Hanai, Kentaro Katsube, Minako Suzuki) Client: Uniqlo; **p149 t r** TBWA/London. Creative Director: Johan Dahlqvist. & Lee Tan. Art Director: Andrew Bloom. Copywriter: Erk Tell. Strategy Director: David Frymann. Brand Leader: Emma Massey. Producer: Justin Martin. Head of Production: Trudy Waldron. Director: Jakob Marky. Production: Academy Films. Digital Production: Perfect Fools; **pp150–51** JWT New York for Diageo (Smirnoff 21). Co-President/Chief Creative Officer, North America: Chief Creative Officer, New York: Executive Creative Director: Matt MacDonald.

Interactive ECD: Justin Crawford. Art Director: Tiffany McKee, Moyeenul Alam. Copywriters: Rick Abbott, Vahbiz Engineer. Planner: Clive deFreitas. Director of Intergrated Production: Cliar Group. JWT Director of Brand Production: Joe Calabrese. Senior Producers: Greg Tharp, Andrea Curtin. Producers: Brenda Fogg, Jennifer Hile. Account Executives: Amy Frisch, Sandra Ciconte. Commercial Production Team: Director: Samuel Bayer. Production Company: Serial Pictures. Post Production: JWT Two/Nice Shoes. Editor: Tony Chang, JWTwo. Editing House: JWTwo. Music: Fall on Your Sword, Art vs Science. Media Agency: Carat. MTV Branded Content Team: Executive Producer: Nusrat Durrani. Director: Arka Sengupta. Producers: Reese Patterson, Emily Anderson. Production Company: MTV. Photographers: K. Peng, Laura Greer; **p153 t** Heimat, Berlin for Hornbach-Baumarkt. Creative Director: Paruj Daorai. Film production: Trigger Happy Productions Gmbh. Director: Pep Bosch. Camera: Paco Femenia. AD: Hendrik Schweder. CD: Guido Heffels. Copy: Sabina Hesse. Edit: Fabrizio Rossetti. Music/Composer: Tijmen Bergman, Maurits Goosens. Executive Producers: Nani Miliane meimeth, Stephen Vens; **p153 b** Agencytwofifteen for Microsoft **p156** SRA Rushmore for Renfe; Executive Creative Director: César Garcia. Creative Director: Paco Conde and Quito Leal. Art Director: Quito Leal. Copy: Paco Conde and Pablo Lucas. Photography Ramon Serrano and Quito Leal; **p157** Client: M.CASSAB; Client Exec: Robério Esteves; Creative Director/Writer: Aricio Fortes; Creative Director/Art Director: Paulo Coelho; Chief Creative Officer: PJ Pereira; Art Buyer: Iron Tavares; Print Producer: Drew Saucedo; Account Executive: Lo Braz; Illustrator: Eduardo Gomes; **p158** BBR Saatchi & Saatchi, Tel Aviv, Israel. Chief Creative Officer: Yoram Levi. Creative Director: Eran Nir. Creative: Aia Bechor, Noam Laist. Producers: Dorit Gvilli, Odelia Nachmias. Account Supervisor: Inbal Rov. Account Executive: Noa Sharf. VP Planning: David Kosmin. Senior Planner : Guy Gordon. Animation Studio: Geronimo. Photographer: Yoram Ascheim. Photoshop: Eyal Orlee; **p159 t** Ogilvy & Mather, Bangkok, Thailand. Executive Creative Director: Wisit Lumsiricharoenchoke/Nopadol Srikieatikajohn. Creative Director: Paruj Daorai. Copywriter. Rudee Surapongraktrakool. Account Manager: Phawit Chitrakorn/Chaowalit Vichay-achakorn. Account Supervisor: Woorawit Yoosawat. Producer: Paiboon Suwansangroj. Art Director: Wisit Lumsiricharoenchoke/Nopadol Srikieatika-john/Gumpon Laksanajinda/Ratapon Houyhong-tong. Illustrator: Surachai Puthikulangkura/ Supachai U-Rairat: Illusion Photographer: Surachai Puthikulangkura: Illusion. Other Credits: Image Composer: Surachai P/Supachai U: Illusion; **p159 b** Client and Job Title: Matt Hunt, Brand Director, Hovis; Creative agency: JWT London; ECD: Russell Ramsey; CD: Russell Ramsey; Creatives: Hannah Ford and Simon Horton; Art Buyer: Romana Kit; Account Director: Isabel Dunbar; Media agency: Starcom; Media planner: Sally Armstrong; Photographer: Andy Rudak; Exposure: National outdoor and press (UK); **p161** Mudra Group. Philips (Flipped City), Nirmal Pulickal (ECD Mudra North & East) and Raylin Valles (Creative Director, Mudra North); **p163** Executive Creative Director: Sr. Stephen Vogel/Christian Mommertz; Art Director & Copywriter: Sabina Hesse/Albert S. Chan; Painter: Remus Grecu; Art Buying: Christina Hufgard;

Photographer: Jo Bacherl; Account Management: Veronika Sikvoelgyi; Advertiser's Supervisor: Claudia Engel **p164** Advertising Agency: The Bridge, Glasgow; Art Director: Simon Parker; Copywriter: Ali Taylor; Designer: Andy Mulvenna; Awards: Roses Advertising Awards 2009, Gold (Best Consumer Direct Mail); **p165 t** Creative: Phil Sanderson; Agency: Denvir Markerting; DM piece created for Chip Shop Awards 2010, winner of 'Best Direct Mail' award, **p165 b** LBi Starring: Mia Robertsson, Mattias Cederfeldt; Fredrik Lundgren, Marlene Hernbrand, Johan Sahlein. Fria Tidningen: Jonas Sandstrom; **p166** Kempertrautmann gmbh Hamburg; **p167** Clemenger BBDO, Australia; **pp168–69** Jung von Matt/Fleet, 7Seas global content management, Dederichs Reinecke & Partner, WWF Deutschland; **pp174–75** Touché Bologna for Sosushi, Italy. Creative Director: Luca d'Alesio. Photographer: Gabriele Corni. Photo retouching: Andrea Giovanelli; **p176** Wieden + Kennedy for Lurpak. Creative Directors: Ben walker and Matt Gooden. Creatives: Matt Joiner and Matt Powell-Perry. Photographer: David Sykes; **p177** BBH London; photo: Nick Georghiou/Wyatt Clarke & Jones; **p178 t** AMV BBDO for The Economist. Tom Ewart and David Sullivan; **p178 b** Saatchi and Saatchi London; **p179 tl** M&C Saatchi for Dixons. Creative: Graham Fink, Simon Dickens, Orlando Warner. Planning Neil Godber. Account Director: Michael Wilton. Head Client: Benj Kaye; **p179 b** BBH London; client: Audi; **p180** Courtesy of People for the Ethical Treatment of Animals, www.peta. org; **p184 t** Creative Juice/Bangkok for M Wrap. Executive Director: Thirasak Tanapatanakul. Art Director: Anchalika Ketwattanachai/Thirasak Tanapatanakul. Copywriter: Natthawut Sittiwara-phan; **p184 b** Wieden + Kennedy London. Creatives: Chris Groom and Sam Heath. Creative Directors: Tony Davidson and Kim Papworth. Photographer: Luke Kirwan; **p185** AMV BBDO for the Museum of Childhood. Copywriter: Mark Fairbanks. Illustrator: Mick Marston; **p187 tl** Rare. Creative Director: Brett Wheeler. Art Director: Brett Wheeler. Writer: Steve Brown and Mitch Mitchell; **p187 tr** Jung von Matt/ Alster Werbeagentur GmbH Hamburg (JvM) for Young Global Leaders; **p187 b** Mudra Group for Bangalore Traffic Police (Talk Them Dead), Joono Simon (ex ECD, Mudra South); **p188 t** Ogilvy & Mather Asia Pacific Singapore for Unilever. Executive Creative Director: Tham Khai Meng/ Eugene Cheong/Todd McCracken. Copywriter: Mike Sutcliffe/Craig Love/Eugene Cheong. Art Director: Adrian Chan/Maurice Wee/Stuart Mills. Photographer: Edward Loh (October Skies); **p188 b** Anomaly London LLP for Diesel. Executive Creative Director: Mike Byrne. Digital Director: Kevin Lyons. Creative Director: Ian Toombs. Art Director: Coral Garvey. Copywriter: Sean McLaughlin. Diesel: Lucinda Spera; **p189 t** Jung von Matt Hamburg for Wüsthof Knives; **p189 b** CLM BBDO (Paris) for Bayer (Alka Seltzer). Executive Creative Director: Gilles Fichteberg, Jean François Sacco. Art Director: Paul Kreitmann/ Copywriter: Alexis Benoit. Account team: Severine Autret, Claire Roy Thermes; **p190 t** Ogilvy & Mather Paris for IBM. Suzanne Assaf, Lily Sorbara and Ann Rubin; **p190 bl** DDB UK for the Financial Times. Photographer Catherine Sanderson; br DLKW Lowe for Marston Pedigree. Creative Team: Richard Prentice and David Adamson. Photographer Laurence Haskell. Model Maker: Jon Steed. Client: Des Gallagher;

THANKS

INDEX

p193 Pierre Berthuel-Bonnes; **p194** Dimitra Papastathi; **p195** Anna Barisani and Frazer Shaw; **p196** Anton Burmistrov; **p197** Concept and Design: Carsten Schneider, Lars Eberle. Illustration: Anna Mentzel. Sound: Taeji Sawai. Programming: Thomas Meyer, Patrick Juchli, Torsten Härtel, Oliver List, Luis Martinez. Backend: Signal 7. Client: Red Bull; **p202** (see credit p121); **p206** Client: Evian; Agency: BETC; Agency Account Management: Marielle Durandet, Dominique Verot, Catherine Clément, Gaëlle Gicqueau, Marie-Josée Cadorette, Olivier Vigneaux, David Roux; Media Strategy Manager: Martine Picard; Founder of BETC and Global Creative Director: Rémi Babinet; Art Director: Agnes Cavard; Assistant Art Director: Gregory Ferembach; Copywriter: Valerie Chidlovsky; Web: BETC 4D; Creative Director: Vincent Vella; Art Director: David Tremayo; Copywriter: Pierre Duquesnoy; Community Management: Alexis Thobellem; TV Producer: Farbice Brovelli; Music Supervisor: Christophe Caurret; Music: BETC Music; Production Company: Partizan; Director: Michael Gracey; Music & Artist: Rapper's Delight by Dan the Automator; **p208** Photo ©Onne van der Wal/Corbis. Photo by Chicasso/Getty Images; **p209** © Louis Moses/Corbis; **p212-23** Lisa Lake/Getty Images; **p214** Anna Barisani; **p215** Anton Burmistrov; **p216 t** Anzhela Hayrabedyan; **p216 m** Luca Grosso; **p216 b** Shesley Crustna; **p224 t** DDB Stokholm; **p224 bl, br** TBWA South Africa; **p227** Leo Burnett Toronto for James Ready Beer. Chief Creative Officer: Judy John. Creative Director: Judy John, Lisa Greenberg. Copywriter: Steve Persico. Art Director: Anthony Chelvanathan. Editor: David Nakata. Producer: Gladys Bachand. Group Account Director: David Buckspan. Account Director: Natasha Dagenais. Account Executive: Jordan Lane; **p232** Jung von Matt/Alster Werbeagentur GmbH, Markenfilm Crossing GmbH Hamburg/Daimler AG

Dedicated to Graham, Willow and Opal

With thanks to those people behind the scenes at various agencies that made this book possible; Harry Barlow, Agustina Palma Cané , Philomena Doyle, Linda Eriksson, Charlotte Evans, Alex Everett, Christopher Forsyth, Emily Halada, Kenneth Hein, Jennifer Jahinian, Sonja Kruger, Johan Ljungman, Annika Messerschmidt, Yuko Nakamura, Neeti nayak, Giorgiana Nuti , Tommasina Panebianco, Petra Peacock, Kershnee Pillay, Hernan Ponce, Roger Pride, Patricia Reta, Siobhan Squire, Carly Wengrover, Janine Zaim.

To the amazing interviewees who gave up their time and expertise; Jamie Barrett, Raphael Basckin, Ergin Binyildiz, Shane Bradnick, Ali Bucknall, Mattias Cederfeldt, Albert S Chan, Mario Crudele, Jon Daniel, Scott Duchon, Steve Freedman, Paul Harrison, Sabina Hesse, Simon Higby, Nicky Hirst, Paul Jordan, Tsubasa Kayasuga, Hiroshi Koike, Leah Mitchell, Angus Macadam, Matt Macdonald, Madeleine Morris, Hiroki Nakamura, Rocky Novak, Shinsaku Ogawa, John Patroulis, Mia Robertsson, Shelley Smoler, Aaron Seymour-Anderson, Nick Stringer, Justin Tindall, Peter Totman, Adam Tucker, Raylin Valles, Brendan Wilkins, Hajime Yakushiji.

To all the Clients and advertising agencies that shared their hard work with me.

To those at Laurence King who helped turn a bunch of pages into a book; Sophie Drysdale, Sue George, Claire Gouldstone, Jo Lightfoot.

Not forgetting the 3rd year Greenwich students from 2011 Anna Barisani, Pierre Berthuel-Bonnes, Anton Burmistrov, Dimitra Papastathi and Frazer Shaw.

And finally to Graham, Trevor, Enid, Giusi and Pasquale without whose babysitting talents and household interventions and patience this book could not have got off the ground.